Governing Child Sexual Abuse

The turn of the 1990s saw a number of high profile public inquiries into the handling of child sexual abuse investigations in Great Britain. *Governing Child Sexual Abuse* examines the implications of these inquiries on the regulation of relationships between families and the state. In so doing, Samantha Ashenden brings a number of contemporary debates in social and political theory to bear upon the governance of child sexual abuse. In particular, drawing on the work of Foucault and Habermas, she looks at:

- The liberal constitution of a boundary between public and private spheres
- The legal and scientific determination of legitimate intervention
- The relation between democracy and expertise in the governance of social life.

This book will be of particular interest to scholars and students of social and political theory, political sociology, the sociology of law and social policy.

Samantha Ashenden is Lecturer in Sociology in the School of Politics and Sociology at Birkbeck College, University of London.

D0219316

Governing Child Sexual Abuse

Negotiating the boundaries of public and private, law and science

Samantha Ashenden

Routledge
Taylor & Francis Group

LONDON AND NEW YORK

First published 2004
by Routledge
11 New Fetter Lane, London EC4P 4EE

Simultaneously published in the USA and Canada
by Routledge
29 West 35th Street, New York, NY 10001

Routledge is an imprint of the Taylor & Francis Group

Typeset in Baskerville by
Keystroke, Jacaranda Lodge, Wolverhampton
Printed and bound in Great Britain by
TJ International, Padstow, Cornwall

British Library Cataloguing in Publication Data
A catalogue record for this book is available from the British Library

Library of Congress Cataloging in Publication Data
Ashenden, Samantha.
    Governing child sexual abuse : negotiating the boundaries of public
and private, law and science / Samantha Ashenden.—1st ed.
        p. cm.
Includes bibliographical references and index.
    1. Child abuse. 2. Child abuse—Social aspects. 3. Child abuse—Law
and legislation. 4. Child welfare. I. Title.
    HV6626.5.A854 2003
    362.76'561—dc21   2003008615

ISBN 0–415–15893–1 (hbk)
ISBN 0–415–15894–x (pbk)

To the memory of Paul Hirst

Contents

Conclusion   203

Acknowledgements

I should like to thank my students at Birkbeck College for their lively curiosity and critical engagement with many of the ideas presented here. I am also grateful to colleagues in the School of Politics and Sociology for their comradeship and good humour. Paul Hirst, in particular, was an important inspiration, as a supervisor and as a colleague. On many occasions he urged me from my 'epistemological pit', produced intellectual challenges and engaged with me in a spirit of exemplary generosity. He also read the whole manuscript and provided invaluable suggestions. I owe much to his honesty, encouragement and support; his recent death is a very deep loss.

Special thanks are due also to David Owen. This book contains many ideas conceived in conversation with him, and owes a great deal, both in general orientation and for many specific formulations, to his critical care and attentiveness. Thanks also to members of the History of the Present research network, in London and elsewhere, for lively discussion of many of the themes presented here. James Brown and Alexandra Hingst have been constant friends. James's intellectual curiosity, willingness to think *à deux*, and his and Lê's culinary generosity through my recent period of nomadism have made finishing this text far more fun than it should have been. Thanks to Kelvin Knight for his encouragement, belief in my capacity to write, and for his astute and constructive criticisms of my arguments. Thanks also to John B. Thompson who supervised an MPhil dissertation on Habermas during which time I began thinking about some of the ideas and questions that were to become motivating concerns of this book. I am also indebted to Mari Shullaw for her patience and encouragement in pursuing the publication of this book despite hiccups and delays.

Jacqui, Chris, Jenny and Suzi Butler have been there through the whole thing. Particular thanks go to Jacqui, whose longstanding friendship, wit and occasional provision of red wine, chocolate cake and 'industrial strength' coffee has sustained me through many personal and intellectual crises. Thanks to Philip Spencer, Jane, Rosa and Reuben Anderson, and to Steve Bastow, Stalo Phylactou and Laïra Phylactou-Bastow, for their inspiration, for all their love and support, and for leaving me their houses, cats and gardens across long summers. Special thanks go to Steve, for helping with the French and for editing out superfluous prose. Tim Edwards has engaged with the issues with directness, and I thank him for his ongoing friendship, and for constructive criticisms of several chapters of this book. Particular thanks are due to my parents, for their practical and emotional support for my pursuing this work, and for their ongoing love. Finally, I would especially like to thank Martin, for his patient reading and assiduous criticism of the whole text, but mostly for meeting me.

Abbreviations

EPO	Emergency Protection Order
NSPCC	National Society for the Prevention of Cruelty to Children
PAIN	Parents Against Injustice
PSO	Place of Safety Order
RAD	Reflex anal dilatation
RSSPCC	Royal Scottish Society for the Prevention of Cruelty to Children
SRAG	South Ronaldsay Action Group
SSD	Social Services Department
SWD	Social Work Department

The case [Cleveland] illustrates how the concept of child abuse craves objectivity

(*The Social Construction of What?* Ian Hacking 1999: 150)

Mark it for a sign, mark it!

(*The Crucible*, Arthur Miller [1953] 2000: 30)

Introduction

This book is a study in the governance of social life and of the way certain specific social theories attempt to account for it. Its aim is to enhance our understanding of contemporary practices of governance by focusing on the analysis of a particular problem: child sexual abuse.

The sexual abuse of children raises stark questions concerning the limits of legitimacy of, and appropriate means for, public interventions into the private sphere of the family. It also raises challenging questions concerning the forms of, and effects created by, legal and scientific knowledge and practice through which social life is organised. Child sexual abuse thus constitutes a site on which tensions in the relationship between public and private spheres emerge, in which law and science meet, and where the interface between democracy and expertise is disclosed. This book aims to bring questions central to contemporary discussions in social and political theory into direct relation with this important social issue, in order to examine what the governance of child sexual abuse tells us about our forms of political reasoning. Rather than focusing on child sexual abuse as such, this book examines how this problem is governed. Its concerns are therefore two-fold: the analysis of contemporary family–state relations, and the interrogation of different conceptual approaches to these relations and their effects. This introduction provides a preliminary outline of how these two frames of reference are figured in the chapters that follow.

A tension exists within modern social and political discourse concerning the nature of the family–state relationship. On the one hand, there exists a widespread assumption of the need to protect children, and on the other, an assumption regarding the importance of safeguarding individual rights and family privacy. By examining recurring calls of 'crisis' in the management of child sexual abuse we can investigate how current social and political imperatives simultaneously requiring the protection of children and respect for family privacy are held in tension and managed by the claims to expertise of legal and welfare professionals. We can also thus examine the problems encountered when these practices of governance are called into question. This book considers this by examining the techniques through which 'normal' family–state relations are re-inscribed following investigations into calls of 'crisis'.

The sexual abuse of children re-emerged as a pressing problem for governance in Britain during the 1980s (see Chapter 1). This book concentrates principally on the cases of Cleveland (1987), where contemporary strategies in the governance of child sexual abuse first emerged as a major public concern, producing changes to legislation in the form of the Children Act 1989; and Orkney (1991), a case which relates explicitly to the failure to have learned the lessons of Cleveland. The dynamics of these cases bring into sharp relief questions concerning the legitimate relationship between public and private life and how this is managed by legal, medical and psychological expertise. These cases provide specific contexts against which to assess the cogency of different theoretical formulations of the problems attending contemporary forms of governance.

There are a number of ways in which the question of child sexual abuse as a problem of governance can be analysed. Prominent among these are liberal political theory, the Critical Theory of Jürgen Habermas, and Michel Foucault's genealogical work. This book engages with liberal and Critical Theory, establishing the limits of looking at state–individual relationships through these conceptual frameworks. It argues that 'crises' in the governance of child sexual abuse take the form they do because of the widespread assumption of a clear division between public and private life, the presupposition of the naturalness and primacy of the family, and the commitment to an idea of the possibility of eliciting and acting beneficially on the truth of the child. Both liberal and Critical Theory assume these parameters. Foucault's work by contrast provides the possibility of addressing problems involved in the governance of child sexual abuse by facilitating a critical engagement with the relation between public and private life and the management of this distinction through expert knowledge and practice within which evidence of child sexual abuse is elicited.

Central to much contemporary social and political theory are debates about the capacity of modern forms of the regulation of state–individual relations to render the agencies that govern social life accountable. This discussion has centred on the relationship between democratic culture, public opinion and expertise. For example, the welfare state is widely regarded as failing its policy objectives and regulatory functions, closing down spaces of critical reflection and producing pathological effects on the body politic (Beck 1992; Bauman 1989; Ginsburg 1992; Habermas 1976, 1984, 1987a, 1996; Offe 1984; Johnson 1987; Luhmann 1990; Mishra 1984; Teubner 1985). Analyses of these issues are varied, ranging from policy-oriented approaches demanding more resources and better procedures, through to theoretical arguments about legitimation crises, the overburdening of law, the opacity of social relations in the face of attempts at prediction and control and so on. The latter are arguments that are suggestive of fundamental problems with the rationality of modern governmental regimes. This book takes up these concerns in the context of a critical examination of the relationship between public and private spheres, as well as issues in the relationships between science and law and democracy and expertise. In giving these concerns substantive focus by examining the emergence of child sexual abuse as a problem for modern forms of governance, the book sets out to investigate the forms of practical reasoning involved in the governance of family–state relations, to delineate the constitution of these forms of reasoning, to demonstrate their effects, and to evaluate the problem of the democratic negotiation of expertise. The relationships between public and private spheres, democracy and expertise form the theoretical horizon of the book; modern forms of the governance of child sexual abuse are taken as the domain of inquiry.

The issue of child sexual abuse has achieved its contemporary public prominence in large part through feminist political practice and through analyses conducted within the framework of theories of patriarchy, work that was spawned by the recognition of sexual violence within family relationships as normal rather than exceptional (e.g. Campbell 1988; Renvoize 1993; Rush 1980; Search 1988). Emerging alongside and in parallel with this has been feminist work in social and political theory (e.g. Benhabib 1986, 1992, 1996; Boling 1996; Butler 1990; Flax 1990; Fraser 1989; Nicholson 1986,1990; Pateman 1988; Phillips 1991, 1995; Sawicki 1991; Smart 1989, 1992; Young 1990). My decision to focus on child sexual abuse as a problem of governance gains inspiration from an engagement with these two dimensions of feminist literature. I will explore this a little further in order to develop the context of and rationale for my own intervention.

Within feminist discussion, to date, there has been little sustained critical engagement with child sexual abuse specifically as an issue for social and political theory (but see Bell 1993a). Rather, thinking within the theoretical framework of patriarchy has tended toward a discussion of the politics of 'denial'. This has centred on the Freud–Fleiss controversy in psychoanalysis, a debate about the status of fantasy, memory and real events in explaining trauma (MacKinnon 1989; Malcolm 1985; Masson 1985; Miller 1985; Scott 1988), and politically on the silencing of children by individual perpetrators and the dominance of patriarchy as a system of oppression (Campbell 1988; Dominelli 1986; Rush 1980). In other words, the political need to establish the fact of child sexual abuse, as opposed to its delegitimation as fantasy, has dominated feminist concerns and perhaps occluded the development of a more wide-ranging critical engagement.

The need for sustained theoretical engagement with the issue of child sexual abuse is illustrated by the limitations of analyses that operate by positing the prior identity of children as 'innocents', therefore asserting that adult–child sex is wrong in some a priori sense (see Renvoize 1993; Rush 1980). Such strategies of argument presuppose what they seek to show: they must posit that adult–child sex is wrong on the basis that children are like 'this', i.e. innocent. This blinds such analyses to considerations of how childhood has come to be constituted in particular ways, ways that in turn locate children as subjects of abuse. Such analyses have a number of deleterious effects. First, they articulate a distinction between innocence and experience within which the sexually abused child inadvertently suffers disqualification (Scott 1988). Second, by prioritising the fact that it is predominantly men who sexually abuse children, feminists have focused attention on abusive sexuality as an extension of 'normal masculinity'; whilst this works to problematise masculine sexuality it obscures the fact that women are also per-petrators of abuse. Third, focus on children's innocence and on problems of patriarchal masculinity has diverted attention from the manner in which the contemporary governance of family–state relations is conducted through particular configurations of authority and expertise, issues equally important to feminists. Given the above limitations, this book seeks to explore the ways in which relations between public and private life, notions of childhood, and conceptions of expertise are constituted, and to question the implications of different ways of thinking through and acting upon these relations and conceptions. It therefore engages extensively with the question of the relation between public and private life and the constitution and management of this distinction through a politics of expertise.

Plan of the book

Chapter 1 examines the context of contemporary concerns with child sexual abuse as a problem for governance by public institutions. It explores the tension within liberal societies between, on the one hand, the idea that the family is a private sphere, and on the other, that the protection of children from harm may require public intervention into this private unit. It looks at the forms taken by periodic calls of 'crisis' in the practices of governance established to negotiate this tension, and provides an overview of the events of Cleveland and Orkney in this context. The chapter then provides some perspective on this set of concerns by examining the historical emergence of contemporary conceptions of childhood and of child abuse, focusing in particular on the ways in which child sexual abuse has been rendered governable through legal and scientific knowledge and practice. It considers the stakes of contemporary debates about childhood in social and political theory and in social policy, and suggests that in order to develop the conceptual tools necessary to examine the governance of child sexual abuse we need a form of analysis that will enable us to theorise the relationship between public and private, and to examine how relationships between law and science configure child sexual abuse as a governable problem.

Following from this preliminary specification of the ways in which child sexual abuse has recently become a problem for governance, the book is divided into two parts. The first part (Chapters 2 to 4) draws out the tools for analysis of the relationship between public and private life, and between law and science, that can be derived from liberal political theory, Habermas's Critical Theory, and from Foucault's genealogy of modern forms of governance. The second part (Chapters 5 to 7) draws on Foucault's work to develop an analysis of the forms of reasoning and acting that underpin and articulate the governance of child sexual abuse by examining the cases of Cleveland and Orkney.

Chapter 2 interrogates liberal political theory. It focuses in particular on characterisations of the distinction between public and private life as a distinction between state sovereignty and individual autonomy, where interventions into the private sphere demand specific justification, and also on conceptions of childhood as a distinct and dependent phase of life requiring special attention to prevent harm and foster autonomy. It argues that whilst liberal arguments are central to contemporary discussions that attempt both to justify and to delimit public interventions into suspected child sexual abuse, the presupposition of a distinction between public and private, and of a naturalised conception of childhood, imply that liberal arguments are fundamentally limited in their capacity critically to question the contemporary governance of child sexual abuse. Specifically, liberalism's constitutive commitment to some version of a public/private distinction and to designations of harm revealed by medicine and psychology impose limits on our capacity to think critically about the governance of child sexual abuse, by tying us to already entrenched patterns of reflection.

Chapter 3 looks at Habermas's attempt to develop a social theory capable of providing a critical explanation of the dynamics of modern societies. In particular, it addresses the extent to which events such as those of Cleveland and Orkney can be understood using his account of the relationship between the state and the family as a conflict between the 'system' and the 'lifeworld'. Developing his suggestions concerning the resolution of the legitimation problems of modern welfare states, the chapter goes on to explore the extent to which Habermas's arguments for further extending democratic governance and the legal regulation of expertise offer a distinct model for the governance of child sexual abuse. The chapter concludes that, whilst Habermas's work highlights a number of important tensions in contemporary state–society relationships, his analysis of the dynamics of these tensions, and proposals for their resolution, are limited to refining our existing conceptions of the problems posed by the governance of child sexual abuse. Insofar as his account is premised on a category distinction between the system and the lifeworld, and on a distinctively modern conception of childhood as a stage of development prior to the autonomy of adulthood, it promises to reiterate the constituent tensions of liberalism and is thus limited in its capacity to provide critical perspective on contemporary practices of governance.

Having established some of the limits of looking at the governance of child sexual abuse through the conceptual parameters of liberal political theory and Habermas's Critical Theory, Chapter 4 turns to Foucault. Foucault's orientation to the practice of social criticism does not presuppose a distinction between public and private life, nor does it engage in prior theoretical determinations of the relations between law and science; it is a mode of analysis that enables us to take these terms, presupposed elsewhere, as phenomena for investigation. In so far as this is the case, this chapter does not proceed in the same manner as previous chapters, outlining a theoretical argument and examining how this works to elucidate or to occlude the dilemmas attending the contemporary governance of child sexual abuse. Rather, this chapter develops this mode of analysis and uses it to reproblematise the governance of child sexual abuse.

The second part of the book takes up Foucault's work to provide a substantive analysis of the contemporary governance of child sexual abuse. It investigates the ways in which assumptions about the delineation of public and private life and the authority of law and science produce a particular form of the problematisation of child sexual abuse, and asks how and with what effects these ideas act upon, inform and constrain us, and what role they play in maintaining intractable problems in this area of governance. Particular attention is given to the implications of the Cleveland Inquiry for the regulation of expert judgement in managing the relationship between families and the state, and to the press discussion of Orkney.

Chapter 5 develops an account of Foucault's suggestions concerning liberalism as a rationality of rule, showing how this account refigures our understanding of the public/private distinction as something orchestrated by and managed through specific practices of governance. It then draws on his account of the relationship between legal mechanisms and scientific knowledge within contemporary forms of rule, to consider how relations between law and science produce forms of practical knowledge and techniques through which the governance of child sexual abuse is conducted, and to examine the public inquiry as a mechanism for governmental reflection and for the renegotiation of formulae for rule where existing practices have been problematised.

Chapters 6 and 7 utilise the analytic framework of Chapter 5, developing an account of the practical deliberations of the Cleveland Inquiry and of the press reporting of Orkney. Chapter 6 examines the role of the public inquiry into the events of Cleveland 1987 in regrounding the possibility of liberal governance in child sexual abuse. This inquiry had an extensive remit and an important impact on the Children Act 1989, reformulating practices of governance in this area. The chapter focuses specifically on the ways in which the inquiry, working within a particular problematisation of child sexual abuse, both assumes and reinvokes a distinction between public and private life, and on the inquiry's negotiation of problems of expert knowledge and practice in this case.

Chapter 7 focuses on the press discussion of Orkney 1991. The Orkney Inquiry had a narrower remit than that of Cleveland and the issues raised by the case were extensively discussed by the press. This chapter therefore focuses on selected press coverage of the issues, exploring how the relationship between the family and the state, and the character of expert knowledge and practice, are presented. The chapter raises for question the extent to which the press provide critical distance on our forms of governance, as compared with the extent to which reporting rearticulates and further entrenches existing forms of governance through its demands. The book concludes by reflecting upon the ways in which the conceptual arguments of Part I, and the substantive analysis of Part II, inform one another.

1 Child sexual abuse as a problem of governance

To state that child sexual abuse is a problem is to state something obvious. As Ian Hacking has recently noted, it is impossible to be 'for' it. He comments, 'We are supposed to be overwhelmed by relativism. It is said that there are no more stable values. Nonsense. Try speaking out in favor of child abuse' (Hacking 1999: 141).[1] To refer to child sexual 'abuse' is already to denote a problem. The concern of this book is to examine how it has been posed as a particular kind of problem, to establish what sort of problem that is, and to assess the ways in which we attempt to govern it.

What sort of problem is child sexual abuse? Whilst it is a problem of many sorts, it is a problem for ethics and a problem for governance in modern liberal societies. The ethical problem denoted by the term 'child sexual abuse' is predicated on the assumption that children are or should be developmentally immature, dependent, vulnerable and innocent or sexually unknowing. Legislative distinctions made between ages of minority and majority demonstrate this assumption. The governmental problem denoted by the term 'child sexual abuse' is based upon a distinction between public and private life, in which children are considered to be the natural responsibility of parents, and where the legitimacy of public intervention into the private family is sanctioned only where there is evidence of harm underwritten by medical and psychological experts and admitted before a court of law.

The ethical evaluation that adult–child sexual relations are wrong, are abusive, depends upon a particular understanding of childhood as a distinct ring-fenced phase of life, an understanding that is historically quite specific. One should be careful here, to state that something is an historical artefact is not to suggest that it is therefore invalid. Child sexual abuse is both a conceptual construct and a reality; it has effects. It is possible to assert that our current conception of childhood is not a natural but an historical artefact without thereby claiming that the contemporary experiences of children, including those who suffer sexual abuse, are not valid. Rather, these experiences are real and at the same time are products of specific processes of historical formation that we can trace. Our classifications of child abuse are institutionalised in law and professional practice, they have entered the public imagination, they have an impact on how children and adults understand themselves, and they have gained moral force.[2] Therefore, whilst the contemporary concept and experience of child sexual abuse emerged at a specific time, in a particular context, and is defined by discourses, this is not to suggest that it can be easily 'undone', or that its effects are any less real.

It is to be inferred from this that child sexual abuse does not just exist as a given problem, but that it is configured in a particular manner, in relation to specific sets of ethical evaluations and in terms of systems of governance. Problems do not simply exist to be 'discovered', rather they are made: problems are identifiable only through a mesh of particular forms of political and professional knowledge and in specific contexts that grant them an appropriate climate of recognition. This is not the same as saying that we can erase child sexual abuse from the social map, or that childhood is a construct that we can reconstruct at whim. There is a great deal of literature on the 'social construction' of social problems. The question to be taken up here is not whether 'child sexual abuse' is 'socially constructed', but rather how has it come to exist as a problem for us, and in particular how it has been given the specific shape and significance that it has within our contemporary governmental and public political imaginations.

In taking child sexual abuse to be a significant issue of concern this book aims to consider what kind of problem in terms of social management it is taken to be, to analyse how concerns over the sexual abuse of children have become located within the remit of modern governance in liberal societies, and to assess the implications of this. My interest, then, is in attempting to map the ways in which what we understand by 'child sexual abuse' has come into being and is governed through the discourses and practices available to us to deal with it. How is it that the governance of child sexual abuse has been 'molded' (Hacking 1991a) in a particular manner?

This chapter examines how child sexual abuse has been located within the remit of modern governance in liberal societies. It does so by delineating liberal welfare rationality as a form of governance prone to calls of 'crisis' with respect to child abuse and by considering some recent historical work on the emergence of contemporary concerns with childhood. Its aim is to throw into relief our contemporary evaluations of child sexual abuse and its governance, in order that we might be able to examine critically the conceptual frameworks that dominate our understanding of this issue and look afresh at this problem. To this end, the first section provides a preliminary specification of the issue of child sexual abuse as a problem of governance. It identifies the manner in which liberal societies attempt to manage the tension between the assumption that family privacy is natural and desirable and the recognition that public intervention may be necessary in order to secure child protection and welfare, a tension managed through professional discourses of child protection. The first section introduces a set of co-ordinates for delineating contemporary calls of crisis with respect to child abuse, and provides a preliminary account of the cases of Cleveland (1987) and Orkney (1991). The second section provides some perspective on these concerns by examining the historical emergence of contemporary conceptions of childhood and of child abuse. Our understandings of childhood and of child abuse, as distinct targets for social policy, are peculiarly modern ones; they are ideas with histories, emerging at specific junctures and institutionalised in particular forms of knowledge and practice. Addressing these concerns will involve a clarification of the specificity of contemporary understandings of childhood, and an examination of the ways in which knowledge of sexual abuse is produced through scientific and legal discussion. The third section concludes this chapter by taking a brief look at the manner in which the figure of the child has become a site of concern within social and political theory and social policy. In summary, the first section of this chapter examines what sort of problem child sexual abuse is as a problem of governance, the second section asks how we got here (how did the 'sexually abused child' emerge), and the third section seeks to address how we might go about developing the tools to analyse this problem further.

Why focus on child sexual abuse as a problem of governance? Sexual abuse has been recognised as a distinct problem more recently than has physical abuse and its governance is more contested. Furthermore, it cuts to the core of our understanding of the privacy of the family more sharply than the issue of physical abuse; where the latter is on a sliding scale from 'reasonable chastisement', the former is regarded as necessarily 'pathological', it has no 'acceptable' level or expression. It is also a more contested cause of intervention: children seldom die as a direct result of child sexual abuse, though they often suffer long-term damage as a result of it. The consequences of mistaken intervention should not be underestimated either. Therefore, part of the contestation over the legitimacy of intervention in suspected cases of child sexual abuse concerns the appropriateness of criteria for intervention into what, within liberal political orders, is considered to be a 'private' domain. Another element in this contestation concerns the parameters and forms of evidence available on the basis of which to intervene. Allegations of physical abuse can usually be grounded in signs that have stable meanings within scientific discourses; this produces evidential clarity.[3] Sexual abuse cases often suffer a lack of such signs, and where proponents have argued that certain signs constitute evidence this has been more highly contested, as in the cases of Cleveland and Orkney, both analysed later in this book. Thus the evidence with which intervention could be justified is often more contested and controversial in sexual abuse cases than in cases of physical abuse. This being the case, we can more easily reveal the grounds that constitute legitimacy in intervention into the privacy of familial relations by examining child sexual abuse cases than by examining physical abuse, by examining what happens when claims to legitimate intervention fail through apparent lack of appropriate evidence.

Family–state relations and 'crises' in the governance of child sexual abuse

Contemporary state–family relations can be characterised as containing a tension. On the one hand, there is widespread recognition of the need to protect children from abuse, and on the other hand a set of assumptions concerning the importance of individual rights and family privacy (Bell 1993b; Frost and Stein 1989). These conflicting assumptions concerning the welfare of the child and the rights of the family reveal a tension between family privacy and state-sanctioned intervention.

Child protection is one set of practices through which relations between families and the state are constituted and regulated. This set of practices enables us to examine the negotiation of the relationship between public and private life. Addressing problems within the context of intimate adult–child relationships today occurs through public intervention into a realm generally regarded as private and outside of, or external to, public scrutiny and concern. Modern management of the legal, social and cultural boundaries between families and the state is effected by the mobilisation of a range of professional forms of knowledge and practice such as law, medicine, psychology and social work specialising in determining where and when intervention is reasonable and legitimate, all of which are premised on the idea of the 'best interests of the child'. How do assumptions concerning the distinction between public and private domains of life and contemporary relationships between law and science configure child (sexual) abuse as an object of governance?

Recognition of problems within adult–child relationships today produces activity from the state or from state-sponsored organisations such as the NSPCC, either to dissolve the family (through, for example, removal of children into care), or to reconstitute the family as a functioning unit (through counselling, family therapy and so on). Most of the time this work goes on unnoticed as part of the normal practice of child protection. However, periodically there are calls of 'crisis' in this set of relationships. Let us specify this a little further.

A series of dislocations in the management of child protection suggest that the relation between the child, the family and the state is an enduring problematic of modern society. In Britain in the last thirty years there have been calls of 'crisis' surrounding the deaths of Maria Colwell (1973, Department of Health and Social Security 1974), Jasmine Beckford (1984, London Borough of Brent 1985), Kimberley Carlile (1986, London Borough of Greenwich 1987), Tyra Henry (1986/7, London Borough of Lambeth 1987), Victoria Climbié (2000, Laming 2003), and also around the events of Cleveland (1987, Butler-Sloss 1988), Nottingham (1988), Epping (1989), Rochdale (1989), and Orkney (1991, Clyde 1992).[4] The first five were cases of child physical abuse in which children died whilst under the supervision of social services; Cleveland centred on allegations of sexual abuse, attention focusing on a rise in the number of referrals to Cleveland General Hospital during 1987 and on the use of reflex anal dilatation as one of a cluster of signs of abuse; the final four cases listed involved allegations of sexual abuse, but became most widely known as 'ritual' or 'satanic' abuse cases. All centred on the legitimacy of particular distinctions between privacy and intervention, on the question of what degree and kind of intervention was appropriate and necessary to secure the well-being of the children concerned. Within this stream of episodes in the management of child abuse, two forms of discourse concerning 'crisis' can be distinguished. These have been expressed in different ways.

First, some cases, such as those surrounding Maria Colwell, Jasmine Beckford, Kimberley Carlile, Tyra Henry, and Victoria Climbié, have been articulated as crises of care and resources. In these cases, children died due to perceived inadequacies in the responsible social workers' training, powers and resources. Social workers were regarded as not having acted when they should. Responses to these failures to act have taken the form of demands for increases in the density and accuracy of knowledge and powers in this arena, rather than a questioning of the efficacy of the knowledge and practices of child protection as such. That is, such cases have led to demands for greater knowledge of the problem area to be produced and disseminated through training, sometimes accompanied by a call for increased powers for those engaged in the task of child protection. Therefore, the first form of 'crisis' connected with the management of child protection is one expressed in terms of resources available to child protection practitioners, in particular relating to the quality of their training and the adequacy of the available legal powers (Clarke 1993; National Institute for Social Work 1982; Parton 1985a). Discussions focused on problems of resources have not fundamentally called into question the rationality of contemporary strategies of child protection. What agencies of welfare should do is not at issue in this form of discussion, rather the question whether social workers are carrying out the job of child protection properly is primarily centred on whether they have sufficient resources, powers and training adequately to fulfil this role.

By contrast, the second form of 'crisis' questions the validity of contemporary child protection strategies. This second type of crisis evaluation involves both a questioning of legitimacy in which the relationship between the family and the state is at issue, and an interrogation of expertise in which the knowledge base and professionalism of agencies of child protection are subject to sceptical questioning. Such questioning raises issues concerning the epistemological adequacy of knowledge and the legitimate exercise of powers within the task of child protection itself. This 'double crisis' renders child protection practice problematic by problematising the grounds of knowledge that legitimate acts of intervention by child protection agencies. Such calls of crisis are exemplified by the events of, and responses to, Cleveland and Orkney.

Cleveland

The Cleveland child sexual abuse case became a national issue in the middle of 1987 when the media took up a dispute concerning the number of children being taken into the care of social services under Place of Safety Orders (PSOs) following suspicion of sexual abuse.[5] During this time, the events unfolding in Cleveland were elaborated by the press as an issue of the family versus the state (Campbell 1988) and a moral panic was created around the issue of parental rights over children, against the power of the state to remove children from families (Bell 1988). This panic centred on the diagnostic procedures used in suspected abuse cases, and focused principally on the medical sign of reflex anal dilatation (RAD) and on techniques used to interview the children. The cases therefore combined questions concerning the definition of appropriate medical truth, the evidential value of disclosure interviews and concerns over the appropriate boundaries of state action.

Concern with and recognition of child sexual abuse as a specific problem had grown amongst social workers, paediatricians and police during the early 1980s and new procedures for addressing this problem were being developed by child protection agencies across the country (Corby 1993; Droisen and Driver 1989; *Feminist Review* 1988). In Cleveland, the increased attention being given to child sexual abuse took the form of attempts to design new systems for joint police and social services investigation of cases, and the appointment in 1986 of a specialist consultant, Sue Richardson, to the Social Services Department. Thus at the time of what became known as the Cleveland crisis in 1987, the different agencies involved in child protection were working toward new procedures for addressing child sexual abuse.

In January 1987, Dr Marietta Higgs was appointed consultant paediatrician at Middlesborough General Hospital; she, together with Dr Geoffrey Wyatt (consultant paediatrician at Middlesborough from 1983 onwards) began using anal dilatation as one of a cluster of signs to indicate potential sexual abuse. Reflex anal dilatation had been suggested as a sign in the clinical diagnosis of child sexual abuse in an article published by Leeds paediatricians Jane Wynne and Christopher Hobbs in the *Lancet* in 1986 (Wynne and Hobbs 1986). This sign had a long history of recognition within forensic medicine. The *Lancet* article suggested that it could be a vital sign, amongst others, in clinical diagnosis. The use of RAD as a clinical sign was criticised by police surgeons involved in Cleveland, including Dr Raine Roberts and Dr Alistair Irvine.

Suspected cases of child sexual abuse in Cleveland rose from twenty-five in January 1987 to 110 by June of that year. Many of the children concerned were admitted to and retained in Cleveland General Hospital under Place of Safety Orders (PSOs) following initial diagnoses, with disclosure interviews used to follow up suspicions of sexual abuse. As the number of referrals increased relations between the police and social services deteriorated, with the police rejecting joint investigations in May. At the same time, parents began to dispute the diagnosis of anal dilatation, and to protest the use of PSOs to detain their children at Cleveland General Hospital. Meanwhile, the children's wards at the hospital became increasingly overcrowded, with the paediatricians refusing to limit the number of admissions pertaining to alleged sexual abuse on the basis that their overriding concern was for the children's welfare.

In June 1987 Stuart Bell, the local MP, gave a speech to Parliament accusing social services and paediatricians in Cleveland of resisting police involvement in sexual abuse investigations, and suggesting that Cleveland social services were empire building. At the same time, parents organised a campaign group that was supported by Bell and the group Parents Against Injustice (PAIN). Bell passed on a dossier of materials on the cases to Tony Newton MP, the then Conservative Government Health Minister.

Overall 121 children were involved. The crisis continued throughout 1987, resulting in the removal of Dr Marietta Higgs from her position as paediatrician at Cleveland General Hospital. In July 1987 a statutory inquiry into the affair was instituted, headed by Lord Justice Butler-Sloss; this reported in July 1988

(Butler-Sloss 1988). In December 1988 Drs Higgs and Wyatt were barred from further sexual abuse work.[6]

The public inquiry that followed the Cleveland events had a wide remit and extensive powers. It set out to examine the arrangements existing in Cleveland in 1987 for dealing with suspected cases of child abuse, paying particular attention to cases of child sexual abuse, and to make recommendations (Butler-Sloss 1988: 4, 1). The inquiry paid close attention to the procedures that had been used in order to take children into care, and to the evidential grounds underpinning the measures taken. To do this, the inquiry set about ascertaining the facts of the case. However, 'the facts' were not just unknown but at issue in the case in the dispute over RAD and the evidential worth of disclosure interviews. The inquiry engaged in a protracted discussion of the evidential problems attending RAD and disclosure. It identified these problems as due to a remediable lack of knowledge; implicitly suggesting that if and when we have sufficient knowledge of sexual abuse, paediatricians and other professionals will concur in their diagnoses and problems of the kind experienced in Cleveland will be avoided in future. However, on the basis of the evidence available to the paediatricians and social workers involved, it concluded that the actions taken in this case had been precipitous.

In addition to recommending more research into child sexual abuse, the inquiry made a number of recommendations to improve child protection procedures. Many of these were incorporated into the Children Act 1989, and into the Department of Health guidelines *Working Together* (Department of Health 1991a).[7] In particular, the Children Act 1989 emphasised the provision of a clear legal framework for child protection policy, replaced PSOs with Emergency Protection Orders (EPOs) limiting the time children may be held in care without corroborative evidence of harm, and providing greater rights for parents to challenge child protection decisions (Bainham 1990a, 1991; Lyon and de Cruz 1993; Parton 1992).

Orkney

The Orkney case began on 27 February 1991, when nine children from four Orkney families were taken into care following allegations of organised sexual abuse. The children were taken into care under PSOs during early morning visits to houses conducted jointly by police and social workers.[8]

The allegations were that 'lewd and libidinous practices' (Clyde 1992: 6.57, 101) had taken place between adults and children, the children allegedly having been sexually abused in organised acts carried out in a quarry on South Ronaldsay. The children were removed to be medically examined and interviewed, while the local Church of Scotland Minister, the Reverend Morris McKenzie, and the children's parents were questioned by the police. The minister and families involved had been trying to help a family whose children had been taken into care earlier and some of the parents believed this was why they were subjected to social work suspicion and 'dawn raids' (*The Times* 1.3.91; Clyde 1992: 2.39–2.43, 23–4).

The children were returned home on 4 April 1991. This followed a hearing on the grounds for referral conducted by Sheriff Kelbie, who judged the proceedings incompetent and dismissed the cases without hearing all the evidence (Clyde 1992: 12.2, 203, 12, 345). While it would have been technically possible for the authorities to continue with the case, Kelbie had indicated that in his opinion the children should returned to their parents and, in view of the difficulty of establishing new grounds for further PSOs, and the adverse effects of the 'enormous media publicity' given to Kelbie's statements on the credibility of any witnesses, those involved did not feel that this was possible (Clyde 1992: 12.2, 203, 12.34, 12.35, 209, 12.25, 207). Kelbie's decision to dismiss the case was nonetheless appealed and his judgement overturned (Clyde 1992: 12.2, 203). In May 1991 any case for the prosecution of parents was dropped; in July the children were removed from the child protection register (Clyde 1992: 12.37, 209–10). Following a preliminary hearing in July 1991, a full judicial inquiry was undertaken, headed by Lord Clyde and lasting from August 1991 until March 1992 (Clyde 1992).

At the end of the 1980s and beginning of the 1990s in the UK a number of cases of alleged sexual abuse of children were accompanied by claims that the victims had been subjected to ritual practices in the course of being sexually abused. The general context of the Orkney case was thus a rise in public and professional concern about organised, 'ritual' and 'satanic' abuse. Whilst the press regularly referred to the Orkney case as involving allegations of 'ritual' abuse, the social workers involved in the case did not regard the term 'ritual' as applicable to the case (Clyde 1992: 15.10, 268); this nonetheless played an important part in the public discrediting of the interventions (see Chapter 7).

La Fontaine has documented the process whereby workshops and seminars on ritual abuse organised in the UK during this period called upon a number of 'specialists',[9] mostly from North America, claiming to be able to assist in the diagnosis of, and providing written material concerning indicators of, ritual and satanic abuse. La Fontaine points out that some of those active in developing ideas and practice around ritual and satanic abuse during this period were fundamentalist Christians, that some were social workers or therapists, but that they constituted a 'heterogeneous category of people with little in common except a committed belief in the existence of satanic abuse' (La Fontaine 1994: 20).

According to press reports the period leading up to the Orkney events involved the growth of religious fundamentalism on the islands in the form of the Orkney Christian Fellowship. This was a Calvinist sect which had broken away from the Church of Scotland 5 years previously and which involved belief in faith healing, the laying on of hands, demonology and speaking in tongues as a method to gain access to the word of God (*The Times* 6.4.91). In the year prior to the Orkney case, rumours of satanic practices, though not involving sexual abuse, had emerged following an Orkney Christian Fellowship summer camp from which children are reported to have returned 'visibly affected', with personality changes, hysteria and so on (*The Times* 17.3.91).

In November 1990, a conference on ritual abuse was held in Aberdeen; the press suggest that this was attended by one of the Orkney social workers (*The Times*

6.4.91). This seminar reportedly brought ideas similar to those involved in the Rochdale case to Orkney.[10] The conference involved lectures by Maureen Davies, described by critics as founder of the 'British Inquisition' and as 'a fundamentalist Christian and self-appointed "expert" on ritual and satanic abuse' (*The Times* 17.3.91). She had advised Rochdale social workers whose allegations of ritual abuse had subsequently been dismissed as 'fantasy' by Mr Justice Brown. Davies was depicted as believing that satanic abuse was widespread in Britain. Her lectures apparently involved discussion of a number of 'satanic indicators' among children that she suggested could be regarded as signs of abuse, such signs included 'writing backwards, mutilating dolls, talking about ghosts and being frightened of police' (*The Times* 17.3.91).

Prior to these events, in 1987 an Orkney man was convicted and imprisoned for the physical and sexual abuse of some of his children;[11] several of the children from this family were within the care network in 1991 as there was evidence of continuing sexual abuse (Clyde 1992: 2.36, 23). This, the 'W' family, was the family to whom the four families involved in the allegations of organised abuse had offered their support, regarding the authorities as uncaring and unreasonable in keeping the children in care. Following the events of February 1991, the parents accused the social workers of running a vendetta against them because they were successful in publicising their concern for the children in care and their mother.

The original allegations leading to the removal of the children came from children from the 'W' family. While in care in February 1991, three of the children made statements indicating that the nine children of the four families involved had been involved in sexual abuse (Clyde 1992: 2.69–2.82, 31–6). A few days later a decision was made to seek Place of Safety Orders for the children; these were granted on the 26 February 1991. The next day at 7 a.m., having sought assistance from the RSSPCC, the police and Strathclyde and Central regional councils' social work departments, four joint teams of police and social workers went to the homes of the four families and removed the children. The children were then flown to placements in Highland and Strathclyde. During their 5 weeks in care they were kept from contact with one another and from their parents. While in care, the children underwent interviews with the RSSPCC and the police.[12] The impetus for the removal of the nine children at the centre of this case in February 1991 were therefore allegations made by children of the 'W' family already in care, rather than from the nine children themselves of from concerned third parties.

Throughout the 5 weeks of the children being in care, and even after the order returning them home, the Director of Social Services, Paul Lee, maintained that the children had been abused and that they continued to need protection. In opposition to this claim, the parents and their supporters had formed the South Ronaldsay Action Group (SRAG), assisted by PAIN, to campaign for the return of the children and claiming a social work vendetta against them. The situation was thus one of social workers acting on the assumption of the truth of children's statements while SRAG, PAIN, and the media countered this assumption with sceptical disbelief. Popular disbelief in children's statements, exacerbated by press presentations of the SWD case as involving allegations of 'ritual' abuse, was then deepened by mishandling of interviews with the children whilst in care and by social work defensiveness in the face of media attention. This culminated in the wholesale discrediting of the case.

First, medical evidence of either physical or sexual abuse gained from examining the nine children proved negative (Clyde 1992: 9.6, 136, 10.7, 148). Lack of medical evidence meant that the social work case had to rely on the children's statements of abuse and the possibility that they may have been subjected to 'simulated sexual intercourse' and 'moral danger' (Gordon Sloan, Reporter to the Children's Panel, quoted in *The Times* 26.3.91). Second, this claim was interpreted by those opposing the removal of the children as unjustifiably defensive social work, presuming that the parents were 'guilty until proven innocent' (Church of Scotland statement in *The Times* 1.4.91). Third, and finally in the process leading to the discrediting of the social work case, evidence emerged that the children had been coached or led into answering questions (Clyde 1992: 14.60–14.101, 252–62).

The abuse of legal procedures concerning the rights of both parents and children to attend hearings of the Children's Panel where PSOs were being discussed led to the immediate release of the children, leaving the question of the truth or otherwise of the allegations unanswered and the case impossible to continue. Proceedings thus came to a halt with Sheriff Kelbie's decision to dismiss the case.

At appeal, Sheriff Kelbie was himself rebuked by three senior Scottish judges for dismissing the allegations without hearing the evidence and for making inappropriate remarks in public which made any attempt to continue the case practically impossible (*The Independent* 13.6.91; Clyde 1992: 12.25, 207). Therefore, the case foundered on the issue of incorrect procedures for taking children from families and conducting interviews, as an issue of the rights of parents and children, rather than directly on evidential issues. This set the tone for the inquiry that followed, which dealt exclusively with procedural issues and the relationships between the professionals involved, avoiding directly confronting the truth or otherwise of the allegations and thereby not providing clear judgement on the guilt or innocence of the parties involved (Clyde 1992: 1.10, 4).

The question of what actually happened in Orkney remains, as in Cleveland, subject to dispute. There has been no final decision as to the truth or otherwise of the allegations. The question of the evidence used by the local authority to bring these cases concerns the question of the value of children's disclosures, video reports, social workers accepting the truth of children's statements, and so on. The Orkney cases were discredited by the media to the point of being impossible to continue, while the focus on social work abuse of procedure within the inquiry left the question of the truth or otherwise of the allegations of abuse unresolved.

*****

Having given a preliminary account of the cases that form the substantive focus of this book, we can return to the distinction between calls of 'crisis' relating to resources and calls of 'crisis' relating to the rationality of practices of child protection outlined earlier. We are now in a position to elaborate this distinction.

We can develop the distinction between 'crises' of resources and 'crises' of rationality through a brief examination of the emergence of official recognition of different forms of child abuse. Hacking points out that child abuse is a 'normalising concept', where 'normal' bridges the distinction between 'is' and 'ought', producing a 'complicated play between what is usual and right' (Hacking 1991: 286–7). This points to the way in which 'child abuse' is an idea established in relation to the distinction between the normal and the pathological, that is, it is an idea generated within discourses of science and resting upon an understanding of 'normal' childhood development. This set of discourses is immanently related to a set of moral ideas concerning what is right, and these we find instantiated in legal frameworks governing child protection practice. Thus the concept of 'child abuse' is simultaneously veridically and juridically constituted, it is both a scientific and a legal concept. This has important implications for the ways in which different forms of child abuse achieve and sustain recognition as appropriately public concerns. It also points to the problematic character of child sexual abuse as compared with physical abuse.

Both physical harm and sexual molestation of children were recognised as issues of concern prior to the 1960s, as evidenced by legislation and philanthropic action in relation to child cruelty and neglect (see below). In America in 1962, Kempe and Kempe identified physical harm to children as 'battered child syndrome', a condition that could be diagnosed through the use of X-rays (Pfohl 1977). This medicalised the problem, providing a stable set of signs for the diagnosis of physical abuse that could be used as grounds for action to protect children.

In this context, the death of Maria Colwell in Britain in 1973 produced an articulation of 'crisis' surrounding child physical abuse against a backdrop of stable scientific understanding of the signs of such abuse.[13] Whilst this event brought increased public and professional attention to physical abuse, the concern provoked by her death did not take the form of questioning what evidence would satisfactorily ground child protection measures, but rather was couched in terms of a series of attacks on the professionalism of social workers. Social workers were perceived to have failed to achieve an established objective, the protection of children from physical abuse and neglect (Parton 1985a). Such attacks were not centred on questioning the efficacy of the knowledge available in order to justify intervention; rather they were focused on inadequacies in existing practices of protection. The central problem was identified by the inquiry as a lack of training, powers and resources on the part of social services adequately to fulfil their responsibilities for child protection.

Thus the death of Maria Colwell was articulated as a crisis of resources in relation to an already established problem, namely child physical abuse. The governmental response to this tragedy was essentially a bureaucratic one. Colwell's death led to increased public concern about the accountability of social workers and to a restructuring of the relationships between the state, the family and social work, in which social workers experienced increased monitoring and control

(Parton 1985a). This trend continued throughout the 1970s, with the establishment of Area Review Committees and Non-Accidental Injury Registers, line management of social workers, and the establishment of closer mechanisms for liaison between social workers and police. Together these developments represent an increased awareness of problems of child abuse, and greater use of statutory powers such as PSOs in dealing with it (Parton and Jordan 1983).

The decade between 1972 and 1982 saw a 20 per cent increase in the use of court orders in admitting children into care (Parton 1985b). This represents a shift to a more impersonal, administrative response to child abuse and protection, and an increasingly adversarial relationship between social workers and families. The deaths, through physical abuse and neglect, of Jasmine Beckford, Kimberley Carlile and Tyra Henry during the 1980s further intensified this set of concerns.

In contrast to the cases of physical abuse discussed above, we have seen that in Cleveland and Orkney concerns about the appropriate use of powers by social workers in relation to suspected child sexual abuse were underscored by contestation over what would constitute sufficient evidence of such abuse. The former concerns took the shape of critical questioning of the appropriateness of the use of PSOs to take children from parents and keep them in care, intensified in Cleveland by a failure to administer the situation appropriately such that the number of referrals to Cleveland General Hospital outstripped its capacity. The latter concern is demonstrated by the critical attention given to the development of the local paediatric practice of using reflex anal dilatation (RAD) as one of a cluster of diagnostic signs in Cleveland, alongside concerns about the veracity of evidence gained through disclosure interviews with the children in both of the cases. In these cases, RAD failed to become established as a sign in the clinical diagnosis of child sexual abuse, and disclosure interviews were contested on the grounds that they constituted the fabrication of evidence by interviewers. In short, in Cleveland and Orkney there was a failure to achieve consensus concerning the meaning and evidential value of RAD and disclosure amongst medical doctors and psychologists. In the absence of stable and agreed understandings amongst experts concerning determinate signs of child sexual abuse, these cases became impossible to sustain.[14] These cases were therefore expressed as crises of rationality: the legitimacy of the interventions was undermined as the expertise underpinning the diagnoses was questioned.

At this point it is useful to make a preliminary specification of the forms of reasoning that converge to produce concern for, and calls of 'crisis' in, child protection. We can do this by reference to the transformation of liberalism produced by growing concerns for welfare from the latter part of the nineteenth century. The increasing importance of a range of scientific discourses within governance from this time, especially in the emerging field of child welfare, transformed classical liberalism. Within liberal welfare rationality, liberalism provides the foundation of legal rationality and concerns for welfare, expressed in medicine, psychology and later in social work, provide scientific knowledge of that which is to be governed. Liberal welfare rationality thus operates through mobilising the vocabulary and values of both liberalism (rights, due process, and so on) and welfare (needs, best interests, and so on).

Liberal welfare rationality contains a tension between a juridical discourse predicated on the division of the political and nonpolitical within which, for example, the notion of parents' rights is articulated, and a range of normalising discourses predicated on forms of knowledge within which the idea of children's welfare and best interests is articulated. The ambivalence contained by liberal welfare rationality can thus be stated in terms of the juridical presupposition of the family as private, as a realm that should in principle be free from state inter-ference, combined with a normalising presupposition of the family as public, focus falling on the needs and interests of children whose welfare is central to the management of the population and future of the state.

Within liberal welfare rationalities, legitimacy in intervention to secure child protection is founded on the idea of competent knowledge, forms of practice and expertise with which to govern in law, medicine, psychology and social work. In other words, the boundary between privacy and intervention is maintained and re-articulated through notions of competency and the possibility of predictive, preventive and therapeutic knowledge of the social domain. Calls of 'crisis' that question not only the resources of agencies of child protection but also the rationality of child protection practice combine concerns with legitimacy, in which the relationship between the family and the state is at issue, and concerns with expertise, in which the knowledge and professional practice of agencies of child protection are subject to interrogation as their efficacy and veracity is questioned. This form of problematisation has led not simply to calls for greater or lesser powers of intervention (though such calls have been present), but has also opened questions concerning the professional knowledge base of the claims to legitimacy of interventionist practices in the governance of child sexual abuse, thus demonstrating the ways in which the distinction between public and private is adjudicated though claims to competent practice based on credible evidence, which in turn assists in sustaining the claim to the possibility of governing reasonably.

If one interprets cases concerning the sexual abuse of children as pointing to a tension in liberal welfare rationality that is most evident in calls of 'crisis' and in ensuing public inquiries, then what is at stake? Arguably, the distinctions and forms of knowledge by which this rationality is articulated: distinctions between the public and private spheres, and between the respective competencies of legal and scientific discourses, and the forms of knowledge that might underwrite these distinctions. Before we examine how adequate are a number of major contemporary theories in analysing these tensions in the governance of child sexual abuse, we need to give some account of how the distinction between public and private life and legal and scientific knowledge have come to configure modern childhood and child (sexual) abuse.

Constituting child sexual abuse as an object of governance: childhood, family privacy and moral reform

> We have had something like our concept of child abuse for less than thirty years. [. . .] Prior to that we had a number of ideas that were kept quite distinct, ranging from cruelty to children to child molestation. [. . .] Since 1962 the class of acts falling under 'child abuse' has changed every few years, so that people who have not kept up to date are astonished to be told that the present primary connotation of child abuse is sexual abuse.
>
> (Hacking 1991: 259)

Child sexual abuse became a fully fledged public issue in Britain as a result of events in Cleveland in 1987. Concern with and recognition of sexual abuse as a specific problem had grown within feminist politics from the 1970s and within social work and paediatrics through the 1970s and 1980s, where it gained increased recognition as part of more general child protection practice (Corby 1993; Droisen and Driver 1989; *Feminist Review* 1988). However, although contemporary concerns about children and sex have taken a specific form, with the term 'child sexual abuse' only recently crystallising in professional and public debate, fears about the connection between children, delinquency and vice were an important part of nineteenth century child-saving. Adult sexual relations with children gained recognition as a criminal offence in England and Wales with the Punishment of Incest Act of 1908. The more recent public prominence of issues concerning children and sex is thus at once the re-emergence of a set of general ambivalences over the relationship between the family and public authorities, evident in a number of different forms in Britain since the late nineteenth century (Ferguson 1992), and at the same time represents the constitution of a new object of governance. The contemporary constitution of concerns about children and sex as 'child sexual abuse' is subsequent to and a product of the organisation of specific forms of knowledge and practice on a particular site; it is an object of governance that has taken shape in the context of social workers' attempts to govern families and in the interstices of legal, medical and psychological ideas about childhood. In order to understand contemporary manifestations of these concerns with childhood and sexual abuse, it is necessary briefly to examine the history of childhood, the constitution of a norm of family privacy, and of the forms of legal and scientific knowledge and practice that underpin modern practices of child protection.

There is a growing literature on the history of the family and of childhood, not least because of an ever-increasing recognition of the difficulties of drawing firm or fixed conclusions about the respective roles of the family and state in connection with the raising of children. Of particular concern here is to elucidate the interrelationship between conceptions of childhood as a distinct and special phase of life, the growth of privacy of familial relations and the emergence of social reform. The development of modern understandings of childhood have been tied to the constitution of the family as a private space and to the development of distinct forms of knowledge and practice concerned with child welfare. The confluence of family privacy and social intervention, guided by legal and therapeutic knowledge, has provided the context within which child abuse is conceptualised and managed and it is this which must be analysed in order to understand the intractable problems surrounding the governance of child abuse and protection, as well as the tenacity of the political rationality of which these practices form a part.

A number of writers have emphasised that concepts of the family and of childhood have changed radically over time. Such work suggests that the private nuclear family as a normative model for parent–child relationships in western countries is very recent (Aries 1962; Flandrin 1979; Shorter 1976). Between the traditional and modern family we can discern a movement toward the social segregation and specialisation of the conjugal unit and an increasing importance attributed to privacy, whereas until the seventeenth century the family was constituted within a domain of wider sociability. This change, the 'privatisation' of the family, is central to our understanding of the modern division of labour between the public and the private spheres in the context of child welfare. The development of a 'private' realm, separate from the 'public' domain of social life, is important in forming the context for the emergence of modern notions of childhood, parenthood and of contemporary concerns over child sexuality and, therefore, possible abuse. These concerns, in turn, lead to 'public' interventions into these 'private' units.

Aries's *Centuries of Childhood* (1962) was a groundbreaking book in the modern concern with the history of childhood, inaugurating a new branch of social history and forming the basis of a number of continuing disagreements within historical analysis and the social sciences more generally.[15] This debate is important to our concerns, because the thesis Aries advances provides a case for recognition of a number of important changes in conceptions of childhood being accompanied by transformations in the relations between public and private life, and by the emergence of novel forms of knowledge of childhood and of family relations. Whilst this book has been subject to extensive critical discussion amongst historians, it has been of enduring importance in emphasising the specificity of modern conceptions of childhood. The main points of Aries's argument will be outlined below and followed by a brief reflection on the work of other historians who have contributed to our understanding of the distinctiveness of modern childhood. In the final part of this chapter we will return briefly to Aries, taking up the dispute his work has caused amongst historians, and within social and political theory and social policy, disputes that demonstrate amply the dominance and tenacity of current evaluations of childhood.

Aries is concerned with the cultural construction of a concept of childhood, with the emergence of childhood as an idea:

> In medieval society the idea of childhood did not exist: this is not to suggest that children were neglected, forsaken or despised. The idea of childhood is

not to be confused with affection for children: it corresponds to an awareness of the particular nature of childhood, that particular nature which distinguishes the child from the adult, even the young adult. In medieval society this awareness was lacking.

(Aries 1962: 128)[16]

Using a range of sources, including paintings, diaries and evidence drawn from the writings of churchmen and pedagogues,[17] Aries documents a shift from medieval society, which he argues had no distinct concept of childhood, children and adults mixing freely from the age of 7 (Aries 1962: 128), to the sixteenth and seventeenth centuries which saw the gradual separation of childhood from adulthood. Thus, the children of the upper classes began to be given distinguishing marks of their own status, such as special costumes. He documents the division of this process between upper and lower classes and also between male and female children. Aries argues that this process occurred first among the upper classes from the seventeenth century, only beginning among the lower classes in the late eighteenth and nineteenth centuries. Female children, due to their exclusion from formal schooling, were only briefly constituted as children; until the seventeenth century girls were considered women by the age of 10, and not infrequently married in their early teens (Aries 1962: 319, 331–2).

The first attitude Aries identifies in this specialisation of childhood from the sixteenth century was 'coddling' (Aries 1962: 131). This developed within the family. Children were seen as sweet, simple and droll, to be enjoyed by their parents and relations. However, once they had passed the age of 5 to 7 they entered the adult world (Aries 1962: 329). By the late sixteenth and seventeenth centuries, a second attitude had developed, appearing outside the family among churchmen and pedagogues attempting to influence families. These moralists and pedagogues were not interested in the child as an object of amusement but rather concerned with its psychological and moral well-being and education (Aries 1962: 131). They emphasised the need to develop the child's capacities of reasoning through formal training. Both groups, parents and pedagogues, showed a new awareness of childhood as a special phase, although the latter regarded children not as toys, but as 'fragile creatures of God' (Aries 1962: 133) who needed safeguarding and reform. Aries suggests that this externally generated attitude in turn passed into family life, as a perception adopted and reinforced by parents.

This moment, which Aries locates as that of the birth of the modern concept of childhood, corresponded with the emergence of modern schooling (Aries 1962: 329), with ideas of a long childhood education and, concomitantly, of adult responsibility for the child's morality and education. This involved a reformed notion of discipline, not as external and extreme violence, but as moral and spiritual formation, seen as having intrinsic value in building a 'good' human being (Aries 1962: 333). Thus, by the eighteenth and nineteenth centuries, children were increasingly receiving supervision in school, while it was expected that parents would respect the school cycle (by not taking children away to work) and also assume responsibility for their children's formation as moral beings. From the eighteenth century onwards, therefore, adulthood and childhood have been increasingly distinguished in terms of autonomy and dependence (see Chapter 2).

This change in attitudes and the increase in the level and amount of schooling corresponded to a shift from life lived in a collective society, a sociality of the street (Aries 1962: 405) with the 'family' basically having the functions of the transference of property and name, the conditions of social life providing little room for the private family, to the eighteenth century decline in sociability as the privacy of the family increased (Aries 1962: 406). On this account, by the late eighteenth century an attitude of protection, reform and a new concern over hygiene and physical health surrounded children as they took a central place within the family (Aries 1962: 411). These themes are echoed in Sennett's account of the ways in which, since the eighteenth century, individuals have sought to defend themselves against social life (Sennett 1978), and in the work of Shorter (1976), and Flandrin (1979), all of whom regard sentiment as increasingly important to the family as it becomes a domain held together through emotional bonds rather than lineage.

Reflecting on this, we can say that the modern family is primarily concerned not with lineage, but with child welfare. The family has become an increasingly important social site as general sociability has decreased (Barrett and McIntosh 1982). From the eighteenth century people began defending themselves against social life and became increasingly concerned to safeguard the privacy of the family (Aries 1962: 406). At the same time, the emergence of the modern family and of schooling removed children from adult society, so that the distinction between adult autonomy and childhood dependence became increasingly marked from this time.

The separation of childhood from adulthood and the development of a private sphere therefore form part of the same process. This is important in providing the context for modern experiences of and concern with child sexual abuse (Droisen and Driver 1989; La Fontaine 1990; McIntosh 1988). Since the seventeenth century increasing appreciation of privacy and emphasis on domesticity has meant the home has been regarded as a haven (Lasch 1977), spawning, for example, the culture of domestic womanhood (Smart 1992), and providing the site for and problematic of child sexual abuse.

Turning from this account of a culturally conceived construction of a concept of childhood to a specifically public construction of childhood as a domain of power, we can fill in important gaps left by Aries's account. Whilst Aries, coming from the *Annales* school and writing a history of *mentalities*, focuses on childhood as a predominantly cultural construct, other writers have been concerned to elucidate the emergence of a distinct conception of childhood in the transformed economic relations of industrialism, and in the emergence of modern legal orders and scientifically grounded medical practice.

Recent work on economic and demographic change suggests that industrialisation did not generate new family structures in Europe, but did have considerable impact on the functions previously carried out by families, that industrialisation transferred production to other institutions, with the family becoming increasingly centred on consumption and the nurturing of children (Hareven 1987; Laslett

1987). Through industrialisation, therefore, families became increasingly privatised and inward looking.

Thane identifies an important gap in Aries's work concerning the impact of economic change on definitions of childhood, arguing that in addition to recognising the impact of Calvinism and the Enlightenment in providing ideas which helped generate a lengthened period of childhood, it is also necessary to examine the effects of the development of capitalism on the need for tighter control over the next generation, both in terms of ensuring that acquired wealth was not dissipated by careless marriage and loose discipline, and in terms of the training necessary to provide the skills to succeed in the emerging commercial society (Thane 1981: 10). Thane argues that these pressures were experienced first by the new entrepreneurial middle classes, later by the landed elite who felt competition from this new group, and by the labouring poor when the changing nature of work produced demands for greater education, discipline and physical efficiency. Aries fails adequately to analyse class differences in developing concepts of childhood due to a lack of attention to economic processes; his account of the emergence of modern conceptions of childhood should be supplemented by an account of economic and wider processes of change.

Cunningham relates transformations in knowledge and concern surrounding childhood to economic processes. He examines how, in the context of the emergence of secular views of children and childhood from the eighteenth century, the industrial revolution changed the character and context of child labour and produced conditions for the increased visibility of poor children, visibility which was a precondition of campaigns for reform and for the development of nineteenth-century child-saving (Cunningham 1995: 187–8).

Transformations in ideas of childhood are evidenced by the emergence of specialised forms of knowledge centred upon the child; particularly important are a series of developments in the practices of law and medicine and the emergence of nineteenth-century philanthropic activity and twentieth-century social work centred on childhood. Within law, there has been a shift from the status of childhood in early modern Europe, where childhood as such received little recognition in legal statutes, to the nineteenth- and twentieth-century production of a range of legal limitations on and protections of children. There have been a number of important transformations and elaborations of the status of the child in legislation from the nineteenth-century Factory Acts onward. Cunningham notes that, while these acts can be seen as the continuation of the legal regulation of child labour provided by a long history of Apprenticeship Acts,[18] so that intervention to regulate child labour was not novel to the nineteenth century, nonetheless nineteenth-century legislation had a distinct character and purpose: 'It was not therefore the principle of state intervention in the child labour market which was the novelty of the period beginning in 1830; that principle was well-established. The novelty was the first voicing of the assertion that children had a right not to work at all' (Cunningham 1995: 138). He goes on to argue that 'a child was becoming defined as someone who was not a "free agent", who was dependent, and therefore in need of protection by law' (Cunningham 1995: 140–1).

Nineteenth-century philanthropy and increased state concern with the physical and mental fitness of the population, at a time of growing fear of a residuum undermining national efficiency, were vital to these developments. Through the latter part of the nineteenth century the Society for the Prevention of Cruelty to Children (from 1889 the NSPCC) campaigned for reform of the criminal law in relation to child abuse and neglect and for the establishment of a child inspectorate.[19] This, combined with the growth of a national crisis concerning the physical and mental fitness of the population for work and for war, and a number of studies of urban poverty, such as Mearns and Preston's *The Bitter Cry of Outcast London* (1883) and the Royal Commission on the Housing of the Working Classes (1884–5) produced a number of Acts of Parliament which more closely defined the conditions of childhood. In this context, the 1880 Education Act made elementary education compulsory and made parents responsible for ensuring that their children attended school. The 1889 Prevention of Cruelty to Children Act brought fines or imprisonment for anyone with custody of a child found guilty of causing unnecessary suffering through ill-treatment, neglect or abandonment. This act also further restricted child employment by making the responsible adult punishable rather than the child. It allowed wives to testify against husbands and provided that child victims no longer had to give evidence under oath (Rose 1991). Provisions were made for the medical examination of children suspected of being cruelly treated and local authorities were given powers to assume parental rights in such cases; the NSPCC established a national network of inspectors on the basis of this legislation. The 1908 Children Act or 'Children's Charter' consolidated these powers and established separate children's courts, with the Punishment of Incest Act in the same year making incest a criminal offence.[20]

Accompanying these legal changes was the development of a number of medical and psychological ideas concerning the specific nature of childhood. Within medical and other literature, the nineteenth and twentieth centuries have seen the emergence of the 'priceless child' (Zelizer 1985), paediatrics, psychology, psychoanalysis and social work being central to this (Armstrong 1983; Hendrick 1990, 1994; Rose 1985, 1990). Medical literature on child-rearing developed from the middle of the seventeenth century, growing rapidly through the eighteenth century (Jordanova 1989). Facilities specifically for children in hospitals emerged during the late eighteenth century, with children's hospitals growing in number in late nineteenth century Britain, accompanied by the development of paediatrics as an organised field of medical knowledge (Cooter 1992; Granshaw and Porter 1989).

Thus we can say that the period between 1880 and 1914 saw the emergence and institutionalisation of a distinctively modern conception of childhood (Hendrick 1994); the growth of laws concerning child protection combined with the medicalisation and psychologisation of childhood within schools, hospitals, children's homes and within families since the late nineteenth century has been important in producing a new domain of truth (Rose 1989). It is in this context that modern social work developed as a practice within which child protection was to gain special significance, and within which the concepts 'child abuse' and 'child sexual abuse' have emerged and gained their current salience.

Through the nineteenth and into the twentieth century, the protection of children from harm was mostly carried out by philanthropic organisations such as the NSPCC. This intervention largely focused on concern with child cruelty and neglect and was a question of 'child rescue' rather than 'prevention', removal of the child being the most frequent course of action (though philanthropic intervention also included attempts to achieve the moral reform of working class parents, see Packman 1981; Parton 1985a). The development of state social work did not come about until the implementation of the Children Act 1948.

The 1948 Children Act established state social work in Children's Departments, separating childcare from the Poor Law and philanthropy and establishing a professionalised approach to child care policy. Underpinning this shift was a new focus on children's emotional, as well as physical, well-being. Important here was work on maternal deprivation, such as Bowlby's *Maternal Care and Mental Health* (1951), which emphasised the importance of uninterrupted mother–infant attachment to the later emotional stability and social responsibility of children. These ideas entered social work training and brought increased emphasis on working with families to achieve prevention and rehabilitation rather than protecting children through severance from the family. The high point of this movement was the Seebohm Report (1968) and the act that followed it which produced Social Services Departments and generic social work training with social workers organised as professionals working within a bureaucratic framework.

Reflecting on developments since 1948 we can say that concerns to prevent harm to children and to rehabilitate families gave much wider scope for the regulation of family life than did previous practices of severance. New ideas and practices of child welfare grounded in medicine and psychology have extended a strategy of power into the family and produced new concepts, including 'child physical abuse' as separate from cruelty and neglect, and 'child sexual abuse' as something distinct from earlier notions of sexual molestation and incest. At the same time, the policy of preventing family breakdown has meant that institutionalised care of children, the point where the state has to take over, has increasingly been regarded as a failure of policy, thus reinforcing the ideal of the natural, biologically based, nuclear family. In the last 50 years, therefore, child protection has involved an increasingly tense negotiation of the relation between public and private life through medically and psychologically derived concepts of 'normal' child development and its underside, the developmentally 'abnormal' child.

The modern notion of the child is accompanied by the idea of the private family and by a range of forms of specialist knowledge of childhood and its problems. Paediatrics, psychology and psychoanalysis focus on the physical, emotional and sexual problems of childhood and, through their organisation within child welfare services, are central to the articulation and maintenance of a distinction between public and private life (Cooter 1992; Donzelot 1979; Rose 1985, 1990). The emergence of the notion of childhood as a special phase is central both to the development of the privacy of familial relations and to the regulation of this privacy, so that today children and the problems of childhood are at the epicentre of relations between the family and the state (Donzelot 1979). In this context, there exists a tension between the idea of the family as a private sphere in itself and as a private sphere constituted and regulated by public concerns, not least by the medically and psychologically constituted object of concern the 'sexually abused child'.

To summarise this brief historical location of childhood and families as foci of concern and intervention, we can see that increased privacy of and within family relationships has been tied to the emergence of movements for social reform and to the development of professional knowledge about child care: privatism and moral reform accompany one another. The importance attributed to privacy and the specialisation of childhood, the idea of children as different from adults and in need of protection, are linked historically and are tied to the development of an interest in the moral reform and supervision of family relationships. In this, children are at once located within the private space of the family and form a central focus for the public regulation of these relationships. These two themes provide the context for a fundamental tension within current state policy between the assumption of the need to protect children and of a need for family autonomy and privacy (Frost and Stein 1989). The tension created by these twin assumptions is managed within liberal welfare rationality through the constitution of a public/private distinction informed by knowledge from legal and scientific discourses.

The stakes of contemporary childhood

This chapter has attempted to delineate the form that child sexual abuse has taken as a problem of governance, and to give some account of how society has come to problematise child sexual abuse in this way, through looking at the historical constitution of contemporary categories of the family, childhood and child abuse. In concluding this chapter, I want briefly to return to the ethical and governmental problems indicated by the term 'child sexual abuse' discussed at the beginning of this chapter. I suggested that the ethical problem denoted by the term 'child sexual abuse' is predicated on the assumption that children are or should be developmentally immature, dependent, vulnerable and innocent, and that the governmental problem denoted by the term 'child sexual abuse' is predicated on a distinction between public and private life, such that children are considered the natural responsibility of parents, but where state-sanctioned intervention is justified in instances where harm is discerned using evidence drawn from medicine and/or psychology. These ethical and governmental concerns are intertwined: the ethical evaluation that adult–child sexual relations constitute abuse underwrites and at the same time is itself partially constituted through those practices of governance that attempt to reconcile the privacy of families and the requirement to intervene where harm is caused to children. The question I wish to raise at this point is the effect of taking these evaluations as they stand.

My purpose in raising for question current valuations of childhood and child abuse arises not from a desire to disregard the pain of those who experience child sexual abuse, nor from an unrealistic assumption that we could abandon the category childhood in modern complex societies, but from a sense that these evaluations, and the practices of governance that they articulate, tie us powerfully into a logic in which it becomes increasingly difficult to think about how we might address these concerns differently. That this should be necessary is demonstrated by reiterations of 'crisis' in the governance of child protection outlined earlier. We can begin to reflect on this by looking briefly at the ways in which childhood is presented within social and political theory and social policy, and by assessing claims and assumptions made about the status of childhood within recent historiographical debates.

Within modern social and political theory the status of childhood is most often assumed. Childhood only rarely appears as a discrete topic of concern, and where it is explicitly theorised debate is most often framed around the question whether children should be accorded rights, or whether some relationship of guardianship and trust between parents/caretakers and children, and between those caretakers and the state, is a necessary consequence of children's dependence (Archard 1993, 1998; Fortin 1998; O'Neill 1989). More interesting is the manner in which most social and political theory simply assumes dominant conceptions of childhood. Such assumptions are rarely fully explicated, but nonetheless have a structuring effect of the main foci of attention; they frame questions concerning the appropriate scope and limits of state action, they implicitly colour the understandings, explanations and evaluations of contemporary state–family relations.

Where it is not expressly theorised within social and political theory, the figure of the child is implicitly endowed with dependence, innocence and potential. Children as potential citizens then become the concerns proper of social and political theory, and in particular the 'property' of welfarist notions of state and family. To elaborate, the conceptual distinction between adulthood and childhood is marked by distinctions between autonomy and dependence, public status and its privation. In making these distinctions, most theorists assume the modern category of childhood as characterised by the developmental models provided by medicine and psychology. As we will see in the chapters that follow, this set of assumptions works to ground and sustain a distinction between public and private spheres, such that social relations are theorised as necessarily divided between the privacy of families and the public realms of social and political life. Such assumptions make it difficult to formulate an analysis that does not itself presuppose some version of a public/private distinction and the modern nature of childhood as constituted by law and science. This will be taken up in more detail in Chapters 2 and 3, at this stage I want simply to raise a question: what are the stakes of assuming this conception and these parameters of childhood?

Here it is useful to return to Aries's thesis. This account has been subject to extensive criticism.[21] The most significant of these criticisms for our concerns is the charge of presentism, that Aries produces 'bad' history by interpreting the past in the light of present concerns. A number of writers have taken Aries to task on this point (Archard 1993; Pollock 1983; Vann 1982; Wilson 1980). This charge is framed, by Pollock (1983) and also by Archard (1993), in terms of a critique of the claim that no concept of childhood existed in the Middle Ages. Archard expresses this succinctly in stating that 'Aries judges that the past lacked a concept of childhood. In fact what the past lacked was our concept of childhood' (Archard 1993: 19).[22] In beginning to assess this, it is important to remember that Aries's concern is to discern the emergence of a 'particular nature' (Aries 1962: 128) attributed to childhood. His is an account of the cultural constitution of a category of childhood that we have supplemented by looking at the economic transformations and legal and medical developments that have produced our understanding of childhood as a distinct phase of life subject to specific forms of governance. To this extent, Archard's point is Aries's also: the past lacked our particular conception of childhood, that is, childhood was conceptualised differently in European societies prior to the nineteenth century.

However, the claim of presentism made against Aries's book should be looked at more closely. By examining the different ways in which this book has been taken up within social and political theory and social policy, we can disclose the high stakes of current debates concerning childhood. Moreover, we can develop both a way of reading Aries's text and a way of addressing childhood and child sexual abuse that will help to take us beyond the misplaced debate about whether childhood and child abuse have been 'invented' or 'discovered'. To do this, we will look briefly at some of the ways in which Aries's work has been taken up, examining the divergent ways in which this work has been interpreted as providing a strongly evaluative account, either of the growth of enlightenment or of domination in relation to child-rearing. We will then clarify the productivity of Aries's argument, and of other accounts that stress the historicity of our conceptions of childhood and child abuse, for our own concerns.

Attached to the charge of presentism in work within social and political theory and social policy is a determination to read Aries's book as a moral message. Some authors detect in Aries's account a trajectory from barbarism to a golden age of childhood: 'Aries subscribes to the historical understanding of "modernity" as the culmination of a long and painful passage to moral enlightenment' (Archard 1993: 21; also Pollock 1983).[23] Others see Aries as documenting a path from 'freedom' to 'confinement': 'Aries can be seen, therefore, as a child liberationist. He would like to undo the chains imposed by this modern concept of childhood and return to a more varied, open and liberated past' (Corby 1993: 8).

These very different readings of Aries's work reveal a determination to read the book as a directly evaluative account. In so doing, these receptions of Aries incorporate his work into current concerns with children as in need either of protection or of liberation, interpretations that say more about the limits and possibilities of current discussions of children's welfare than they do about Aries's text. The text provides no clear moral or political message. Rather, it points to a complex range of changes which have produced the special nature of childhood as a legally, medically and psychologically distinct phase of life. Thus, while it is clear that Aries does begin with the present, recent writers' reflections on the book import teleology to it so that it is read as a value-laden study.

In this context it is worth making the distinction between a value relation and a valuation: something may have a relation to value in being considered worth knowing, without this necessarily involving the imposition of a particular value judgement (Weber [1918] 1991). For example, one may acknowledge that, within complex societies dependent on the skills acquired through formal education, childhood is necessarily construed as a specific and dependent phase of life, without thereby claiming that this is in itself either 'good' or 'bad'. I take Aries to be engaged in the former exercise rather than the latter, staking out an account of how our conception of childhood has come into being, how it has become a particular locus of value for us, without making a firm value judgement concerning the merits of this.

Seen from this perspective, the insistence of contemporary writers in reading Aries's book in terms of present valuations is ironic, since the very writers who have charged Aries with 'presentism' are engaged in a presentist activity themselves. In other words, recent readings of Aries as providing a moral message illustrate his argument very well; that is that contemporary concerns with childhood are a distinctly modern phenomenon. The importance of Aries's work, however, lies not in its provision of a story of the past as barbaric or golden, it goes without saying that there have been both loving and neglectful parents in every generation, but in its focus on the transformation of conditions of life, a focus which reveals the historicity of current concerns with childhood and child abuse (see Bellingham 1988; Jordanova 1989). Its importance lies in its demonstration of the historical and cultural specificity of nineteenth- and twentieth-century European conceptions of childhood. Here, despite some important errors and omissions, Aries's work is valuable in highlighting the historical and social significance of contemporary configurations of the distinction between public and private life and in pointing to the development of a specific nature attributed to childhood evidenced within new forms of knowledge and practice.

The importance of recent work that has stressed the historical specificity of modern conceptions of childhood therefore lies not in any overblown claim that 'no' concept of childhood existed in the past, but in pinpointing the historical and cultural particularity of nineteenth- and twentieth-century European conceptions of the child. Such work points up the ways in which our concepts of childhood are specific valuations; in so doing it helps to dislodge the naturalness of our assumptions and enable us to examine how these assumptions underpin our conceptions of the relations between public and private life and the intractable problems of attempting to govern child sexual abuse within liberal polities. In this context, our concern is not whether childhood and child abuse have been 'discovered' or 'invented' but, rather, to map how childhood and child abuse have become problems for governance and to examine the specific domains of knowledge and practice that constitute the problem of 'child sexual abuse'.

At this point it would be well to clarify what I am not saying. Arguing for the historical specificity of modern conceptions of childhood and of child abuse does not license relativism. It is possible to hold that contemporary concerns with adult–child sexual relations, for example, are recent historical phenomena, and at the same time to take seriously the potential damage caused by such relations. There are very good reasons for thinking that within current contexts, the set of experiences named 'child sexual abuse' are almost bound to be destructive, and seriously so. Nor is this injunction to examine critically current valuations of childhood and practices of intervention to suggest that intervention into suspected cases of child sexual abuse could be grounded successfully through discovery of objective and permanent 'facts' standing outside all evaluative schemas, as if that were possible. The facts of child sexual abuse are always already valuations in relation to existing norms of childhood development. One might conclude that our contemporary evaluations and the practices that they underpin and articulate are the best that we can do. The point of elaborating the historical specificity of our contemporary conceptions of childhood is, in a small way, to unlock the hold they have on our capacities to conceptualise the problem, to enable us to look again at the ways in which child sexual abuse has become a problem for us.

The need to ask new questions is evidenced by reiterations of cries of 'crisis' in the governance of child protection, and by theoretical debates that assume and re-entrench contemporary evaluations. If we interpret problems concerning the governance of child sexual abuse as indicative of tensions within liberal welfare rationality, then we need to examine the distinctions and forms of knowledge by which that rationality is articulated: distinctions between the public and private spheres, and between the respective competencies of legal and scientific discourses. That is, we need a form of analysis that does not presuppose a distinction between public and private life but that enables us to examine how this is constituted and reconstituted within our practices of governance, and how the authority grounded in legal and scientific knowledge and practice configures and reconfigures child sexual abuse as a governable problem. It is to these concerns that we now turn.

Part I

Conceptual frameworks

2 Dilemmas of liberalism

Child, family and state through the public/private distinction

The distinction between public and private life is foundational to liberal politics and is constitutive of current dilemmas surrounding the management of child abuse. Chapter 1 set out a difficulty attending the government of child sexual abuse in terms of the simultaneous recognition of children as the 'property' or concern of their parents and as a locus of public concern for social welfare. Child abuse in general and sexual abuse in particular raise in sharp form the question of the demarcation between privacy and intervention within liberal democratic welfare states.

The concern of this chapter is to explore the distinction between public and private life as this has taken shape within liberal political thought, to provide some preliminary indications concerning how this has come to structure liberal forms of governance, and to highlight the tensions to which this gives rise by opening up the problem of the legitimate authority of interventions into the private sphere. The purpose here is to elaborate the tension attending the distinction between state sovereignty and individual autonomy within liberal political thought. This tension problematises public interventions into the private sphere of the family and raises the issue of how such interventions are to be legitimated within liberal political discourse. As we will see in later chapters, within liberal political regimes this relationship is negotiated by a number of forms of medical, psychological and legal expertise in the field of child welfare.

The chapter does not question the cogency of liberal political philosophy as a whole,[1] rather it focuses specifically on the ways in which liberal political reasoning presupposes a distinction between public and private life and its consequent inability adequately to analyse and account for this distinction. Chapter 5 returns to the theme of liberalism, considering liberalism as a political rationality or rationality of rule. At this stage, I am concerned only to highlight some of the constituent tensions attending liberal political theory. To this end, the first section of this chapter examines the emergence of liberal political ideas and the place of the distinction between public and private within this. The second section discusses the ways in which, within liberal political thought, concepts of autonomy give shape to the scope and delimitation of the public and private aspects of childhood, before considering how liberal political theorists attempt to justify public interventions into the private realm of the family. The chapter concludes by briefly examining feminist criticisms of the public/private distinction as this has been drawn within liberal political thought and practice, criticisms that point to some of the problems attending liberal assumptions for our concern with the governance of child sexual abuse. This then forms the springboard for questions raised in the subsequent chapters of this part of the book concerning how we are to analyse contemporary relations between families and the state.

Liberalism and the distinction between public and private life

Writers within the liberal political tradition have assumed that it is both possible and desirable to divide societies into public and private spheres or domains of responsibility.[2] This is rooted in the idea that political association serves the primary function of defending private individual interests and is associated with the idea of limits to legitimate public intervention and the recognition of the need for a private sphere of relationships free from state or other public intrusion. This idea implies recognising the legitimacy of a realm defended against state interference in an individual's private life, which has included familial relationships.[3]

A distinction between public and private life is thus central to liberalism. This can be traced historically, in the emergence of the idea of a quasi-natural sphere of economic relations in commercial society and in the notion of a realm beyond the state of private individual conscience. It can also be specified analytically, in terms of the importance accorded to equality (Dworkin 1986) or impartiality (Rawls 1973) within liberal political philosophies that argue the necessity of a division between the right and the good in order to maintain neutrality in the operation of justice in plural societies.[4]

Before examining the conditions of emergence of specifically liberal versions of the public/private distinction, we examine the etymology of the terms 'public' and 'private'; doing so will help to clarify the distinctiveness of the ways in which these terms are figured within liberal arguments. The Latin *pubes* indicates the age of maturity, of being qualified for public things, *Publicas* means pertaining to the people as a whole (Elshtain 1997: 167). The term *privatus* means withdrawn from public life, and *privare* is to bereave or to deprive (Williams 1976: 203). Williams points out that from the sixteenth century in English 'private' also implies privilege, and that from late eighteenth century it comes increasingly to denote that which is personal and secluded from others. Reflecting on this, we can say that public judgements and actions relate to collective or general, as opposed to particular or individual concerns, and that such judgements and actions are properly political. We can also note that public indicates an open or accessible sphere or set of relations, and is counterposed to that which is hidden or withdrawn from public life. Moreover, we can say that the term public indicates a modality of agency in which the individual or self is understood as mature or autonomous, as capable of making public judgements.

So what form does the liberal distinction between public and private life take? As a preliminary, we can note that liberalism combines two understandings of the distinction between public and private life; one distinction falls between the state (public political) and the market (private social), the second falls between the intimate (private personal) and the impersonal (public social). The first is a distinction between the sphere of government and an autonomous sphere of social life; the second is a distinction between social life and individual privacy, freedom of conscience and the right to personal retreat (Kymlicka 1990). The second distinction is important to the development of modern notions of selfhood and to the idea of an inner world of conscience presupposed, for example, within psychoanalysis.[5] Whilst 'liberalism' is not a unitary phenomenon, but rather includes a number of different and arguably incompatible ideas,[6] it is possible to identify some core features of liberal political thought. Gray identifies four such features:

> It [liberalism] is *individualist*, in that it asserts the moral primacy of the person against the claims of any social collectivity; *egalitarian*, inasmuch as it confirms on all men the same moral status [. . .] and denies the relevance to legal or political order of differences in moral worth among human beings; *universalist*, affirming the moral unity of the human species [. . .] and confirming a secondary importance to specific historical associations and cultural forms; and *meliorist* in its affirmation of the corrigibility and improvability of all social institutions and political arrangements.
>
> (Gray 1995: xii)

Of these features, individualism is central to the growth of a modern distinction between public and private life, while the egalitarianism, universalism and meliorism of this tradition open space for the emergence of a conception of human agents and societies as capable of reform and improvement. These two themes are central in providing ground for the emergence of modern social relations that combine a strong emphasis on the distinction between public (state) and private (individual and family) spheres with concerns about and techniques of education and social reform.

How does one account for the liberal distinction made between public and private? Liberalism, logically and historically, can be regarded as a response to the problem of political obligation, to the question of the scope and limits of the sovereign authority of the state. Logically, the issue of the scope and limits of public authority is posed as a problem for liberalism because liberals propose principles of individual liberty and state sovereignty that are, prima facie, incompatible. The historical antecedents of the liberal separation of public and private lie in a series of seventeenth-century debates concerning the origin and character of political authority in the context of civil and religious war and seventeenth- and eighteenth-century discussions of the emergence of commercial society and the appropriate place of political authority in relation to this 'civil' sphere (Hont and Ignatieff 1983; Skinner 1989; Wolin 1960). We can clarify these developments in turn by outlining the impact of reformed Christianity on social and political relations, and by reference to the economic transformations brought about by the breakdown of feudalism and the emergence of commercial society.

The liberal principle of toleration arose in part as a response to pan European civil–religious warfare. Individualism was an unintended consequence of Protestantism, given the priority it accorded to individual conscience. The Protestant understanding of the individual's relationship with God dispensed with intermediaries. This had a number of effects: it facilitated the replacement of traditional ideas of descending authority by more incisive concepts of sovereignty, it dislocated theocratic justifications for authority and thus necessitated secular justifications of political authority, and it encouraged the prioritising of private life, both morally and materially.

Turning to economic transformations, the (partial) separation of economic from political power brought about by the growth of the market had a number of consequences. One was greater individualism and scope for contractual relations, which in turn necessitated a stronger and more extensive system of law, especially with regard to private property. A concomitant of this was the progressive concentration of political power in the hands of the modern, sovereign state.[7] Another consequence of the growth of the market and of industrialism was the decline of the household economy. All of these factors are aspects of an increasing division between, and reformulation of our understanding of, public and private spheres.

In the context of civil and religious wars in seventeenth-century Britain, liberal thinkers posed a solution to the problem of political order. This solution took a number of forms but manifested itself centrally in the idea of limits to the legitimate authority of the state (public) and the securing of a space of individual freedom of conscience and of commerce (private). In contractarian arguments, this was formulated in terms of the idea that political authority gains legitimacy from a hypothetical contract between individuals in a state of nature coming together and consenting to government in order to secure a limited freedom. Thus, Locke is often cited as a progenitor of the liberal tradition in relation to his refutation of Filmer's account of the origin of political authority.[8] Where Filmer regarded authority as having a single, patriarchal, origin in God the Father, Locke argued for the distinctive character of political authority as only properly founded on the rational consent of those governed. Whilst the idea that patriarchalism was displaced by liberalism occludes a number of complexities, not least that much of the language of patriarchy was adopted by early liberalism, and that 'paternalism' recurs in later liberal thought,[9] seventeenth-century debates concerning the origin and character of political authority heralded a conception of human beings as rational, as having an individual relationship to God, and as the bearers of equal rights.[10] The emergence of the idea of the individual as the bearer of rights and of government as limited, secular and based on contract, consent to government, were important in the development of civil society as a realm separate both from government and from family relations from the eighteenth century onwards. In non-contractarian accounts, the separation of state and society was formulated in terms of ideas of the natural sociability of man and of the opacity and self-sustaining character of social relations, which implied limits to government in order that society could be self-regulating. This can be seen, for example, in the work of the writers of the Scottish Enlightenment (Berry 1997; Hont and Ignatieff 1983; Seligman 1992). Both contractarian and non-contractarian forms of argument suggest limits to the state and that government should be conducted in the name of society. These ideas therefore converge around a critique of the idea of society as coterminous with government and of the possibility of the transparency of society entailed by this understanding.

The seventeenth and eighteenth centuries, therefore, saw the formation of a modern understanding of the distinction between public and private life. Whereas there is a longstanding distinction between domestic and public life within western political thought, coming from Aristotle, the distinction between public and private life made by the progenitors of modern liberalism is a distinction between the public power of the state as a centralised site of impersonal authority, law-making and coercion, and the private relations of individual conscience, commerce in civil society and the natural relations of the family (Hont and Ignatieff 1983; Skinner 1989; Spruyt 1994). From the eighteenth century onwards, the distinction between public and private life is constituted as a distinction between state sovereignty and individual autonomy, within which questions concerning the boundaries of legitimate public intervention into social and personal life are raised in new ways. Thus, liberalism adopts the language of the public/private distinction, as this helps to solve the problem of political obligation, and gives this a novel inflection.

It is possible to locate the liberal problematic of individual autonomy and state sovereignty more specifically by comparing these themes in the works of Hobbes and Locke. A number of scholars (e.g. Oakeshott 1975; Strauss 1963) have argued that Hobbes be regarded as a founder of modern liberalism on account of his individualism and affirmation of the equality of persons in the state of nature. This positioning is bolstered by the observation that, in relation to the patriarchalism of Filmer, Hobbes and Locke stand on similar ground in asserting the conventional character of political association. Nonetheless, when we compare Hobbes and Locke on questions of sovereignty and autonomy, important differences emerge; these differences clarify the ways in which, for liberalism, the limits and character of state sovereignty, and the question of individual autonomy and its attainment, become particular and enduring concerns.

If Hobbes and Locke both stand at the beginning of the liberal tradition, they do so rather differently. Both make clear distinctions between public and private power and argue that public power only comes into being as a result of an act of consent on the part of those governed; however, as we shall see, public regulation of the family does not figure as a problem in Hobbes's account, rather family privacy is a kind of remainder left over once the sovereign has legislated. Locke, on the other hand, introduces a two-fold conception of sovereignty through developing a distinct account of individual autonomy. This enables him clearly to distinguish parental and political power, generating one conception of sovereignty that is grounded in rational consent to civil government, and another that is grounded in the natural relations of the family. In Locke's account, the contrast between individual autonomy and state sovereignty produces state and family as two distinct and differently grounded spaces of rule.[11] Examining these differences a little more closely will help to disclose the ways in which questions of sovereignty and those of autonomy and its attainment are figured as particular sorts of problems for liberalism.

Both Hobbes and Locke distinguish public political and private power (Hobbes [1651] 1996: 155; Locke [1698] 1988: II, §2–3, 268). However, they do so to different ends. Hobbes's account is one of appetitive individualism, of the equality of individuals in the state of nature, and of the social contract as the foundation of government. Importantly, this is couched within a conception of sovereignty such that the absolute power of the sovereign is regarded as compatible with the liberty of the subject, 'nothing the Soveraign Representative can do to a Subject, on what pretence soever, can properly be called injustice, or Injury' (Hobbes [1651] 1996: 148).[12] Furthermore, in so far as all are subject to sovereign authority, there is in principle no distinction between the mode of subjection of the child and that of the adult. Locke introduces two elements of disjunction into this.

First, where Hobbes's argument, as a justification for absolutism, requires the transfer of sovereignty,[13] Locke's ruler is a trustee. In Locke's account of civil government, that is, sovereignty ultimately remains with the people; they do not forfeit this on entry into the compact, and therefore retain a right to revolt (Locke [1698] 1988: II chapter XIX, 406–28). In Locke's account, therefore, sovereignty is counterpoised to and strictly limited by individual liberty. Second, Locke introduces a clear distinction between the subjection of the child and that of the adult. He does this by developing an account of autonomy as the capacity to discern natural law. Whereas for Hobbes liberty consists simply in 'absence of Opposition' ([1651] 1996: 145) and pertains as much to the irrational and inanimate as to rational creatures (Hobbes giving the example of water not being at liberty when held from spreading by a vessel), for Locke liberty is irreducibly tied to reason, or rather, to the capacity autonomously to discern the law of nature: 'Thus we are *born Free*, as we are born Rational; not that we have actually the Exercise of either: Age that brings one, brings with it the other too' ([1698] 1988: II §61, 308, emphasis in text).

We can therefore note two features of Locke's account that are not present in that of Hobbes: first, with the concern to limit public power, Locke counterpoises individual liberty and state sovereignty, opening an enduring tension that liberal political theory and practice has attempted to manage ever since; and second, by yoking together reason and autonomy, Locke opens up a problem space for thinking about how we become rational and the extent of our freedom until this time.

These two different accounts of sovereignty and autonomy result in distinct accounts of the relation between public political power and the power of parents. Both Hobbes and Locke distinguish paternal and political power, and argue that the former exists in the state of nature. However, where for Hobbes sovereignty is a zero-sum game, 'For the Father, and Master being before the Institution of Common-wealth, absolute Soveraigns in their own Families, they lose afterward no more of their Authority, than the Law of the Common-wealth taketh from them'

([1651] 1996: 163), Locke opens up a two-fold conception of sovereignty so that: '*Parents in Societies*, where they themselves are Subjects, retain a *power over their Children*, and have as much right to their Subjection, as those who are in the state of Nature' ([1698] 1988: II §71, 314, emphasis in text).

For Locke, sovereignty in the political realm is founded on the consent of the governed and concerns the right of public law-making, sovereignty in the family is founded on the natural right of the child to receive care and on the corresponding duty of the parent to provide ([1698] 1988: II § 56, 65, 67, 74, 305, 310, 312, 316). Moreover, in Locke's account, both political and paternal sovereignty are limited by the continued existence and applicability of natural law within the context of civil government, in the former case providing a right to revolt and in the latter providing a limit on parental power such that this can only legitimately be used in order to foster the child's capacity to become autonomous (see below).

In other words, the zero-sum character of Hobbes's argument is a product of his conception of the move from the state of nature to political society as one of total rupture, in which sovereignty is transferred delivering natural law absolutism. Whilst this produces a division between the natural and the conventional, any distinction between public and private or limitation of the public is dependent on the will of the sovereign, and therefore this account does not produce a problem regarding political regulation of the family. This is not a problem for Hobbes because, first, individual liberty is what is left over once the sovereign has acted and, second, Hobbes does not hold any necessary connection between autonomy and reason. For Locke, however, the distinction between the family and the public or commonwealth is between two spheres of sovereignty, where this distinction articulates differently organised spaces of rule. That is, it is Locke's and subsequently liberalism's articulation of different principles of rule, conceived as public political rule and private individual and familial rule, that produces a problem of legitimacy regarding public intervention into the private domain.

We can sum this up by noting that within liberalism the public/private distinction becomes a distinction between a domain of state sovereignty and one of individual liberty and that this is articulated through the notion of autonomy. We can see this when we examine liberal justifications for paternalism in relation to children and others considered lacking the requisite capacities for reason, and in liberal articulations of legitimate grounds for public intervention into family relations.

The limits of liberal reflection

The division of society into public and private domains of responsibility, and the conception of the autonomous individual as the basic unit of society that is central to liberalism,[14] give rise to two immediate problems in relation to thinking about the governance of child abuse. The first is a problem concerning how to conceptualise childhood using liberal assumptions about the individual; the second is a problem concerning the legitimacy of intervention into the private sphere of the family given the presupposition of a distinction between public and private life as realms of state sovereignty and individual autonomy, respectively. These two themes are interrelated.

Autonomy and paternalism

The sexual abuse of children raises in specific form the general problematic of how to think about childhood using liberal assumptions about the individual. The idea of the rational autonomous individual is central to liberalism (Archard 1993; D'Agostino 1998; Hindess 1996a; Pateman 1988). So, therefore, is the question of when and to what degree children are rational and autonomous. Hindess notes that there is ambivalence within liberalism concerning the understanding of the individual as autonomous; the autonomous individual is simultaneously presupposed by liberal political theory and is an accomplishment of liberal techniques of government directed at the formation and preservation of autonomous subjects capable of regulating their own behaviour (1996a: 73). This ambivalence is, as might be expected, played out particularly closely with respect to children.

Central to the ways in which liberal thinkers have attempted to conceptualise childhood is in terms of a temporary stage of dependence prior to the full autonomy of adulthood, where the movement from childhood to adulthood is marked by coming to reason. That is, in liberal accounts the figure of the child is counterposed to that of the adult, this distinction being marked by the capacity for reason. Here, autonomy is a normative assumption that distinguishes adulthood from childhood, and it is an ideal to which the child (and its parents for it) aspires. We find this in Locke's idea that the capacity for reflection grows with age:

> *Children*, I confess are not born in this full state of *Equality*, though they are born to it. Their Parents have a sort of Rule and Jurisdiction over them when they come into the World, and for some time after, but 'tis but a temporary one. The Bonds of this Subjection are like the Swaddling Cloths they are wrapt up in, and supported by, in the weakness of their Infancy. Age and Reason as they grow up, loosen them till at length they drop quite off, and leave a Man at his own free Disposal.
>
> ([1698] 1988: II §55, 304, emphasis in text)

We might usefully compare this with Rawls's affirmation of 'the equality of children as future citizens' (Rawls [1997] 1999: 601). Rawls ascribes equal rights to children, whilst noting that their lack of knowledge and understanding implies that they 'cannot with reason doubt the propriety of parental injunctions' (1973: §70, 463), and that therefore 'the child's morality of authority' whose 'prized virtues are obedience, humility, and fidelity to authoritative persons . . . is temporary, a necessity arising from his [*sic*] peculiar situation and limited understanding' (1973: §70, 466–7).

We can elaborate on this by noting that, in these accounts, autonomy is presupposed, and is an ideal or hoped for outcome of liberal practices of governance.

It is presupposed in the notion of the child as a potential adult. However, in so far as the child is only potentially autonomous, then autonomy becomes an ideal to be pursued as the intended outcome of practices of education and training. In this second moment, in which autonomy is regarded as an achievement or hoped for outcome of liberal governance, paternalism is justified; our coming to reason may involve others exercising power over us.

In liberal arguments then, concern for the potential for autonomy of the individual may justify paternalism in relation to those deemed not to be autonomous individuals; in the case of children it justifies parental authority.[15] We can once again turn to Locke here. Locke couches a justification for paternalism in terms of an individual's capacity to discern the law of nature. In so far as children are born to but not in equality, they lack reason, thus the child is 'to be guided by the Will of his Father or Guardian, who is to understand for him' (Locke [1698] 1988: II §59, 307; also §57, 305–6). Therefore, Locke makes autonomy the foundation of a distinction between childhood and adulthood and suggests that the subjection of the child is necessary in order that the child may achieve autonomy in adulthood. It is worth quoting at length on this point:

> The *Power*, then, *that Parents have* over their Children, arises from that duty which is incumbent on them, to take care of their Off-spring, during the imperfect state of Childhood. To inform the Mind, and govern the Actions of their yet ignorant Nonage, till Reason shall take its place, and ease them of that Trouble, is what the Children want, and the Parents are bound to. [. . .] whilst he is in an Estate, wherein he has not *Understanding* of his own to direct his *Will*, he is not to have any Will of his own to follow: He that *understands* for him, must *will* for him too; he must prescribe to his Will, and regulate his Actions; but when he comes to the Estate that made his *Father a Freeman*, the *Son is a Freeman* too.
>
> ([1698] 1988: II §58, 306–7, emphasis in text)

From this passage, we can see how for Locke '*natural Freedom and Subjection to Parents* may consist together, and are both founded on the same Principle.' ([1698] 1988: II §61, 308, emphasis in text), that principle being the law of nature as dictated by reason. Here, the 'imperfect state of childhood' is compared with that of the 'freeman' able to 'direct his own will', that is the incapacities of childhood are compared with those of a (hypothetical) perfect reasoner. Autonomy thus functions as a normative presupposition and as an ideal state to which the child should aspire. In this move, the adult–child distinction becomes one of the central means by which Locke constructs a distinction between autonomy and heteronomy, public reason and private passion.

The slippage between autonomy as something presupposed and as something which emerges under the auspices of liberal practices of governance is taken up by Valverde (1996) in discussing the way in which, in the work of J.S. Mill, the notion of 'habit' reconciles the concern for individual autonomy with liberalism's pessimistic understanding of human beings' capacities. That is, the idea of the correct formation of habits forms a bridge between the 'despotic' governance of the child and the liberal political order that Mill advocated as appropriate to mature adults. Naturalised assumptions about the status and (in)capacities of childhood figure strongly in Mill's introduction to *On Liberty*:

> It is, perhaps, hardly necessary to say that this doctrine is meant to apply only to human beings in the maturity of their faculties. We are not speaking of children, or of young persons below the age which the law may fix as that of manhood or womanhood. Those who are still in a state to require being taken care of by others, must be protected against their own actions as well as against external injury.
>
> ([1859] 1989: 13)

Valverde elaborates on the way in which liberalism operates through a distinction between public and private where this articulates distinct and incompatible spaces of rule, and through appeal to naturalised kinds such as childhood as a state distinct from adulthood. From the foregoing, we can see that both moves are articulated through the principle of autonomy.

We might add to this that the idea of the inculcation of the correct habits of reason through education is the point of potential reconciliation between Locke's political theory and his psychology. Whereas his political theory grounds the claim of human autonomy on the capacity to discern the law of nature, his psychology is empiricist in its suggestion that infants are empty vessels to be filled with sense experience. The elision of this tension in Locke's notion of the child coming to reason is indicative of the ways in which liberal political thought and practice takes as natural phenomena forms of individuality that are in fact artefacts of government. More generally, in figuring the nature of childhood as faulty adulthood, as potential adulthood, and as (in some variants of liberalism, though more properly in Romanticism) innocence, liberalism itself produces the notion of childhood as a specific phase. We might say that within liberal arguments the adult–child distinction becomes necessary in order to stabilise the counter-pulling between the individual capable of autonomy and his/her passionate, sensuous nature.

Within liberal arguments, the adult–child distinction is constructed through an account of autonomy in which the condition of childhood, an historical product (see Chapter 1), is naturalised. In liberal orders children are recognised as persons, they have legal personality, but are not regarded as fully formed, they essentially lack legal capacity, and therefore have to be moulded into fully autonomous personhood. Liberalism simultaneously presupposes autonomy and has to find ways to bring this into being. Liberal strategies of governance are thus not simply governing childhood as a natural object, although this is often liberals' self-conception of the task, rather liberal forms of governance (and the ideal of autonomous adulthood) have themselves produced the conditions of childhood: childhood is an historical artefact and the history of this is repressed by liberalism as the status of childhood is assumed.[16]

The hypothetical perfect reasoner of the liberal imagination perhaps achieves his/her maturity in Rawls's *Theory of Justice* (1973). This text provides a useful contemporary reworking of the distinction between childhood and adulthood specifically around the 'problem of paternalism' (1973: 248). Rawls specifies the relation between the potential for autonomy of the child and the need for parental authority in addressing the priority of liberty and its relation to paternalism. Rawls states that 'the precedence of liberty means that liberty can be restricted only for the sake of liberty itself' (1973: §39, 244), and goes on to justify paternalism in terms of what the parties to the original position would acknowledge as necessary to protect themselves against 'the weakness and infirmities of their reason and will in society' (1973: 249). He states: 'Others are authorized and sometimes required to act on our own behalf and to do what we would do for ourselves if we were rational, this authorization coming into effect only when we cannot look after our own good' (1973: 249). Children's powers of reasoning are undeveloped and as such 'they cannot rationally advance their interests' (1973: 249). In this situation, Rawls argues that we should 'try to get for him [*sic*] the things he presumably wants whatever else he wants' (1973: 249), that is, paternalism is justified only by an 'evident failure or absence of reason and will' on the part of the individual concerned, so that 'paternalistic principles are a protection against our own irrationality' (1973: 250) and must be oriented toward the autonomy of the individual to whom they are applied.

One way out of the ambivalence attending the distinction between child-hood and adulthood is to accept a libertarian position in relation to childhood. Libertarian arguments, emerging since the 1970s, have taken the form of a demand that children be accorded the same rights as adults. This demand is based on the claim that withholding rights from children is unjustifiable since age-related criteria do not map on to capacities, so that to withhold rights from children is a form of paternalistic domination (Farson 1978; Franklin 1986; Harris 1982; Holt 1975).[17]

These criticisms have drawn attention to the somewhat arbitrary character of legal age cut-offs in respect of minority–majority and have highlighted the potential for despotism in the assumption that parents or caretakers can be relied upon to act in the child's 'best interests'; they also do much to reveal the problematic status of the notion of autonomous adulthood, however they have had little direct impact on the practices of liberal governance. Rather, in recent liberal arguments concerning children's rights this liberationist position is attenuated; first, by the recognition that children often need specific facilities in order adequately to represent their views or to have these views represented; second, by the argument that it is important to distinguish between enabling children to represent their views and taking these into consideration when making decisions, and ensuring that children's views are acted upon (Fortin 1998; Fox-Harding 1991). In contemporary debates 'children's rights' are articulated as rights to protection and (some degree of) voice. This latter understanding of children's rights replicates the structure of early liberal arguments and is a position that regards children as potentially autonomous beings requiring care and education in order to achieve this potential;

that is, it is a view that explicitly recognises that autonomy is something that develops over time. In turn, this potential for autonomy requires that children have a trust relationship with parents or guardians until autonomy is achieved. This is underwritten by expectations written into law that parents will act as trustees in the relationship so that at majority the new adult is endowed with capacity to cut the umbilical cord of the 'bare trust' relationship and so move from being beneficiary to fully autonomous person with power to become a trustee him/herself. This relationship of trust is combined with age-related thresholds of autonomy and with criteria of harm justifying different degrees and kinds of public intervention appropriate to different stages in a child's development.

Within liberal arguments, therefore, the notion of autonomy and its development gives shape to the scope and delimitation of the public and private aspects of childhood. The achievement of autonomy, as the child moves from childhood to adulthood, is a move from private to public in terms of voice, capacities, and so on, and is at the same time a move from public to private in terms of liberty to live as one wishes (within the limits of prevailing norms of adult autonomy).

We can clarify this by examining the ways in which childhood is understood within liberal legal reasoning. Liberal legal orders ascribe to children rights to receive care and protection in order that their potential for autonomy is not hindered. We might call this passive autonomy. Passive autonomy is ascribed to individuals from the point of birth (if not before this, for example, in jurisdictions where there exist proscriptions against or time limits on abortion); that is, in being recognised as an individual a child has a right to be protected in full from harm, that is to have equal protection to that of an adult (though at the time of writing this is compromised in the UK context by the continued recognition of parents' rights of chastisement, see Fortin 1998: 228–38). Passive autonomy can be counterposed to active autonomy which is something that children are regarded as acquiring with the growth of capacities for decision-making, responsibility, the capacity to distinguish truth and falsehood, and so on. Active autonomy thus conveys rights to make decisions regarding one's own life and, concomitantly, responsibilities for one's actions.

If we examine the relation between these concepts of passive and active autonomy and the designations public and private, we find that within liberal legal orders children are simultaneously the most private and the most public of individuals. On one hand, they are archetypically private in so far as children are assumed dependent upon the care of their parents and have no independent right of access to public institutions on their own behalf (until they reach reason, or at least until they reach school age in contemporary liberal societies with compulsory education systems). Children are thus deprived of access to the public sphere. This privacy and dependence on parents is borne out, for example, in the assumption of the Children Act 1989 that the interests of parents and those of their children are usually to be considered consonant with one another and that parents will best fulfil their obligations if allowed to do so without undue interference (Bainham 1990b, though the 1989 Act also recognises that children have the right to have their voices heard in relation to decisions that affect them). On the other hand, children are the most public of individuals if we mean by this that they generally lack a sphere of personal retreat from the social context of their families, or if we examine the condition of childhood in terms of the state's interest in and powers over children's welfare.

The passive autonomy that children have from birth within liberal political orders confers a right to protection by the state *erga omnes*;[18] this involves recognition by public agencies with concerns for children's welfare, but in this conception children remain private individuals in so far as they are deprived of the right of making their own decisions. This situation is slowly reversed as children develop capacities for active autonomy. That is, recognition of an individual's capacity for active autonomy comprises recognition that s/he is an accountable but private individual in relation to decisions concerning how s/he chooses to live his/her life, and a public individual in so far as s/he is deemed capable of exercising the public rights and duties of citizenship (voting, being legally responsible, and so on). The point at which a child is deemed actively autonomous varies depending on the activity in question and on the legal jurisdiction in which the child lives. However, despite these variations, within liberal polities childhood constitutes a specific phase of life in which the individual in question is recognised as requiring protection from the exigencies of life and from others, but is not yet recognised as capable fully of exercising rights. Childhood is thus understood as a temporary evolutionary phase of dependence prior to the acquisition of the full autonomy of adulthood.

The legitimacy of public intervention into the private realm

By examining the ways in which liberal writers articulate the notion of autonomy in relation to childhood we have begun to disclose how it is that within liberal political orders children are excluded from public life themselves and are, simultaneously, central to public concerns. Turning to the second theme noted at the beginning of this section, that of the legitimacy of public interventions into the private sphere, we can further clarify the stakes of liberal political theory in relation to childhood and the governance of child abuse.

Within liberal political orders the family is regarded as a paramount locus of privacy. One commentator, reflecting on the Children Act 1989, has recently suggested that 'The family may be likened to a state within a state; interference by the public state within family affairs is a grave matter, comparable to interference by one state with the internal affairs of another' (Fortin 1998: 10). However, as we have already noted, this privacy is conditional and is checked in relation to concerns for the interests of children. Let us look more closely, first at the suggestion that liberalism grounds a two-fold conception of sovereignty, and then at the way in which liberal writers legitimate breaching the privacy of family relations in contexts of concern for children.

To clarify the manner in which liberal writers conceive the family as private we need to return to the ways in which liberals counterpoise individual autonomy and state sovereignty. Here, Fortin is correct in identifying liberal conceptions of the family as akin to a 'state within a state'. It is the concern for autonomy that plays a decisive role in liberalism's two-fold conception of sovereignty. We have seen, for example, that both Locke and Rawls make autonomy the foundation for a distinction between adults and children, where autonomy in adulthood is achieved through submission to parental will as a child. Autonomy is also the principle upon which the limits of state sovereignty are articulated, in so far as the liberal concern with privacy is a concern with autonomy or freedom from the state and other public intrusion. The liberal conception of the autonomous individual, sovereign over him or herself, requires a limitation of public authority, and this has included the right to family privacy. However, we need to examine a little more closely the meaning of the distinction between the family and the state as separate spaces of sovereignty. The two-fold conception of sovereignty characteristic of liberalism is not simply a distinction between different spaces of rule or jurisdictions; it is a distinction between different principles of rule. That is, liberalism articulates differently grounded and incompatible spaces of rule: the natural(ised) relations of the family, and the conventional relations of the polity.

This is clearly articulated in Locke's differentiation of political and parental power. We have already noted Locke's argument that, '*Parents in Societies*, where they themselves are Subjects, retain a *power over their Children*, and have as much right to their Subjection, as those who are in the state of Nature' ([1698] 1988: II §71, 314, emphasis in text). He goes on to point out that this could not be the case if paternal and political power were the same; rather, he argues that these two forms of power are distinct:

> these two *Powers, political* and *Paternal, are so perfectly distinct* and separate; are built upon so different Foundations, and given so different Ends, that every Subject that is a Father, has as much *Paternal Power* over his children, as the Prince has over his.
>
> ([1698] 1988: II §71, 314, emphasis in text)[19]

We will return in a moment to the limits Locke places on parental autonomy. First, it is important to note that the distinction between the natural and the artefactual has been formed on shifting ground in liberal accounts. For Locke the family, grounded in nature, pre-exists the polity. In modern liberal arguments such as that forwarded by Rawls, the family is not regarded as straightforwardly pre-political, but is conceptualised rather as an outcome or artefact of political decision. Rawls states that:

> A domain so-called, or a sphere of life, is not, then, something already given apart from political conceptions of justice. A domain is not a kind of space, or place, but rather is simply the result, or upshot, of how the principles of political justice are applied, [. . .] the spheres of the political and the public, of the non-public and the private, fall out from the content and application of

the conception and justice and its principles. If the so-called private sphere is alleged to be a space exempt from justice, then there is no such thing.
([1997] 1999: 599)

However Rawls, whilst recognising the artefactual character of family relations as the outcome of political decision, nonetheless holds to the notion of a difference of kind between the family and the political sphere: 'We wouldn't want political principles of justice – including principles of distributive justice – to apply directly to the internal life of the family' ([1997] 1999: 598). He makes it clear that he does not intend the principles of political justice to apply directly to the family, or to that of other associations such as churches, but rather argues that they impose constraints on these institutions and thus guarantee the basic rights and liberties of all of their members ([1997] 1999: 597). Rawls bases this distinction between the political sphere and that of the family on the argument that different principles guide our behaviour in these two realms, that is the political sphere and that of the family are regarded as differently grounded spaces of rule:

> These principles [the political principles of justice] do not inform us how to raise our children, and we are not required to treat our children in accordance with political principles. Surely parents must follow some conception of justice (or fairness) and due respect with regard to their children, but, within certain limits, this is not for political principles to prescribe. Clearly the prohibition of abuse and neglect of children, and much else, will, as constraints, be a vital part of family law. But at some point society has to rely on the natural affection and goodwill of the mature family members.
> ([1997] 1999: 598)

As one of the central institutions of the basic structure of society, Rawls suggests that 'a central role of the family is to arrange in a reasonable and effective way the raising of and caring for children, ensuring their moral development and education into the wider culture' ([1997] 1999: 596). Making the disclaimer not to be able to deal with the complexities of family relations in a discussion of public reason, Rawls states that he 'assume[s] that as children we grow up in a small intimate group in which elders (normally parents) have a certain moral and social authority' ([1997] 1999: 596).

Whether the family is regarded as pre-political or as an outcome of political decision, within liberal arguments, it figures as a distinct arena in terms of the appropriate principles guiding its internal organisation. That is, within liberal arguments the family features as a naturalised (if not strictly natural) domain of privacy in which the sovereignty of parents over children is required in order to produce autonomous individuals. The privacy of family relations is both assumed and aspired to. This raises the problem of how to justify intervention into this private sphere. Here, concern for autonomy is once again important.

We have seen that concern for individual autonomy produces a bifurcated conception of sovereignty within liberalism, and that this produces a problem regarding the legitimacy of public intervention into or regulation of private familial relations. Parents are regarded as requiring privacy defended against the state, both to protect their own liberty and in order that they are able to raise children. However, liberal writers are also sensitive to the fact that children require care and protection in order that their potential for autonomy is nurtured. How do they manage this tension? How is public intervention into the family justified within the terms of liberal arguments?

In the discussion of autonomy and paternalism above, we noted that within liberal political thought autonomy is simultaneously presupposed and is a hoped-for outcome of liberal practices of government. Paternalism is justified where individuals are regarded as lacking in the required capacities for reason. This legitimates parental power over children, in so far as children are regarded as less than fully formed. However, it also provides potential justification for overriding the rights of parents in relation to children where parents 'abuse' their power, for example where they exercise power and authority in a manner inimical to the development of the capacities for autonomy of the child. Again, we can turn to Locke here.

Locke's argument displaced older notions of political authority based on the model of the family, such as Filmer's descending thesis of political authority, founding sovereignty in relation to the political realm on consent or compact. At the same time, Locke constructs a second domain of sovereignty, that of paternal or parental authority over the household.[20] The autonomy of the family (i.e. control by parents) is then regarded as necessary to the proper functioning of family as a unit. This raises the problem of how to legitimate public intervention into this private sphere. However, concern with autonomy also produces a check on the power of parents, in so far as children are regarded as potentially autonomous and therefore as individuals endowed with rights.

We can clarify this by looking at how Locke assumes and invokes a duty of care on the part of parents. Locke assumes the naturalness and efficacy of parental power over and care for children (as does Rawls, as we have just seen). Locke argues that

> The Nourishment and Education of their Children, is a Charge so incumbent on Parents for their Childrens good, that nothing can absolve them from taking care of it. And though the *power of commanding and chastising* them go along with it, yet God hath woven into the Principles of Humane Nature such a tenderness for their Off-spring, that there is little fear that Parents should use their power with too much rigour; the excess is seldom on the severe side, the strong byass of Nature drawing the other way.
>
> ([1698] 1988: II §67, 312, emphasis in text)

At the same time, this authority does not go unqualified. Locke describes paternal authority as a 'temporary Government, which terminates with the minority of the Child' ([1698] 1988: II, §67, 312). He makes it clear that 'the *Father's Power* of commanding extends no farther than the Minority of his Children, and to a degree only fit for the Discipline and Government of that Age' ([1698] 1988: II, §74, 316, emphasis in text). As such, he suggests that parental power is more properly described as 'the Priviledge of Children, and Duty of Parents, than any Prerogative of Paternal Power' ([1698] 1988: II §67, 312). In this account parents are under an obligation of the law of nature to preserve, nourish and educate their children, not as their own work, but as the workmanship of God ([1698] 1988: II §56, 305). Parental authority is therefore grounded in the obligation that parents have to care for their children. Moreover, Locke comments of the father of a family that 'when he quits Care of them, he loses his power over them' ([1698] 1988: II, §65, 310). That is, a parent may forfeit the power s/he has over a child, but cannot alienate it ([1698] 1988: I, §100, 214).[21] In this conception, children have rights to nurturance that apply under natural and civil law ([1698] 1988: II , §59, 307); Locke assumes that parents will fulfil this role, but indicates that where they do not they forfeit their power and that the power appropriate to a parent by virtue of their exercising a duty of care falls to any foster parent who assumes these duties ([1698] 1988: I, §100, 214).

From this account we can see that Locke assumes that parental propensity to care is natural. However, he also qualifies parental power through recognising that children are born to equality (though not in it); that is, Locke recognises the rights of children as potentially autonomous individuals and grounds these rights in natural law.[22] This in turn limits the power of parents, this power being directly tied to a duty of care:

> *Paternal* or *Parental Power* is nothing but that, which Parents have over their Children, to govern them for the Childrens good, till they come to the use of Reason, or a state of Knowledge, wherein they may be supposed capable to understand that Rule, whether it be the Law of Nature, or the municipal Law of their Country they are to govern themselves by.
>
> ([1698] 1988: II, §170, 381, emphasis in text)

A similar move is made by Rawls. Whilst for the most part being content to assume that parents care for children, he also builds into his account a justification for paternalism that can accommodate public intervention into the private life of the family in order to protect children (and others), in so far as this is understood as protecting an individual's potential for autonomy; where this is the case the concern for individual autonomy overcomes the concern for family autonomy. In considering the family in his recent work, Rawls puts this in the following way:

> political principles do not apply directly to its [the family's] internal life, but they do impose essential constraints on the family as an institution and so guarantee the basic rights and liberties, and the freedom and opportunities, of all its members. This they do [. . .] by specifying the basic rights of equal citizens who are the members of families.
>
> ([1997] 1999: 597)

He continues:

> Just as the principles of justice require that wives have all the rights of citizens, the principles of justice impose constraints on the family on behalf of children who as society's future citizens have basic rights as such. [. . .] The equal rights of women and the basic rights of their children as future citizens are inalienable and protect them wherever they are.
>
> ([1997] 1999: 598–9)

In these accounts the family, normally outside government in order that the autonomy of the individuals involved be respected, has limited rights with regard to bringing up children, though the state or other public agencies may be justified in intervening to protect children's interests. That is, concern regarding the future capacity for the autonomy of children may override parental rights to privacy, in so far as this privacy is the cause of harm to children. Locke provides a justification for such intervention through the argument that children have natural, i.e. inherent, rights. The issue remains relatively unexplored by Rawls, but can be derived from his account of the basic rights of children and from his justification of paternalism in contexts where this will foster individuals' capacities for autonomy. It is, however, J.S. Mill who articulates the principles underpinning this position most clearly and explicitly.

Mill's account of the sovereignty of the individual over him/herself, provided at the beginning of *On Liberty* is well known: 'the only purpose for which power can be rightfully exercised over any member of a civilised community, against his will, is to prevent harm to others. [. . .] Over himself, over his own body and mind, the individual is sovereign' ([1859] 1989: 13).[23] Intervention into the private sphere of an individual's life is therefore only justified by the 'harm' principle: individuals are at liberty to do as they please in so far as this causes no harm to others. In situations where an individual's action causes harm to others, intervention is justified. In elaborating this point Mill reflects specifically on the family. He suggests that, within Europe, the family is the site for a misplaced sense of liberty:

> A person should be free to do as he likes in his own concerns; but he ought not to be free to do as he likes in acting for another, under the pretext that the affairs of the other are his own affairs. The State, while it respects the liberty of each in what specially regards himself, is bound to maintain a vigilant control over his exercise of any power which it allows him to possess over others. This obligation is almost entirely disregarded in the case of the family relations, a case, in its direct influence on human happiness, more important than all others taken together.
>
> ([1859] 1989: 104–5)

In explicitly articulating the 'harm' principle implicitly at work in other accounts, Mill sharpens the need to clarify and untangle the relationship between individuals and the families of which they are a part, and by implication to spell out the role and limits of state intervention.

Whilst Mill asserts that sovereignty over one's actions does not apply to children, since they 'require being taken care of by others' ([1859] 1989: 13), he challenges the idea that children are the property of their parents, suggesting that the state has direct, if unrecognised, responsibilities toward children:

> It is in the case of children that misapplied notions of liberty are a real obstacle to the fulfilment by the State of its duties. One would almost think that a man's children were supposed to be literally, and not metaphorically, a part of himself, so jealous is opinion with the smallest interference of law with his absolute and exclusive control over them.
>
> ([1859] 1989: 105)

Mill thus provides a clear account of the state's responsibilities toward children, articulating a position that regards children as separate from their parents and as bestowed with individual rights. However, at the same time he reiterates the theme of parental, rather than societal, responsibility for children:

> It still remains unrecognised, that to bring a child into existence without a fair prospect of being able, not only to provide food for its body, but instruction and training for its mind, is a moral crime, both against the unfortunate offspring and against society; and that if the parent does not fulfil this obligation, the State ought to see it fulfilled, at the charge, as far as possible, of the parent.
>
> ([1859] 1989: 105)

Mill rejects the notion of the family as an unhindered space of privacy, reflecting and contributing to the movement toward increasing individualisation of rights during the nineteenth century.[24] If we look at *The Subjection of Women*, we find a characterisation of the family as currently constituted as a 'school of despotism' (Mill [1869] 1989: 160) in so far as home is an arena of 'unrestraint' ([1869] 1989: 153) for potential male violence. However, alongside this suggestion of the need for a radical reform of family relations Mill goes on to argue that, justly constituted, the family would be 'the real school of the virtues of freedom' ([1869] 1989: 160). That is, Mill's account provides a critique of the current constitution of the family, whilst at the same time rearticulating an ideal of the justly constituted family. He suggests that whilst it will 'always be a school of obedience for the children, of command for the parents' ([1869] 1989: 161), properly formed the family would be a 'school of sympathy in equality [. . .] between the parents. [. . .] and a model to the children' ([1896] 1989: 161).

Reflecting on Mill's argument, we can see that this is a moment when the tension between individual rights and the idea of the family as a space of privacy and parental autonomy is sharpened, but that within this a naturalised understanding of childhood as a phase of dependency prior to the autonomy of adulthood is maintained. Here, the 'harm' principle as the criterion of legitimate intervention signifies that the public/private distinction is both presupposed and that this is figured as a distinction between state sovereignty and individual and familial autonomy, where familial autonomy is only justifiable where the family is 'justly constituted'.

At this point we can note an assumption and an aspiration animating liberal arguments. The assumption is that the family is founded on a set of relations that are natural, and that privacy is necessary to its functioning. The aspiration following from this is that of the properly founded family, that is the family headed by an autonomous individual, acting to secure the best for his/her children.

It is important to note that where classically liberal conceptions of rights are rights against intrusion into individual privacy, this is complicated with regard to children because children are regarded as potentially autonomous and in need of care. This justifies parental control over children, but also produces arguments for children's rights to protection that may in turn compromise parents' rights against intrusion. The potential for autonomy of children is a concern with children's 'best interests' ideally provided for by parents, but where this parental authority is limited and may be unseated by concerns that a child is being harmed.

Liberal thinkers since Locke have based the legitimacy of public intervention into the private aspects of a person's existence on the principle of 'harm', and have endlessly debated what is covered by this principle. 'Harm' is a necessarily unstable designation that, within liberal political orders in recent years, has come to include recognition of child physical and now sexual abuse. In relation to children and child abuse therefore the 'harm' principle, variously defined according to available evidence, for example from paediatric medicine and child psychology, combined with age-related criteria providing thresholds for active autonomy, articulates the public/private distinction by providing appropriate criteria for determining whether intervention is appropriate in a particular case, and what form that intervention should take.

Developing the liberal designations of public and private as, respectively, domains of state sovereignty and individual autonomy, we can see that children are private in lacking active rights-bearing status and in being positioned within the privacy of the family, with parents standing between them and the state. However, they are also public within this private sphere, both in respect of their parents or guardians understanding of their 'good' (children have little by way of a zone of negative privacy) and in respect of the state's interest in their well-being. The latter concern in turn compromises parents' rights of privacy. That is, within contemporary relationships, children are effectively excluded from public life and constituted as a central element in private family relations. Children, and therefore families, then become a focus of public concern on the part of others.

Several important features of these accounts can now be clarified. Liberal political thought assumes a distinction between public and private life, this is naturalised in liberal accounts as a distinction between differently grounded spaces of rule. However, this distinction is an artefact of liberal reasoning and a product of liberal practices of government in which the privacy of family relations is both assumed and aspired to. In turn, liberal arguments assume and invoke an understanding of childhood as a distinct phase of life in which the individual is dependent, less than fully formed as an individual, but nonetheless endowed with rights as an individual. Liberalism treats of childhood as a natural object, that is, it assumes the characteristics of this condition, and at the same time reproduces this conception. In turn, parents have rights in respect of their children, but also responsibilities for organising their welfare in an appropriate manner. Public intervention is justified where harm is or is likely to be suffered by the child concerned, where criteria of 'harm' and those of the 'best interests of the child' are determined by particular forms of knowledge of what constitutes childhood and appropriate child development.

We can conclude this section by noting that autonomy is an organising concept of liberal political thought: the public/private distinction as a distinction between the public powers of the state and the rights of the individual to privacy is articulated through the principle of autonomy. The autonomous individual is both presupposed within liberal political theory and is an accomplishment of liberal techniques of government structured around concerns to produce autonomous individuals. Children figure in these accounts as potentially autonomous individuals requiring care and education to the point of autonomous adulthood. Family privacy is assumed necessary both to secure the autonomy of adults within it, and in order that those adults act as parents producing appropriately autonomous offspring. Justifications for intervention into the privacy of family relations are framed in terms of harm or potential harm to existing or future capacities for autonomy.

In these accounts the understanding of the family as a separately grounded private space of rule and of childhood as a specific, dependent phase of life work as naturalised historical products. Liberal political reason both assumes a separation between public and private life and provides grounds for reworking this distinction through developing accounts of harm premised on specific understandings of the characteristics of childhood. Attention therefore centres on where to draw the boundary between the public and private aspects of life, and on justifications for particular delineations of this distinction.

Feminist re-readings of liberal political theory

Recent work within feminist political theory has demonstrated some of the limits of liberal political thought. Recognising problems attending the liberal tendency to split public and private into unconnected and differently grounded spheres, there has been a debate within feminism about how to conceptualise the relationship between the private and the public and also discussion concerning what should be done to change this relationship (Boling 1996; Elshtain 1981,1982; Landes 1998; Lister 1997; Millett 1977; Pateman 1988, 1989; Phillips 1991, 1995; Smart 1989). What is at stake here? We have noted that within liberal political discourse this distinction has signified a distinction between individual autonomy and state sovereignty where individual autonomy signifies an unregulated 'private' sphere counterpoised to the regulated 'public' sphere; this is the basis for the view of private relationships as relationships 'free from' intervention. Feminist work has shown how public life is constituted in relation to private life, demonstrating that these realms are interdependent or mutually constituted.[25] For example, the legal premise that the family is naturally private unless and until intervention is justified by a breach of specific legislation constructs a boundary and in so doing forms a 'private' set of relationships, while law is regarded as concerned with the 'public' or 'regulated' sphere. Yet, in constructing this boundary, law (in contemporary societies often, as in child protection practices, backed by a range of scientific ideas) defines both public and private by identifying what will be the scope of intervention and what will be left private: what is left unregulated is as significant as what is regulated. The idea of privacy or of a sphere beyond legitimate public intervention may legitimate the continuation of other norms and power relations, for example the 'patriarchal' ordering of the private family (Pateman 1988). The traditional liberal conception of this division is inadequate as a description and as a normative account of social life because it is unable fully to grasp child sex abuse as a problem occurring largely in a paramount site of privacy: the family.

Feminist arguments have done much to highlight problems attending the use of liberal political thought to analyse the contemporary governance of child sexual abuse. However, in paying attention to the ways in which liberalism presents an understanding of public and private as separate spheres, feminists have done little to elucidate the ways in which liberalism as a strategy of government mobilises the family in the service of the production of autonomous individuals. To consider this we can turn to Pateman's argument that in the liberal division of public and private spheres the family is 'forgotten' (1988: 12). Pateman provides a critique of liberal contractarianism as a continuation of patriarchy in its modern form. She examines how, in the story of the social contract, civil society is created through a compact between autonomous individuals that takes those participating from a 'state of nature' to 'civil government' (1988: 25–8). She points out that by beginning with the autonomous individual liberal contractarianism assumes, but does not disclose, a prior contract, the sexual contract, a contract between men over the ownership and exchange of women and children. Pateman argues that, in contractarian accounts, the family is both presupposed and forgotten as the natural and necessary foundation of civil and public life (1988: 12). For example, in discussions of the appropriate place of the state versus civil society which dominate liberal accounts the role and dynamics of familial relations are obscured; the family is for the most part occluded from analysis and public and private are treated as separate spheres, despite the fact that patriarchal familial relations play a constitutive role in making possible the form of public envisioned by liberal political theorists, a public of autonomous individuals.

What does it mean to argue that in the liberal separation of public and private the family is 'forgotten'? We should remember that the force of Pateman's argument is that the family is occluded as the underside of the autonomous individual making the contract that founds political society. In this respect, Pateman's analysis is insightful in providing a critique of the ways in which, in attempting to ground an argument for political obligation, liberal contractarian arguments work, and indeed begin, with the assumption of the rational, fully-formed individual. However, as we have seen, it is not clear that liberalism 'forgets' the family. Rather than being forgotten, within liberal strategies of argument the family is repositioned; that is, the family ceases to be seen as the appropriate model for government, and becomes instead an instrument of government (this theme is followed up in Chapter 5). Within liberalism, the question of paternal authority and that of political authority are separated from one another, paternal (and later parental) authority being justified by reference to arguments concerning the differential strength and capacities for reason of adults and children.[26]

Within liberalism, therefore, the family is not forgotten, nor is it treated as unproblematically hierarchical (Gobetti 1997). Rather, the family is an instrument and agent of liberal governance, a means of producing autonomous individuals, and only able to function as such given the requisite degree of privacy. Rather than forgetting the family, therefore, liberal political thought prioritises it as a paramount site of privacy and invests this site with expectations. Liberal theorists and political regimes engage in endless discussions concerning where to draw the line between public and private life; in so doing, liberals both assume and continuously problematise the distinction between what is public and what is private. This is the context in which calls of crisis concerning the governance of child sexual abuse take shape, are played out and in which patterns of governance are established and reconfigured. This is the ground that we need to reproblematise.

Conclusion

From the brief sketch of the emergence of modern conceptions of childhood and of the modern family in Chapter 1 and from the discussion of liberal political thought in this chapter we have seen that within contemporary patterns of governance childhood is understood as a natural stage of dependence, prior to the attainment of autonomy in adulthood. Children are effectively excluded from public life and constituted as a central element within private familial relations. Children then become a focus of concern on the part of others. Liberal theorists have attempted to cope with this ambiguous position of children, either by suggesting that children be granted rights or by proposing that adults be appointed as guardians of their welfare (Archard 1993; Franklin 1986; Harris 1982; O'Donovan 1993; O'Neill 1989). These strategies of argument, whilst being in their own terms quite different from one another, can be seen to operate with the notion of a distinction between public and private domains as realms of state sovereignty and individual autonomy respectively, simply providing different modes of mediating this distinction in order better to protect and/or represent children within liberal practices of government.

Noting the way in which modern conceptions of childhood, privacy and moral reform form parts of a single constellation is important in providing grounds for criticism of the idea of the private as an unregulated or 'free' sphere as supposed in liberal political thought and, as will be shown, within contemporary Critical

Theory, both of which have tended to characterise the family as a haven. Instead it becomes possible to see that the emergence of the privacy of the modern familial relations has been accompanied by regulation under the liberal state; that is, privacy is a notion conditional upon and conditioned by the maintenance of social norms within this sphere. These related developments demonstrate the inadequacy of the public/private distinction as it has been formulated within liberal political discourse. A central concern of liberalism is the question of where to draw boundaries between public and private life; as such liberalism presupposes this distinction and cannot consequently reflect on the politics of this distinction, that is the way this distinction operates to underpin a particular kind of political rationality.

One of the central arguments of this book is that thinking critically about child sexual abuse requires that we are able examine how particular notions of childhood have come into being and are considered natural at the same time as being continuously re-entrenched by particular practices of government; that is, how childhood functions as a naturalised historical product. Furthermore, we need to be able to theorise the relation between public and private spheres as central to the problematic of discourses of child welfare. We need a form of analysis that does not presuppose a division between public and private and consequently focus attention on where to draw the boundary between these domains. Rather, what is required is a form of analysis that is capable of examining how this distinction emerged and its role in constituting and maintaining intractable problems in the governance of family relations. Liberal political theory is limited in its capacity to provide a way to think through the relation of public and private, as this distinction is foundational to liberalism itself.

In summary, the analytical categories of liberalism prevent a full examination of the problems that emerge in connection with child sexual abuse. As a theory, liberalism tends to reify the privatism and familialism identified as distinctively modern in Chapter 1 into foundational categories of political thought. In the process, a set of historically contingent social configurations are taken as given and form the basis of numerous articulations of the public/private distinction. This limits the capacity of liberalism to give a critical and distanced account of the relation of public and private or the discourses of science and law through which this is articulated and managed. Liberal ideas are not alone in this, as the next chapter demonstrates.

3 From liberal to Critical Theory

Child, family and state through the system/lifeworld distinction

In the context of liberalism's presupposition of a public/private distinction and naturalised understanding of the status of childhood, a question arises concerning how to theorise the public and the private and the relationship between them. This is important in order to account for the problematic and shifting concern with child sexual abuse and its management. Jürgen Habermas, the leading contemporary exponent of Critical Theory,[1] presents a critical diagnosis and normative reframing of state–society relations that attempts to address and respond to the dilemmas of liberal democratic welfare states. His recent work accords a central place to the analysis of state–family relations in understanding the dynamics of conflict in modern societies, and provides clarification of the relationship between expertise and democratic decision-making that might have a positive impact on the governance of child sexual abuse.

Habermas seeks to produce a systematic social theory with a practical intent; central to this is the aim to provide a framework for the analysis of the emergence and contemporary dynamics of modern state–society relations. In particular, he provides a socio-theoretical account that aims to explain the development of modern social 'pathologies', using examples from the field of child welfare to do so.

The aim of this chapter is both to elucidate the ways in which Habermas's work can inform an understanding of conflicts in state–family relations, and to demonstrate the limits of framing an analysis of the governance of child sexual abuse wholly in Habermas's terms. Habermas's theory, whilst useful in highlighting some of the features of recent 'crises' in the governance of child sexual abuse, is limited in its capacity to account for such problems of governance. This is because the theory is grounded on a foundational distinction between the 'system' and the 'lifeworld', and on naturalised assumptions concerning the status of childhood. Habermas's analysis reiterates liberal arguments in a sociological guise, and thus, rather than providing an alternative to such arguments in the analysis of the governance of child sexual abuse, it succumbs to similar limits. While his account provides several proposals that could help to refine child protection law and practice, so as to lead possibly toward more sensitive handling of cases that might avert conditions of 'crisis', this is limited to refining the understandings and practices of governance that we already have.

Habermas's work addresses many issues of central concern to contemporary social and political theory and jurisprudence. His account has developed significantly since *The Theory of Communicative Action* (1984, 1987a), but the framework of concepts for the analysis of modern societies established there continues to underpin the main parameters of his project. Therefore, this chapter begins by considering the argument laid out in this earlier work, showing how this provides a possible way of analysing conflicts concerning the governance of child sexual abuse, and drawing out its limitations. The chapter then moves on to consider how some of these problems are overcome while others resurface in Habermas's more recent work, principally *Between Facts and Norms* (1996).

Rethinking the public/private distinction: system and lifeworld in *The Theory of Communicative Action*

We can begin by examining how Habermas refigures conventional understandings of the public/private distinction. To do this we need to outline his account of action types, processes of rationalisation, and the concepts 'lifeworld' and 'system'. Fundamental to Habermas's account of modernity is the analytic distinction he makes between two categorically different types of action and processes of rationalisation. Running through the work is the distinction between communicative action and purposive rational action. The first action type, communicative action, takes place essentially through language and refers to the interaction of at least two subjects. Such action is oriented toward reaching an understanding (Habermas 1984: 86). In contrast, purposive rational action is action oriented to success: 'the actor attains an end or brings about the occurrence of a desired state by choosing means that have the promise of being successful in the given situation and applying them in a suitable manner' (1984: 85). With this framework of two action types, Habermas reformulates Weber's conceptualisation of the process of social rationalisation, proposing two separate potential evolutionary dimensions corresponding to the two action orientations.[2]

The theory of social evolution that Habermas develops to explain the rationalisation processes of modernity leads him to develop a two level concept of society, corresponding to the two action orientations: those of the lifeworld and the system. The modern lifeworld is formulated as 'a reservoir of taken for granteds, of unshaken convictions that participants in communication draw upon in cooperative processes of interpretation' (1987a: 124). The lifeworld is reproduced through communicative action and serves as a background source of situation definitions, it is 'always already intuitively present to all of us as a totality that is unproblematized, nonobjectified, and pretheoretical – as the sphere of that which is daily taken for granted, the sphere of common sense' (1992: 38). The rationalisation of the lifeworld takes the form of a disenchantment consequent upon the secularisation of world views. Previously unquestioned relations of authority break down, are opened to question, and require justification through argument. The lifeworld therefore undergoes rationalisation in terms of the attainment of 'communicatively achieved understanding' as opposed to 'normatively ascribed agreement' (1984: 70). Enlarging on previous sociological concepts, Habermas argues that the lifeworld is symbolically reproduced and structurally complex, involving the processes of cultural reproduction, social integration and socialisation, functions that have been differentiated out through evolution (1987a: 152). For Habermas, the lifeworld consists in the private nuclear family and the public political sphere.

In contrast, Habermas claims that the system or sphere of material production and purposive rational action is progressively differentiated from lifeworld contexts of symbolic reproduction through the process of rationalisation. The concept of 'system' refers to those mechanisms in modern society that have been 'uncoupled' from the communicative context of the lifeworld and are coordinated through functional interconnections via the media of money and power (1987a: 50). System integration concerns the material reproduction of society and is organised principally through the institutionalisation of purposive rational action within the modern economy and state. These institutions are separated from lifeworld contexts of communicative action through rationalisation as differentiation and increasing complexity require systems for the coordination of action separated from the need for normative agreement (1984: 72). In contrast to the lifeworld then, the rationalisation of systems can be regarded as an increase in their bureaucratic complexity and 'steering capacity' (1987a: 152). The system, for Habermas, comprises the modern economy and state administration.

Habermas suggests that we conceive of society as 'a system that has to fulfil conditions for the maintenance of sociocultural lifeworlds' (1987a: 151–2). While the lifeworld and system have different developmental logics and are progressively 'uncoupled' in modern society, they nevertheless remain interdependent. The system remains anchored in the lifeworld and is dependent upon the structural possibilities and limitations which develop with the rationalisation of the lifeworld (1987a: 148). It is from this sphere that the economic and political subsystems differentiated originally and which continues to be the basis of their normative support and reproduction, even as they become increasingly bureaucratic and divorced from the lifeworld context.

We can now specify the way in which Habermas reformulates the public/private distinction. Habermas posits two distinct but interrelated public/private distinctions in modern societies: one lies within the lifeworld, between the public political sphere and the private family, the other runs between the state and the private commercial relations of the capitalist economy. Whereas liberalism figures the question of legitimation in terms of appropriate limits to the state and public political sphere in relation to the economy and family, for Habermas the question of legitimation and its problems are drawn between, on one hand, the lifeworld of public political discourse and the private family organised principally through communicative action, and on the other hand, the system coordinated spheres of the modern economy and state. This can be represented in the following manner:

	Public	*Private*
System	state	economy
Lifeworld	public political sphere	family

Where liberals draw the question of legitimacy vertically, emphasising the importance of limits to public power per se, Habermas draws the question of legitimacy horizontally, namely emphasising the importance of limits to systems centred on material reproduction and organised through money and power in relation to lifeworld institutions that are symbolically organised. Thus, Habermas's concern is not with the traditional liberal question of the appropriate limits of public authority as such, rather the question is framed in terms of the appropriate limits of the system and its attendant rationality. This reframing of the public/ private distinction helps to elucidate what Habermas calls the crisis tendencies of democratic welfare states, by figuring problems associated with such states as problems of the 'mediatisation' and 'colonisation' of the lifeworld by systems imperatives.

What are the dynamics of the relations between the system and the life-world? For Habermas the functional coordination offered by systems is required by the need to manage problems produced by the increasing complexity and differentiation of modern societies. In such societies world views are progressively decentred and there is an increasing risk of disagreement, so that norm-free system coordination of action becomes necessary (1984: 69, 72). This, however, produces tensions in the relationship between the lifeworld and the system. Habermas explains this through developing the concepts mediatisation and colonisation.

The lifeworld becomes mediatised to the extent that money and power are used to relate the system and the lifeworld. This process occurs through the social roles of employee, consumer, citizen and client. In assuming these roles, actors detach themselves from the lifeworld and adapt to formally organised domains of action (1987a: 185). Monetarisation and bureaucratisation supplant communicative action with purposive rational action, 'driv[ing] moral–practical elements out of private and public political spheres of life' (1987a: 325). According to Habermas, this mediatisation of the lifeworld takes on the form of an 'internal colonisation' when the delinguistified media of the system take over the essential symbolic reproduction functions of the lifeworld itself, thereby 'objectifying' or 'reifying' social relationships (1987a: 305).

Colonisation occurs where 'media-controlled subsystems of the economy and the state intervene with monetary and bureaucratic means in the symbolic reproduction of the lifeworld' (1987a: 356). This has a double implication: reification of relationships within the lifeworld itself, which involves loss of meaning and, as a consequence of this, the production of deficits of legitimation and motivation necessary for the maintenance of the legitimacy of the economy and state systems.

According to Habermas, the internal colonisation of the lifeworld produces pathological effects as the lifeworld has some essentially symbolic functions, that is it is concerned with socialisation, social integration and understanding, all of which rely on communicative action and thus cannot be successfully replaced by the delinguistified media of money and power (1987a: 364). The lifeworld is an arena of authenticity and consensual understanding, necessary to and different from the bureaucratic purposive rational character of the system. A focal example of colonisation, one used by Habermas in *The Theory of Communicative Action* (1987a), is state intervention into the internal structure of family life through welfare policy. Before we attend to this example, we need to say a little more about how law and science are conceived within this framework for the understanding and critical diagnosis of modern societies.

Habermas recognises that the colonisation thesis is very abstract. He suggests that it may be tested by examining evidence of the 'juridification of communicatively structured areas of action' (1987a: 356). Habermas uses the term 'juridification' to refer to 'the tendency toward an increase in formal (or positive, written) law that can be observed in modern society' (1987a: 357). He draws a distinction between increasing density of law in the form of more detailed statements and the extension of law into previously informally regulated areas of social life. In volume 2 of *The Theory of Communicative Action*, he is primarily concerned with the latter, locating the pathological consequences of colonisation as a 'symptomatic consequence of *a specific kind* of juridification' (1987a: 357, emphasis in text), that is the juridification of previously informally organised domains of action.

Legal codification or juridification is the means through which system and lifeworld differentiated, with 'formally organized' relations being those 'constituted in the form of modern law' (1987a: 357). Habermas discerns four stages in the extension of law, culminating in the institutionalisation of the democratic welfare state. The first stage of juridification took place with the establishment of the bourgeois state under the absolutist regimes of Europe; this regulated sovereign monopoly over coercion and provided contractual rights for private persons as a condition of free enterprise in emerging market economies. With this first stage of juridification, the economy and the state were differentiated from the lifeworld and became subsystems organised through the media of money and power (1987a: 358). The second stage of juridification took place with the formation of the bourgeois constitutional state; this regulated individual rights to life, liberty and property against the political authority of the monarch. The third stage of juridification brought political emancipation through the formation of the democratic constitutional state in the wake of the French Revolution. Finally, the fourth stage of juridification consisted in attempts to secure social rights from the state in the form of the twentieth century democratic welfare state.

In the first two stages of juridification, Habermas argues that the operation of law was internal to the regulation of systems of money and power; as such he regards these developments as freedom guaranteeing. In the third stage, that of the formation of the democratic constitutional state, Habermas detects an 'ambiguity in the rationalization of law' (1984: 270). While participatory rights guarantee freedom their bureaucratic implementation curtails possibilities for 'spontaneous opinion formation and discursive will formation' (1987a: 364). According to Habermas, this is a problem not of the form of law itself but of its implementation. Ambivalences attending the introduction of the form of law itself accompany the fourth stage of juridification: in this phase, law as a medium of state administration supplants communicative contexts of action with monetary compensation and therapeutic assistance. In such contexts, the independent organisation of the lifeworld is threatened by the colonising tendencies of the system, spreading 'a web of client relations over the private spheres of life' (1987a: 364). The 'pathological side effects' of this form of juridification are a result of the fact that the extension of legal mechanisms that this involves formalises previously informal and communicatively organised relations, as such it constitutes a 'bureaucratization and a monetarization of core areas of the life world' (1987a: 364).

> The *dilemmatic structure of this type of juridification* consists in the fact that, while the welfare-state guarantees are intended to serve the goal of social integration, they nevertheless promote the disintegration of life-relations when these are separated, through legalized social intervention, from the consensual mechanisms that coordinate action and are transferred over to media such as power and money.
>
> (1987a: 364, emphasis in text)

For Habermas, in so far as juridification supplants a communicative context of action with law as a medium, this is linked to the colonisation thesis. In *The Theory of Communicative Action* (1987a), Habermas uses the example of legal intervention into family life through welfare policies as an instance of juridification leading to pathological colonisation. This is because, according to Habermas, the situations regulated by welfare policy are 'embedded in the context of a life history and of a concrete form of life' that necessarily suffers 'violent abstraction' if it is to be dealt with within a legal and administrative, that is 'formal', framework (1987a: 363). Thus the dilemma of increasing the scope of welfare legislation is that such guarantees destroy 'consensual mechanisms that coordinate action' (1987a: 364), transforming them over to administration through the media of money and power.

At the centre of Habermas's argument concerning the juridification of family life through the intervention of the welfare state is the hypothesis that the establishment of legal principles such as the child's rights against those of his/her parents means 'not increasing the density of an already existing network of formal regulations, but rather, legally supplanting a communicative context of action through the superimposition of legal norms' (1987a: 369). Legal intervention into the family fundamentally transforms the social relations within it and therefore, from Habermas's perspective, precipitates pathological effects as 'in these spheres of the lifeworld we find, *prior* to any juridification, norms and contexts of action that by functional necessity are based on mutual understanding as a mechanism for coordinating action' (1987a: 369, emphasis in text).

Habermas is less explicit in formulating an account of the role of scientific knowledge in the forms of governance that accompany the welfare state than he is about the role of law. However, we can develop an account of this from what he does say about modern science and other expert cultures to show how the splitting off of science into expert cultures segmented from lifeworld contexts of everyday communication can imply, for Habermas, a reification and cultural impoverishment of the lifeworld. To do this, we need to return to Habermas's account of social evolution and specifically to his account of rationalisation as a process of differentiation.

For Habermas, differentiation is something set in train by modernisation, and this brings with it the break down of previously unified narratives. That is, the totalising unity of mythological, religious and metaphysical narratives that comprised one interpretive system 'up to the threshold of modernity' (1992: 17) have been broken down under the impact of processes of modernisation. Habermas documents how, from the seventeenth century in the natural sciences, and the eighteenth century in moral and legal theory, totalising thinking has been progressively displaced by procedural rationality (1984: 72; also 1992: 33). This is expressed as a process of disenchantment whereby modernisation produces a 'linguistification of the sacred' (1984: 141). Rationalisation produces a differentiation of religion (morality and law), science (knowledge) and art (aesthetics), such that each develops its own internal criteria of validity (1984: 197–215).

> The basic concepts of religion and metaphysics had relied upon a syndrome of validity that dissolved with the emergence of expert cultures in science, morality, and law on the one hand, and with the autonomization of art on the other. [. . .] Since the eighteenth century, the forms of argumentation specializing in objectivating knowledge, moral–practical insight, and aesthetic judgement have diverged from one another.
>
> (1992: 17)

Whilst this is progressive in producing increasing rationality in each of these value spheres, one of the implications of this process is the danger that expert cultures become segmented from the lifeworld, with the resultant effect of what Weber called loss of meaning and what Habermas terms reification and cultural impoverishment. Habermas documents this thus:

> As traditional problems are divided up under the specific viewpoints of truth, normative rightness, and authenticity or beauty, and are dealt with respectively as questions of knowledge, justice, or taste, there is a differentiation of the value spheres of science, morality, and art. In the corresponding cultural action systems, scientific discourse, studies in moral and legal theory, and the production and criticism of art are all institutionalized as the affairs of experts. [. . .] In consequence of this professionalization, the distance between expert cultures and the broader public grows greater. What accrues to a culture by virtue of specialized work and reflection does not come *as a matter of course*

into the possession of everyday practice. Rather, cultural rationalization brings with it the danger that a lifeworld devalued of its traditional substance will become impoverished.

(1987a: 326, emphasis in text)

Through the process of rationalisation the cultural value spheres of morality, science and art are separated from each other and segmented from the lifeworld as they become entrenched within expert cultures (1987a: 327, 331). Habermas comments that, 'It is not the differentiation and independent development of cultural value spheres' as such 'that lead to the cultural impoverishment of every-day communicative practice, but an elitist splitting-off of expert cultures from contexts of communicative action in daily life' (1987a: 330). That is, in so far as specialist discourse is split off from everyday practice, this produces disjunctions between reasoning in formally organised domains of action and in informally regulated lifeworld contexts, providing the grounds for what Habermas calls 'frag-mented consciousness': 'everyday consciousness' is 'thrown back onto traditions whose claims to validity have already been suspended' or becomes 'splintered' (1987a: 355). This is the context in which Habermas argues the 'conditions for a *colonization of the lifeworld* are met' (1987a: 355, emphasis in text).

The conditions of 'pathology' diagnosed by Habermas as the result of systemic mechanisms penetrating the symbolic reproductive sphere of the lifeworld, and the fragmentation of consciousness such that everyday consciousness suffers a dis-junction from expert cultures, are regarded as the result of 'selective' or one-sided rationalisation where media steered subsystems are 'objectified into a norm-free reality beyond the horizon of the lifeworld' (1987a: 327): law as a medium of state administration introduces the 'delinguistified' media of money and power into the private family and public political sphere, and expert discourses of science fail to connect with the everyday communicative practice of the lifeworld.

Habermas argues that what is needed is a shift in this balance; that the purposive rational orientation of systems is not inherently harmful, but that it must be brought under the control of the communicative rationality implicit in the lifeworld. He suggests that there is a need to retrieve the potential for rationality of practical and communicative activity, and that therefore the possibility of an undistorted intersubjectivity 'must today be wrung from the professional, specialized, self-sufficient culture of experts and from the system imperatives of the state and economy which destructively invade the ecological basis of life and the communicative infrastructure of our lifeworld' (1985: 210; also 1992: 18, 51). Habermas locates the possibility for such resistance in the public political spheres of civil society, specifically in social movements emerging along the seam between the system and the lifeworld.

This account suggests that the major channels of conflict in modern capitalist societies are not class conflicts, but the results of the self-destructive consequences of system growth. The major lines of conflict in modern societies arise and exist along the seam between the system and the lifeworld as the result of lifeworld responses to the threat of colonisation.

Assessing *The Theory of Communicative Action* in the light of problems in the governance of child sexual abuse

Habermas's account provides a number of useful insights into contemporary problems in the governance of state–family relations. He highlights problems attending the formalisation of family relations through juridification, raises questions concerning the relationship between expert cultures and everyday communicative practice, and makes the provocative suggestion that we understand modern welfare states in terms of delinguistified steering mechanisms penetrating the lifeworld, producing a pathological colonisation of its core functions. We will assess each moment in this account.

First, we can note that Habermas's comments on the juridification of family life as a result of welfare law and policy do much to highlight contemporary questions concerning the capacity of the state effectively to intervene to secure welfare. This way of posing the problems attending state intervention into families elucidates ambivalences noted by a number of scholars that often state interventions to secure welfare are accompanied by new forms of dependence. Habermas comments that, 'The protection of the welfare of the child as a basic right can be implemented only by giving the state possibilities to intervene in parental privileges, once regarded as untouchable' (1987a: 369). He goes on to cite an empirical study of child custody laws in the (pre-1990) Federal Republic of Germany that he suggests highlights the 'dilemmatic structure of the juridification of the family' (1987a: 369). He quotes the study approvingly:

> However indispensable state services may be, they not only bring advantages for individual family members, but simultaneously bring about increasing dependence. Emancipation within the family is achieved at the cost of a new bond. In order to constitute himself [*sic*] as a person, the individual family member sees himself compelled to make claims on the assistance of the state. What therefore, at first sight, is sometimes presented as an instrument for breaking up domination structures within the family, proves on closer examination to be also a vehicle for another form of dependence.
>
> (Simitis and Zen 1975, quoted in Habermas 1987a: 369–70)

Anyone familiar with feminist writing on the dilemmas of welfare states will recognise the ambiguity that attends the move from dependence within private family relationships to dependence upon the state.[3] More specifically in relation to child welfare, this comment is consonant with contemporary unease about the sometimes deleterious effects of intervention as itself prone to producing damaging effects on individuals, that is with the idea that intervention may itself do harm. We will return to Habermas's concern with the impact of juridification on family relationships below in discussing the colonisation thesis, before doing so we can note that he suggests that 'replacing the judge with the therapist is no panacea; the social worker is only another expert, and does not free the client of the welfare state bureaucracy from his or her position as an object' (1987a: 370).

Habermas's suggestion that the social worker is 'only another expert' brings us to the second issue raised by his analysis, that of expert cultures sealed off from everyday communicative practice 'making their way into the lifeworld from the outside – like colonial masters coming into a tribal society' (1987a: 355). What are we to make of this claim? This is certainly how paediatricians and social workers in Cleveland, and even more so the social workers involved in Orkney, were depicted in press reports. Press accounts of the social workers involved in Orkney presented them as invading the natural contexts of action of the families and community, bringing about its destruction through bureaucratic interference, and as would-be professionals out of step with the predominant and accepted cultural understandings of the communities concerned. By contrast, the press presented local Orkney GPs as repositories of sanity and commonsense experience, as 'home grown' experts able to mesh the local value system with their professional activity (see Chapter 7). In a different tone, the report of the Cleveland Inquiry was critical of the professionals involved for acting precipitously on insufficiently founded knowledge of the signs of child sexual abuse, and for failing properly to balance priorities in order to ensure that the goal of child protection was met without the production of a crisis in the management of resources (see Chapter 6).

These criticisms might be interpreted as evidence for Habermas's argument. His account of the elitist splitting off of expert cultures such that professionals' understandings clash with the horizon of values presented by the lifeworld is certainly valuable in highlighting the stresses caused by the dislocation of experts' judgements from everyday communicative contexts of action. However, this analysis runs the risk of overemphasising the split between expert cultures and lifeworld contexts. Experts, after all, participate in lifeworlds as laypersons also.[4] What Habermas diagnoses, then, is at least in part more properly described as a tension that arises within the notion of legitimate expertise. The claim to legitimacy of the expert is predicated on a claim to ethical neutrality or disinterestedness, experts are supposed to discern the 'facts' of a case, and to act according to those facts. As such, experts are supposed to leave behind their own ethical concerns, or at least not to let these cloud their professional scientific judgement. This is borne out by the Cleveland Inquiry's criticism not just of the paediatricians and social workers who took the children into care, but also of the police surgeons involved, for being overly evaluative and non-neutral in their presentations of evidence countering the diagnoses of sexual abuse (see Chapter 6). Therefore, where the professionals involved in Cleveland and Orkney were concerned, it appears that their expertise was compromised by their taking overtly moral and evaluative positions in relation to the issue of child sexual abuse that were not in accordance with dominant norms of either the system or the lifeworld, and by the break-down of consensus amongst experts concerning the 'facts' of the cases concerned, rather than simply by their outstepping the conventions of lifeworld understandings of family dynamics.

Moving to the third issue raised by Habermas's analysis of modern state–society relations further important features of this account can be drawn out. The idea of the system colonisation of the lifeworld suggests that family–state relations are central to the crisis dynamics of modernity, and that organisations such as parents' rights groups might be considered to be lifeworld protests against system over-extension. Habermas's thesis is that the colonisation of the lifeworld by systems imperatives produces responses to this threat from the lifeworld itself, that colonisation creates a zone of conflict along the seam between the system and the lifeworld with protest aiming to defend the lifeworld from intervention by the system. In the context of the politicisation of modern child protection practice, a number of movements have emerged that suggest that this may be the case.

Since the 1970s a number of different organisations have, in diverse ways, contested the right of the state to intervene to protect children. Groups such as Parents Against Injustice (PAIN), founded in 1985 in Britain, and other similar movements elsewhere, have attempted to secure the rights of families to privacy in the face of interventionist states. Claims have centred on concerns that intervention can itself cause harm to children to the point of being abusive, and that professionals in child protection often have discretionary powers that can leave parents and children in limbo. Such organisations have contested the medical and psychological evidence used to bring cases of suspected child sexual abuse into the remit of governance, and have fore-grounded the rights of parents and children to privacy in family relations, to be free from state intervention, frequently stressing that where intervention does take place it should be within strict procedural limits and with attention given to the guilt or innocence of parents.

Habermas's account of the colonisation of the lifeworld by the system helps to highlight and to explain the emergence of such organisations. From Habermas's theoretical perspective, the seam between system and lifeworld is a central channel for conflicts within democratic welfare states, and we can understand movements such as PAIN as lifeworld responses to, and attempts to reclaim social life from, unwarranted or overzealous intervention. This is how organisations such as PAIN present themselves and are presented in the press, as groups organising to claim back autonomy from an overintrusive and insensitive bureaucracy (see Chapters 6 and 7).

PAIN was particularly important during the events of Cleveland and Orkney. It proved a powerful vehicle for parents' voices, helping to frame the issues to be dealt with by the public inquiries in these cases, and having an important impact on the way the events were portrayed by the media. In both cases, PAIN campaigned for the recognition of the rights of parents and children against the power of the child protection system, on the basis that intervention was unjustified as the evidence supporting the cases was unfounded. PAIN articulated responses to Cleveland and Orkney in terms of the need to reclaim the rights of parents and children to family privacy, against the bureaucratic power and administrative discretion of child protection practitioners.[5] Within PAIN's position, therefore, there is a critique of the bureaucratic character of state intervention to protect children that resonates with Habermas's diagnosis of state intervention into the privacy of family life as 'pathological'.

However, while the colonisation thesis provides an explanation for movements aiming to defend the family against intrusion, it is less able to conceptualise feminist and other concerns voiced from within the 'lifeworld' for the need to uncover child sexual abuse, to establish recognition of its existence, and to achieve more effective intervention. Habermas's formulation of the problems attending state intervention into family life as one of colonisation of the lifeworld by the system, followed by lifeworld reaction, seems only to allow for and to make sense of movements against intervention. This is in large part because the colonisation thesis assumes that lifeworld protests are in essence 'reactions' to systems imperatives, such protests are theorised as emerging from the lifeworld and as directed against the encroachment of the system.

Habermas could claim that feminist and other concerns to politicise child sexual abuse are movements from within the public political sphere of the lifeworld, aimed at further rationalising the lifeworld by drawing critical attention to abusive practices taking place within it. That is, movements within the public political sphere attempting to achieve recognition of child sexual abuse as a problem existing principally within the private family could be regarded as attempts within the sphere of communicative action to bring about progressive change.[6] This, the dynamic of relationships between the public political sphere and the private family, remains undertheorised in *The Theory of Communicative Action* with its overriding emphasis on examining relations between the system and the lifeworld. Accepting this interpretation, we would simply have to insert into Habermas's discussion an account of the relationship between the public political sphere and the family in order to accommodate feminist and other concerns to achieve better practices of intervention. There is a problem, however, with this interpretation. It would require that Habermas theorise the lifeworld as itself a locus of power, something he does not do (see below; also Fraser 1989; Honneth 1991). In fact, in *The Theory of Communicative Action* Habermas's conclusion is that 'the juridification of communicatively structured areas of action should not go beyond the enforcement of principles of the rule of law, beyond the legal institutionalization of the *external* constitution of, say, the family' (1987a: 370–1, emphasis in text). Whilst feminist and other concerns to establish recognition of child sexual abuse and to find effective ways of addressing this do not necessarily presuppose legal intervention into the family, this is likely to be an important part of any strategy aiming to deal with this as a problem. Habermas's account though stresses the need for the family to be ring-fenced from legal intervention in order that it be able to organise its affairs informally; this puts aside the insight of the authors quoted by Habermas that 'emancipation within the family' may be necessary (see above) and can only be read as advocating recognition of the family as a domain outside of and prior to intervention. At this point we can note the similarity between Habermas's position and that forwarded by Rawls (as discussed in Chapter 2). As such, there is little room in *The Theory of Communicative Action* for an account of how and why the public political sphere might generate demands for rationalisation within the lifeworld.

In *The Theory of Communicative Action*, Habermas claims that intervention into the family by the state constitutes the system colonisation of a private realm of the lifeworld, which has necessarily 'pathological' effects due to the 'functional necessity' of symbolic ordering within the lifeworld. This account has two immediately deleterious effects in terms of conceptualising child sexual abuse and its management. First, positing a one-way relationship of the 'colonisation' of the lifeworld by the system provides an inadequate understanding of the relationships involved in battles over child abuse, witnessed for example in the conflict between feminist and other demands for more and better forms of intervention as against movements and organisations demanding rights to family privacy. Second, Habermas's claim that system intervention into the lifeworld produces 'pathological' effects is dependent upon a foundational distinction between system and lifeworld as, respectively, the inside and outside of power (Honneth 1991).[7] As such, Habermas's line of thought eclipses the possibility of recognising power relationships within the family (Fraser 1989). The family becomes a haven or consensual ground only disrupted by interventions from outside. The investigation of child abuse by public bureaucracies must then be regarded as akin to all other attempts by the system to intervene in family relationships. This is a very severe limitation on an analysis that would otherwise have the merit of bringing to the foreground conflicts concerning the management of child sexual abuse as central to the understanding of the tensions in the governance of modern societies. Within the framework provided by *The Theory of Communicative Action*, such conflicts can only be theorised as the result of lifeworld responses to the overzealous involvement of the state threatening the destruction of the norms of family life. This analysis thus obscures the family as itself an important site of power relations, within which violence and abusive sexuality may take place as part of the ordering of this institution.

Habermas's depiction of a consensual lifeworld threatened by colonisation from outside has been brought into question by feminist analyses highlighting the existence of power relations within families, and by analyses insisting on an understanding of the relations between the modern state and private family as mutually constitutive and supporting (Fraser 1989; Nicholson 1986; Pateman 1988; Ray 1993). Such accounts problematise the idea of a foundational difference between 'system' and 'lifeworld'. In the context of these criticisms it becomes clear that the colonisation thesis, and its posited 'pathological' effects, is directly dependent on a concept of the intimate sphere as prior to and outside legal regulation, and as informally and consensually regulated; that is, it is dependent upon an idea(l) of the private family as a domain outside power. Therefore, while Habermas's account helps to thematise important conflicts in modern societies, his way of pursuing the explanation and resolution of these in *The Theory of Communicative Action* is unhelpful.

Regrounding the public/private distinction: deliberative democracy and expertise in *Between Facts and Norms*

Habermas's recent work (1996) offers a more nuanced and dynamic account of the role of law in the relation between the state and the public political sphere than that provided in his earlier work. This does much to resolve the first problem identified above, the unidirectional account of systems mechanisms colonising the lifeworld. However, this account resituates and sustains rather than resolving the second problem noted earlier, the foundational character of a distinction between the system and the lifeworld within Habermas's account.

The central concern of *Between Facts and Norms* (1996) is to provide a theory of law and democracy capable of grounding more fully the claim to legitimacy of the constitutional state. Habermas is disturbed by 'lack of constitutional controls on administrative activity' (1996: 431). He locates the origin of this problem in the shift from the liberal meaning of legal order where the rule of law protected the legal freedom of the citizen from encroachment by the state, to the emergence of social welfare legislation the effect of which has been to produce a form of regulatory state in which strategies of risk prevention imply that much regulation is future-oriented and expansive. In this situation, control over administrative regulation does not admit of a return to a 'liberal understanding of government by law' (1996: 434). Instead Habermas proposes that we reconceptualise the relation between law and democracy. To this end, he outlines a procedural paradigm of law that he argues overcomes problems with previous understandings of law in modern society (1996: 419), and in which law gains its justification through public discourse or deliberative democracy.

This argument therefore reformulates the understanding of law found in *The Theory of Communicative Action* (1984, 1987a). In place of the more simplified understanding of law as a medium of the system that dominates this earlier work, law is now explicitly theorised as combining facticity (positive laws have coercive force) and validity (law gains legitimacy through its links with structures of communicative reason rooted in the lifeworld).[8] Rather than being framed as a central mechanism in the colonisation of the lifeworld as such, Habermas now grants legitimately produced law a more positive role in the coordination of complex societies:

> The legal code not only keeps one foot in the medium of ordinary language, through which everyday communication achieves social integration in the lifeworld; it also accepts messages that originate there and puts these into a form that is comprehensible to the special codes of the power-steered administration and the money-steered economy. To this extent the language of law, unlike the moral communication restricted to the lifeworld, can function as a transformer in the society-wide communication circulating between system and lifeworld.
>
> (1996: 81)

Habermas distinguishes between legitimate law and instrumentalised law in terms of a point where empowerment is turned into supervision. He suggests that the legitimation of law, including social welfare legislation, can be achieved through further institutionalisation of its democratic basis. This in turn suggests furthering democratic controls over expertise. The problems associated with law and with the forms of knowledge and practice generated within expert cultures are considered to stem from their inadequate grounding in processes of democratic will formation, an inadequacy that has become more acute as the burden of legitimacy has increased with the development of welfare states.[9]

This weakens the colonisation thesis, suggesting that the problems attending legal and scientific intervention into the family are not the formalisation that this brings per se, but rather the route this has taken. With this move, the problem of colonisation is reframed as a problem of the instrumentalisation of law by administration: 'law, having been *instrumentalized* for political goals and deprived of its internal structure, degenerates in the eyes of an independent administrative system into one more means of solving problems of functional integration' (1996: 429, emphasis in text). Similarly, where there is a redefinition of normative questions as technical issues to be addressed by experts, Habermas suggests this collapses values into facts and forecloses the democratic deliberation and adjudication that would be necessary in order adequately to establish norms justifying particular applications of expert knowledge (1996: 351).

In this context Habermas suggests that as law becomes increasingly important to the tasks of 'political steering and social planning, the greater is the burden of legitimation that must be borne by the *democratic genesis* of law' (1996: 428, emphasis in text). He therefore sets out a framework for the procedural justification of law, achieved through links to the public spheres of the lifeworld, suggesting that in this way law can provide a '*legitimation filter* into the decisional processes of an administration still oriented as much as ever toward efficiency' (1996: 440, emphasis in text).

This answers the first problem highlighted above, that of theorising struggles for more or better forms of intervention into the family. From Habermas's recent account these can be seen as demands orchestrated from within the diverse public spheres of the lifeworld, aimed at politicising aspects of family relations and challenging the legitimacy of ill-grounded administrative intervention, rather than simply as 'resistance' to intervention. This is particularly apt given that feminist concern has been to give publicity to the issue of child sexual abuse and that feminist demands are not simply or even for more state intervention (especially given growing recognition of 'institutional abuse'), they are for better principles and practices of intervention. Habermas's account now, therefore, more fully captures the complexities of struggles around the extension of law and expertise into intimate relations and focuses attention on the question of the legitimacy or illegitimacy of such interventions. This work refines the question of how and where to draw a distinction between public and private life, suggests closer links between public opinion formation in the lifeworld and the formal domain of the state in order more adequately to legitimate law and policy, and explicitly recognises that boundaries between intervention and non-intervention will shift as societal consensus changes in relation to newly identified issues.

What happens if we attempt to think through problems in the legitimation of child protection law and practice in terms of Habermas's proposals? To examine this, we need to outline his suggestions concerning the grounding of legitimate law and professional practice in deliberative democratic processes. With this account, Habermas aims to clarify the ways in which the potential for communicative rationality of the lifeworld can be brought into a constructive ongoing relation with formally structured systems.

Using *Between Facts and Norms* to articulate procedures for the governance of child sexual abuse

If we accept Habermas's account of the problems of legitimacy produced by the instrumentalisation of law and technocratic application of expert knowledge, and his proposals for the discursive relegitimation of these relations, what can we say about the procedures whereby a consensus concerning the governance of state–family relations, and therefore concerning the governance of child sexual abuse, could be achieved? Habermas's account of the discursive legitimation of law serves two purposes: it aims to ground the autonomy of law in rational principles, and it can be achieved only through procedures that facilitate the participation of those affected in the generation of just legal norms. This account has some potentially positive insights in relation to building an improved framework of legitimacy in the governance of child sexual abuse.

For Habermas, the legitimacy of positive law is derived not from a higher moral law but from procedures of rational will formation (1996: 457). He therefore seeks a means more adequately to ground the legitimacy of law in discursive practices of justification. On Habermas's account, the framing of just laws requires that the '*affected parties themselves*' (1996: 425, emphasis in text) conduct public discourses; this is something that cannot be delegated to judges, officials, or even to elected legislators (1996: 426). Here, the 'normative key is autonomy' (1996: 418):

> Individual self-determination manifests itself in the exercise of those rights derived from *legitimately produced* norms. For this reason the equal distribution of rights cannot be detached from the public autonomy that enfranchised citizens can exercise only in common, but taking part in the practice of legislation.
>
> (1996: 419, emphasis in text)

Under the account given in *Between Facts and Norms*, a legitimate balance between state intervention and family privacy in relation to child welfare and protection could be forged by building mechanisms through which all of those concerned could engage in public deliberation to achieve a consensus as to the appropriate measures to be taken in specific sorts of situations. This process of public deliberation would be aided by scientific evidence made available by experts. The deliberative process could then generate an account of legitimate legal regulation in this area by specifying the conditions under which the state, through experts secured in communicative contexts of culture, should intervene, and the ways in which they should intervene, in family life.

We can begin to specify the conditions for this by returning to Habermas's account of rationalisation and noting that, on his account, the rationalisation of communicative action in the lifeworld decentres the world views of subjects; rationalisation breaks down previously unquestioned relations of authority, opening them to scrutiny and requiring that they be justified through argument. In such contexts, Habermas argues that moral norms can be justified only through post-conventional moral reasoning (1979: Chapter 2, 1984: 260, 1992a: Chapter 7, 1993: Chapters 1–3, 1996: 71, 79–80, 97–8, 113–18). This requires that subjects take a reflexive relation to their claims in processes of open-ended and critical argumentation in which the aim is the impartial resolution of conflict through rational agreement.

To ground his argument that discursive democratic procedures could deliver legitimate law, Habermas develops a theory of argumentation that aims to discern the idealising presuppositions inherent in communicative action. He suggests, 'Anyone who seriously engages in argumentation must presuppose that the context of discussion guarantees in principle freedom of access, equal rights to participate, truthfulness on the part of the participants, absence of coercion in adopting positions, and so on' (1993: 31, also 56). In such contexts, participants take a hypothetical stance toward their claims, engage in impartial, reasoned debate about their own and others' points of view, and arrive at judgements that can be defended through arguments (1996: 113–18). It is important to note that this account of the presuppositions of argumentation operates as a regulative ideal; Habermas does not suggest that these conditions are usually realised in practical discourse, but rather that they are logically presupposed by entering into discourse at all and thus provide a counterfactual against which to assess actual discourses.

How is this discursive grounding of the legitimacy of law to be framed and take place? Habermas addresses this by distinguishing two stages of deliberation, the discursive justification of law and the discursive application of law; both are relevant to child protection law and policy.

The discursive justification of child law

Discourses of justification are concerned to ground and elaborate general norms. In such discourses, participants are required to abstract from their specific ethical perspectives to consider the good of all. Habermas specifies this in terms of the discourse principle 'D': 'just those action norms are valid to which all possibly affected persons could agree as participants in rational discourses' (1996: 107). This principle establishes a procedure for legitimate law-making in the idea of communicatively achieved agreement and rests on a principle of universalisation (1993: 32, 1996: 108–9).[10] A universalisation test requires that, 'every valid norm must satisfy the condition that the consequences and side effects of its *general* observance can be anticipated to have for the satisfaction of the interests of *each* could be freely accepted by *all* affected (and be preferred to those of known alternative possibilities for regulation)' (1993: 32, emphasis in text).

Habermas recognises that within political decision-making pragmatic discussions often take place about possible programmes for dealing with a problem, but argues that the formation of a reasonable will concerning the adoption of a particular programme involves more than this. If we accept that in relation to governmental decisions concerning child protection 'distribution of [. . .] life opportunities, and chances for survival in general are at stake' (1996: 165), then a morally relevant issue is at stake. This, according to Habermas, requires a discourse of justification that 'submit[s] the contested interests and value orientations to a universalization test' (1996: 165).

Habermas states that 'in discourses of justification there are in principle only participants' (1996: 172). However, 'justification depends primarily on a correct interpretation of the situation and the appropriate description of the problem at stake, as well as on the flow of relevant and reliable information' (1996: 164). Therefore, 'a certain expert knowledge is requisite, which is naturally fallible and rarely value-neutral, that is, uncontested' (1996: 164). It would therefore be necessary for experts to provide knowledge and information to the deliberative process.

A discourse of justification of norms concerning child welfare and protection might thus comprise a forum in which individuals and families affected or likely to be affected by child protection legislation and practice, informal organisations from the various public spheres of the lifeworld, including concerned individuals and campaign groups organised within civil society, accompanied and informed by professionals such as paediatricians, social workers, psychiatrists, psychologists and child lawyers, would debate the measures that would be appropriate given specific definitions of harmful situations. The process of justification of legal regulation in the field of child welfare would require the participants to abstract themselves from their own substantive ethical starting points and to engage in deliberation over available knowledge and ethical positions in order that they reach agreement over procedural rules. This kind of discussion might produce a set of general principles concerning the rights and needs of children, the rights and obligations of parents/guardians, and it might well privilege autonomy and therefore justify intervention when this is likely to be impeded, for example through 'abuse' as defined by prevailing scientific understandings.

Notably, Habermas assumes that in discourses of justification differences of power between participants are bracketed, so that the discussion takes the form of a deliberative argument delivering the possibility of a rational (because unforced) agreement. While he states that in discourses of justification there are in principle only participants, indicates that the role of expertise is to be limited to providing knowledge and information to deliberative processes, and specifies that such processes will involve a 'political evaluation of expertise and counter-expertise' (1996: 164) in an open argumentative process concerning different alternatives for addressing a problem, arguably his account does not fully address the importance of being able to frame what constitutes relevant knowledge and information (e.g. of 'abuse') in the first place. We should perhaps therefore note that some participants are likely to have more power and influence in determining the relevant features of specific situations likely to cause harm than are others.

Putting this limitation to one side for a moment, Habermas argues that discourses of justification provide only indeterminate general norms, they do not guarantee justice in individual cases; this is necessarily so due to the unforeseeable character of future situations and events (1996: 162, 217). Also, the discursive justification of norms says nothing about the application of such norms; that is, it leaves open the possible problem of professionally dominated interpretation of communicatively generated norms in the context of their application to specific cases. Habermas addresses both of these problems by suggesting that the application of norms must be institutionalised in a different manner from that of their justification.

The discursive application of child law

The indeterminacy of norms produced through discourses of justification requires that they be complemented by discourses of application. This latter form of discourse relies on the principle of appropriateness to a given case (1996: 162). 'Discourses of application refer not to the norm's validity but its *appropriate reference to a situation*' (1996: 217, emphasis in text). Such discourses require a decision about 'which of the valid norms is appropriate in a given situation whose relevant features have been described as completely as possible' (1996: 172). Habermas suggests that this would require that the parties concerned present 'all the contested aspects of a case before a judge who acts as the impartial representative of the legal community' (1996: 172). It also requires a 'distribution of responsibilities according to which the court must justify its judgement before a broad legal public sphere' (1996: 172). Therefore whereas in discourses of justification that seek to ground legitimate law expert determinations of situations are restricted to the capacity to provide knowledge and information to the discursive process (though, as noted above, this may in itself be key), discourses of application refer to the appropriate execution of an already legitimate law and as such will involve professional judgement.

This brings us to the second issue not dealt with by discursive practices of justification, namely the possibility of professionally dominated interpretations of norms in contexts of their application. On this point Habermas is emphatic, 'the population supposedly has the role of author, is a public of citizens – and does not just play the role of client' (1996: 395) and as such there is need for more than a 'self-legitimating code of professional ethics' (1996: 225). Thus the administrative power of professionals in their role as experts implementing the law must be tied to communicatively generated power. This means that administration must be able to 'carry out its tasks as professionally as possible, yet only under normative premises not at its disposal: the executive branch is to be limited to *employing* administrative power according to the law' (1996: 188, emphasis in text).

Habermas suggests several mechanisms for improving the accountability of professionals in relation to the exercise of their powers. He suggests the institutionalisation of a legal public sphere, stating that the 'burden of legitimation could be partly satisfied by additional obligations for courts to justify opinions before an enlarged critical forum specific to the judiciary' (1996: 440). However, he is also aware that 'juristic discourses of application must be visibly supplemented by elements taken from discourses of justification' (1996: 439) and, therefore, from lay involvement. He suggests that the appropriate arrangements for this could only be developed through 'cautious experimentation' (1996: 441), listing participation by clients, ombudspersons, quasi-judicial procedures, and hearings as possible arrangements (1996: 440).

What implication does this account of the discursive application of legal norms have for child protection practice? We can note certain similarities between Habermas's proposals for mechanisms to improve the accountability of professionals in the application of law through the institutionalisation of lay involvement in expert panels and the existing modes of operation of case conferences and magistrates hearings within the English and Scottish child protection systems. Habermas's proposals might suggest that parents (and possibly children, but see later in this chapter) should have direct and unlimited access to such decision-making fora.[11] However, this still leaves intact the question of who ultimately has power to define what constitutes an adequate description of the situation at hand. In particular, it raises issues concerning the respective weight given to different experts, and likely to be given to lay members of such decision-making fora as compared with those deemed experts, in making decisions concerning particular cases (this is considered in more detail in Chapters 6 and 7).

To elaborate, whilst Habermas's concern to tie administrative power to the law is consonant with the direction taken by the Children Act 1989 in its limiting of the discretionary power of child protection practitioners, his suggestion that this would overcome the problem of the professional determination of cases supposes that the normalising power of experts can be eliminated through a properly functioning juridical framework. One might, arguably with equal justification, suppose that the proposals outlined by Habermas would produce a greater capacity for normalisation through more thoroughly articulating experts' understandings of the dynamics of family life to a broader audience.[12] Ironically, this might further 'juridify' (and 'scientise') individuals' everyday understandings of their relations with one another – something that would go against Habermas's desire, as expressed in *The Theory of Communicative Action*, to dejudicialise family conflict (see above and Habermas 1987a: 370–1).

In stressing the need to bind administrative power to democratically sanctioned norms this part of Habermas's argument might be read as in large part a clarification and reiteration of the principles of liberal constitutionalism. However, in attempting to regulate more precisely those normalising and future oriented aspects of governance that attend welfare provisions, it has a number of interesting implications for the field of child protection. For example, the suggestion that experts should be limited to employing administrative power according to the law suggests that any proactive move on the part of professionals that extends their remit of governance, by for example identifying previously unregulated or informally regulated issues as issues for intervention, is illegitimate unless already grounded in the communicative power of discursively generated and sanctioned norms. This goes further in wishing to curtail the power of experts than the findings and recommendations of the Cleveland Inquiry. This was critical of the proactive stance taken by the paediatricians involved in so far as they actively looked for abuse, but its main points of criticism concerned the use of RAD and disclosure interviews to justify intervention in suspected sexual abuse cases, on the grounds that these techniques were insufficiently grounded in consensus amongst experts for the evidence from them to be used to justify intervention (see Chapter 6).

The principal gain for child protection legislation and practice that could come out of Habermas's account of the discursive justification and application of laws is the insertion of more deliberation into existing practices of governance. Despite the queries just raised, we can note two potentially positive features of this account for the legitimacy of attempts to govern child sexual abuse. First, it holds out the hope of more sensitive legal formulations by specifying close connections between everyday communicative understandings and formal processes of law-making. Second, it recognises the contestability of scientific knowledge, the problems this can produce for democratic governance, and attempts to deal with this.

Turning to the first point, Habermas's formulation for arriving at just laws ties their formation to communicative understandings within the lifeworld, whilst simultaneously placing strict procedural constraints on the conditions of discourse itself (it must take place with principles of equality, respect and openness in mind), and on the outcome (a norm only achieves justification by surviving a test of universalisation). Although this might limit the outcome of such a discourse to the provision of a general normative framework, it has the benefit of suggesting that the formulation of just norms must be grounded in participation amongst those affected, or likely to be affected, and therefore suggests the possibility of a more sensitive framing of general principles. In so far as 'the public sphere draws its impulses from the private handling of social problems that resonate in life histories' (1996: 366), then one should expect that closer links between individuals as citizens, informally organised civil associations, and the making of legislation would produce greater sensitivity to new issues and more responsive handling of established ones.

As regards the second feature of Habermas's account, it attempts to deal with the problems for democracy posed by expertise through suggesting a range of institutions that could act as bridges between expert discourses of science, processes of public deliberation, and the broader political culture. Whilst Habermas regards the regulatory activities of the welfare state as necessarily implying reliance on professionally generated information and technical expertise (1996: 435), he argues that this does not mean that solutions to legitimation problems can be found within a technocratic framework: 'The technocratic denial and empiricist redefinition of normative questions in no way leads to a matter-of-fact treatment of administrative problems' (1996: 436). Rather, as we have seen, his solution to this problem of legitimacy is to further institutionalise constitutional principles and underpin them with deliberative democratic processes.

Habermas articulates a fruitful account of the role of scientific knowledge in relation to democratic legitimacy, suggesting that while science provides necessary statements of a factual nature, these cannot in themselves ground values: 'one cannot explain the rightness of normative judgements along the lines of a correspondence theory of truth, for rights are a social construction that one must not hypostatize into facts. "Rightness" means rational acceptability supported by good reasons' (1996: 226). Therefore, whilst the validity of a particular judgement presupposes that it is based on reliable empirical information, whether a judgement is valid 'cannot be clarified by direct access to empirical evidence or to facts [. . .], but only discursively, precisely by way of a justification that is *carried out* with arguments' (1996: 226, emphasis in text).

This understanding of the relationship between facts and values is useful in framing some of the dilemmas posed by the actions of the paediatricians in the Cleveland case and by the social workers in Orkney. This is especially clearly posed by the actions of Drs Higgs and Wyatt in Cleveland. They argued to the inquiry that, on the basis of the evidence available to them in relation to the children suspected of having been sexually abused, they had no choice but to act to protect those children (see Chapter 6). Habermas's account of the relation between facts and values in the contemporary operation of expertise points up the problem that whilst well-grounded facts about a phenomenon might be a necessary basis for action (and leaving aside the question whether the evidence in these cases could be called well-grounded), such facts are never in themselves sufficient to compel action; rather the justification for one particular course of action as opposed to another is something that requires a normative structure. Within the self-understanding of Habermas's account this would be a discursively grounded norm justifying intervention, applied by a panel able to assess the relevant features of the particular cases and therefore to sanction appropriate action.

In the light of Habermas's discussion, one could say that the problems leading to 'crisis' in Cleveland and Orkney were produced by a dislocation between the judgement of the professionals involved, and the views both of other experts in the field and of a broader base of public opinion. That is, despite the fact that a general normative framework justifying intervention on grounds of suspicion of sexual abuse was already available to child protection practitioners in these cases in terms of the broadly (if not discursively in Habermas's sense) agreed principle of the priority of the 'best interests of the child' and accompanying statutory powers, there was little effective way, within the existing configuration of child protection law and policy, for the issues raised by the emergence of a new set of issues to be discursively ventilated, other than when things reached a point of 'crisis'. On Habermas's argument, justification for intervention into cases of child sexual abuse (or anything else) cannot be achieved simply by appeal to adequately grounded knowledge of such abuse, though this may be apposite; rather, sustaining the legitimacy of interventions into families suspected of child sexual abuse requires broad normative agreement about the forms of intervention that are justifiable in such cases.

At this point Habermas's account of the need for more thorough processes of deliberation articulating the relationship between knowledge about a particular phenomenon and evaluative grounds for action has purchase. Habermas suggests that the knowledge of specialists cannot be separated from values and moral points of view: 'As soon as specialized knowledge is brought to politically relevant problems, its unavoidably normative character becomes apparent, setting off controversies that polarize experts themselves' (1996: 351). That is, questions of functional coordination are intertwined with moral and ethical questions, therefore, from the point of view of both cognitive adequacy and legitimacy, 'it is advisable that the enlarged knowledge base of a planning and supervising administration be shaped by deliberative politics, that is, shaped by the publicly organized contest of opinions between experts and counter experts and monitored by public opinion' (1996: 351).

Developing Habermas's insights into the importance of deliberative processes in grounding the legitimacy of law and practice might therefore help to avert the reproduction of 'crises' in child protection, by more closely aligning expert judgements and public opinion, and by more rigorously delimiting the autonomy of experts. Having briefly investigated some of the ways in which Habermas's recent attempt to solve the legitimation problems of welfare states could help to refine the governance of child sexual abuse, the remaining part of this chapter examines the limitations of this way of conceptualising these problems.

Reiterating the constituent tensions of liberalism

The account of the relationship between law, the public political sphere and expert discourses of science put forward by Habermas in *Between Facts and Norms* provides more constructive ground for addressing problems in the governance of child sexual abuse than did *The Theory of Communicative Action*. However, this account continues to assume that a foundational distinction between system and lifeworld can and should be drawn and engages our attention to examine the legitimacy of particular formulations of such a distinction. That is, within Habermas's recent work, we find a continuation of the treatment of the system and the lifeworld as essentially different from one another. This is now more clearly formulated in terms of the distinction between purposive rational and communicative action. As we will see, this restates rather than resolving the second problem noted earlier in this chapter, the separation of the system and the lifeworld as the inside and outside of power, as a move necessary to Habermas's critical project. We will look first at the foundational role of the system/lifeworld distinction in Habermas's recent work, and then at his account of the place of the private family and of childhood in this.

The claim that there exists a fundamental distinction between system and lifeworld and their attendant forms of rationality operates in Habermas's work not only as an analytic and descriptive device, but also as a normative distinction. This is the basis of the claim to provide a distinctively *Critical* Theory (Habermas 1979, 1984, 1987b). That is, the claim of a category difference between communicative action and purposive rational action is a logical and structural requirement of Habermas's claim that the lifeworld and its attendant rationality are, of necessity, radically distinct from the system. This claim grounds his earlier argument that the juridification of family relationships takes the form of a pathological colonisation. It also underpins his later suggestion that the legitimacy of law can be secured by grounding legislation in the structures of communicative reason found within the domain of an undisturbed lifeworld. The claim that colonisation has pathological effects, or in his later account, that instrumentalised law produces legitimation deficits that can be overcome through the institutionalisation of deliberative democratic procedures, depends upon the claim that the family and public political sphere are lifeworld institutions different in kind from the institutions of the system. Habermas's theory, even in its later formulation, requires a foundational formulation of the system/lifeworld distinction in order to work.

We can see that Habermas's account presumes the continued autonomy of the lifeworld from the system if we more closely examine what grounds his formula for the solution of legitimation problems in democratic constitutional welfare states. Habermas grounds the possibility of legitimate law-making in the idea of 'spontaneous inputs from a lifeworld whose core private domains are intact' (1996: 417):

> Legitimate law reproduces itself only in the forms of a constitutionally regulated circulation of power, which should be nourished by the communications of an *unsubverted public sphere rooted in the core private spheres of an undisturbed lifeworld* via the networks of civil society.
>
> (1996: 408, emphasis added)

That is, the concept of a lifeworld substantially free from power continues to ground Habermas's specifically Critical Theory in the potential for autonomy and communicative rationality that, he argues, exists within this sphere.

In pursuing this line, we have seen that Habermas offers a critical perspective on the operation of contemporary welfare states as not involving those subject to its provisions in processes of decision-making. His account also rejects the positivism of much recent work within legal studies by thematising the relation between facts and values and the internal relation between legitimate law and democracy.[13] My criticism is not that this is not how law now works, this makes Habermas's account valuable in clarifying the ideals of constitutionalism; my concern is rather the limits of this as a theoretical horizon. In positing that the lifeworld constitutes an 'undisturbed' sphere, Habermas's account is tied to the dominance of a juridical mode of thinking, as such it assumes a liberal political architecture. Habermas's theory presupposes a foundational distinction between the system and the lifeworld and therefore cannot highlight this as something to question. He gives us an account of the constitution of this distinction, but places normative value upon it, considering it an evolution; as such the account of the historical constitution of this distinction becomes itself the ground of a value.

In developing his social theory Habermas transforms a hypothesis about the historical differentiation of spheres into a foundational claim. That is, there is a movement within Habermas's work between an appreciation of the historical constitution of different spheres of life, of the development of system and lifeworld, and the reification of these categories into quasi-transcendental opposites. The claim that the system and the lifeworld have differentiated from one another through rationalisation is not just a claim about a process of historical development; it is a claim about a process of social evolution. By taking a process of historical development and then placing normative value on the spheres of life constituted through the processes of rationalisation, Habermas places in jeopardy the capacity of his theory to explain the mutual constitution of these spheres. In this process critical purchase on the idea that the 'lifeworld' institutions of the private family and the public political sphere are historical categories, formed in relation to the development of the liberal state, is eclipsed. In effect, Habermas's theory operates in a similar manner to conventional liberal accounts, constructing a sociologised version of the public/private distinction, framed here as a system/lifeworld distinction, and constituting the lifeworld as a realm of freedom, authenticity and consensual action. We can more fully appreciate the impact of this if we examine what Habermas has to say about the private sphere of the family in *Between Facts and Norms*, and if we reconstruct the role that a modern conception of childhood and of the distinction between childhood and adulthood plays in his account.

The 'undisturbed lifeworld' (1996: 408) of Habermas's theory is composed of an autonomous public sphere and the private relations of the family, where the former is grounded in the latter. That is, on Habermas's account the conditions for an autonomous civil society have a 'tight connection' with an 'integral private sphere' (1996: 368):

> 'The constitutional protection of 'privacy' promotes the integrity of private life spheres: rights of personality, freedom of belief and of conscience, freedom of movement, the privacy of letters, mail, and telecommunications, the inviolability of one's residence, and the protection of families circumscribe an untouchable zone of personal integrity and independent judgement.
>
> (1996: 368)[14]

Habermas assumes that the private sphere of the family has a certain structure and role. As such, and as we have already noted, he does not attend to the problem of power relations within families. The above quotation, in suggesting an 'untouchable zone' of privacy that includes families, even suggests that we should not attend to such problems. I do not, however, think this is what Habermas intends. From his premises it would be easy to develop the grounds for a normative justification for intervention to protect children from adult–child sex: accepting that the 'normative key' to his project is autonomy (1996: 418), and accepting the views of contemporary professional practitioners that adult–child sex causes harm, one would say that child sexual abuse is something requiring intervention as this implies conditions of systematically distorted communication and is likely substantially to affect the capacities for the realisation of autonomy on the part of the child concerned. The question whether Habermas could recognise the harm of child sexual abuse is not at issue. The problem is rather that Habermas assumes the model of a 'reasonably functional family' (1993: 114) in order to make his argument run, and then seeks to entrench the principle of legal freedom in a private sphere (1996: 399).

This entrenching of the principle of privacy, necessary as it is to Habermas's location of the possibilities for a rational redemption of modernity through communicative action in an undisturbed lifeworld, implies that his position reiterates some of the constituent tensions of liberalism. It assumes a distinction between public and private life, provides grounds for intervention to protect children from harm where this is demonstrated through appropriate expert knowledge of harm, and where intervention is justified through the discursive valuation of the potential for rationality of the child as a future adult. One can note the similarity with Rawls's account of the appropriate place of the principles of justice in relation to the family in the following statement: 'legally demarcating an "inviolable domain of private life-plans" can only mean that restrictions in this domain must be justified by especially weighty reasons on a case-by-case basis' (1996: 400).

This places severe limits on Habermas's account. We can note, first, that this formulation presupposes a view of the family as a 'natural' communicative context where intervention is justified only by a 'pathological' event or relationship; the account rests on the presupposition of communicative action within the 'core private spheres of an undisturbed lifeworld' (1996: 408). Second, it presupposes that existing scientific descriptions are the most appropriate ways of describing 'harm' in any given situation, at best suggesting that those involved in a specific case should together agree the correct way forward through a full and sensitive reading of the situation. But this is already to frame the situation in a particular manner, and, broadly speaking, within existing terms of reference. This is also the case with Habermas's conception of childhood.

Congruent with Habermas's concern legally to demarcate a sphere of private life plans and defend a zone of privacy that includes the integrity of the internal structure of the family is his view of childhood. Habermas's account is premised on a distinctively modern conception of childhood.[15] This can be seen in the way that he grounds his account of deliberative democracy on an ideal of discourse amongst those who have the capacity for post-conventional moral reasoning (they are able to abstract themselves from the immediate contexts of life and achieve a moral point of view through engaging in critical argumentation with others); this, the capacity for post-conventional moral reasoning, is, for Habermas, a condition of being a competent participant in contexts of communicative action. Habermas explicitly formulates his account of post-conventional moral reasoning through extending the work of Kohlberg and Piaget. He uses the work of these two developmental psychologists to provide an account of individual moral and cognitive development, and also to generate an account of societal development.[16] A distinctively modern view of childhood as a series of stages of progressive development toward adulthood is thus a systematic requirement of Habermas's theory.

This has two notable effects: first, in so far as those involved are required to have communicative competence, to have achieved the capacity for post-conventional moral reasoning, children themselves are excluded from discursive processes of decision-making. This might not be a bad thing, but it certainly implies that Habermas's claim that the right to participation cannot be delegated has to be qualified (see above and Habermas 1996: 426). Second, in so far as Habermas's account assumes autonomous subjectivity produced through socialisation within intact lifeworlds, so that actors in communicative contexts of justification have already achieved autonomy, childhood becomes the constitutive outside this. Other things being equal, children can 'come to reason', so they are not excluded as individuals for all time, but the child as such figures as the heteronomous other of the moral reasoning subject. A particularly modern understanding of childhood as a state of dependence prior to the full autonomy of adulthood thus forms the constitutive outside Habermas's account, the child figures as the 'other' of the post-conventional reasoner. His account is therefore dependent on the modern distinction between childhood and adulthood and thus can only provide us with a framework for refining the practices of governance that we already have.

To put this differently, Habermas assumes the category of childhood as described by modern developmental psychology. This category then underpins his account of the intersubjectively organised ability of the adult to engage in post-conventional moral reasoning, an account that assumes as its model an autonomous human being whose development is complete. Habermas states that the moral intuitions reconstructed in discourse ethics are available to 'anyone who has grown up in a reasonably functional family' (1993: 114). This works to ground and sustain a distinction between the system and the lifeworld, the state and other public power and private families, since parents or guardians require autonomy in the form of a private ordering of family relations both in order to ground their own autonomy and in order to bring children from a state of dependency to one of autonomous subjectivity, capable themselves of participating in public life: 'a robust civil society can develop only in the context of a liberal political culture and the corresponding patterns of socialization, and on the basis of an integral private sphere' (1996: 371).

In this process, what Habermas's account occludes is the way in which the ideas of child–family and family–state relations that he assumes must be the case are artefacts constituted and maintained through governmental techniques, that is, by specific ways of thinking about and acting upon the child, the family and the state. Instead, Habermas makes these ways of thinking and acting foundational to his account. One might think this perfectly reasonable for a theorist concerned with the legitimation problems of modern democratic welfare states, given that one has to assume certain categories and concepts in order to bring others into question. But this imposes severe limits on Habermas's Critical Theory in relation to its capacity to explicate the dynamics of the governance of child sexual abuse, in so far as it leaves him able only to refine the understanding and the tools that we already have. So long as we assume that childhood is a natural stage of dependency best described by the language of developmental psychology, and that the family is by nature and essential functions a private lifeworld institution, then we always already face a conceptualisation of the problem as one of where to draw the line between public jurisdiction and family privacy, where this can only be resolved through appeal to expert knowledge of child development. We might manage to refine the governance of child sexual abuse using this model, but in so far as Habermas assumes a system/lifeworld distinction and an understanding of childhood derived from developmental psychology, this is all we can hope to do.

Habermas's first published book, *The Structural Transformation of the Public Sphere* ([1962] 1989), provides an historical sociology of the emergence of the liberal public sphere in late eighteenth century Europe, and its subsequent transformation under the pressure of commercialisation of the mass media and the development of welfare states. In this text, Habermas gives an account of the emergence of a specifically modern intimate sphere of the patriarchal conjugal family as a condition of the emergence of the notion of 'humanity' as such, and as a prerequisite for the emergence of the bourgeois public sphere. Many of the themes of this book are reflected in his later sociological and philosophical work. However, our modern conceptions of intimacy, and of the private conjugal family, are phenomena disclosed as products of a distinct historical formation in this early book. In Habermas's later work the specifically historical character of these relations is repressed and Habermas takes the modern form of these relationships as necessary, grounding them in an explicitly evolutionary account. In so doing, this account takes our historical horizon as a necessary one. Habermas's work has distinctively modern understandings of the relationship between state and society and of childhood as a condition of dependence as its historical condition, construes these as universal, hypostatises the relationship between the state and public political sphere and the family, and the condition of childhood, in their modern forms, and therefore at best can help us to refine existing practices of governance.

Conclusion

In conclusion, we can note that Habermas's argument makes some advances over liberal accounts of the public/private distinction: by theorising this distinction in terms of the relationship between the system and the lifeworld and by challenging the dominance of the purposive rational orientation of the system, Habermas opens up a space in which to consider the ways in which the politicisation of family relations does not immediately or necessarily have to take the form of a demand for increased state intervention. By thematising the importance of the public political sphere of the lifeworld Habermas challenges the reduction of politics to administration and asks us to consider, as political questions, issues that for liberalism remain largely prepolitical or apolitical (see Chapter 2).

However, in so far as Habermas makes this move by positing the absolute difference between communicative action and purposive rational action, he reinvents one of the constituent tensions of liberalism. Where liberalism figures the public/private distinction in terms of a distinction between state sovereignty and individual autonomy, Habermas's concern centres on clarifying the appropriate boundaries between the system and the lifeworld and posits grounds for the assertion of a set of normative criteria through which we can ascertain the appropriate relationship between the state, the family and the public political sphere of civil society. In pursuing this line, his account presupposes a distinction between the system and the lifeworld, purposive rational action and communicative action, and thus a sociologised version of the public/private distinction. As we have seen, he also assumes a naturalised understanding of childhood. Together, these features of Habermas's theory produce a similar understanding of the dynamics of the governance of child sexual abuse as those provided within liberal analyses, counterpoising the public/system as a realm of intervention and control with the private/lifeworld as one of freedom, and suggesting that the governance of child sexual abuse takes place through the mobilisation of expert knowledge of child development and its aberrations, where this is grounded in discursively legitimated legal procedures.

Both liberal political theory and Habermas's Critical Theory imply foundational commitments to versions of the public/private distinction; liberal political theory in terms of the need to defend a realm of life free from the state, Critical Theory in terms of maintaining critical purchase on the potential of communicative rationality. In each case, the realm of the private or lifeworld is regarded as one of freedom and authenticity that can be threatened by public or system intervention. That is, the public/private and system/lifeworld distinctions act within liberal and Critical Theory, respectively, not just as descriptions but also as normative assumptions about the world. Both of these frameworks for examining problems in the governance of child sexual abuse presuppose foundational distinctions between the state and the family, and assume naturalised models of childhood dependence. Both therefore direct attention toward reframing existing practices of governance in more appropriate ways, promising to reiterate, and perhaps to refine, what we already have, rather than enabling us to examine these distinctions and categories more critically for the work that they do in maintaining existing patterns of governance.

These founding distinctions and categories of liberal and Critical Theory are problematised by the issue of child sexual abuse. From within the parameters of these theories we cannot fully address questions concerning the historical constitution of current notions of public and private, or how these notions are maintained and reiterated through practices of governance. Yet it is the distinction between public and private and the forms of knowledge and practice that articulate this that are brought into question by the emergence of child sexual abuse as a public problem, as a problem of modern governance.

The recognition of child sexual abuse as problem of governance raises questions concerning the distinction between the state and the family and how this is managed through relationships between law and scientific knowledge. In order to examine this, we need a form of analysis that does not presuppose a public/private distinction, and which does not rest on naturalised assumptions about the characteristics of childhood. Rather, we need a form of analysis that will enable us to bring these categories into question, in order that we can ask what role they play in maintaining existing patterns of governance.

4 Reproblematising the governance of child sexual abuse

Foucault's practice of social criticism

Chapters 2 and 3 have been concerned to elucidate the theories forwarded by selected liberal political theorists and by Habermas, and to assess the respective contributions of the work of these theorists to the analysis of the governance of child sexual abuse. We now turn to examine the work of Michel Foucault and the ways in which this might help us to analyse the governance of child sexual abuse. Here we find a step-change in orientation. Foucault is not concerned to provide a theory of modernity that can drive empirical observation and accommodate its results. Rather, he is concerned with modernity as a critical attitude centred on the investigation of how we have become what we are and with the examination of the concepts and practices that hold these definitions and understandings in place (Foucault 1984a).

Some of the specific domains of Foucault's work are examined in Chapter 5. The aim of the present chapter is to sketch this orientation in thinking at a general level, both to provide an outline for the account which follows and in order to show that, rather than presupposing an account of the relations between public and private life or of the relations between law and science, Foucault's work suggests that we take these features of our epistemological and political landscapes as questions to be addressed. The work that these ideas do, the practices in which they are exhibited and their effects upon us require investigation.

Foucault's work does not provide a set of normative criteria with which we might specify correct practices of intervention or the legitimate boundaries between public and private life. Where others have regarded this refusal to provide normative grounds for his social criticisms as a serious limitation or failure of Foucault's work (Habermas 1987b; Fraser 1989; Fraser and Nicholson 1988; McNay 1992), this chapter attempts to show the productivity of this approach for the analysis of the governance of child sexual abuse. The importance of Foucault's work lies in its capacity to destabilise the assumptions held in place and reiterated by other analyses of child sexual abuse, in particular assumptions concerning distinctions between public and private life, and concerning the role of legal and scientific knowledge in constituting and regulating the conditions of contemporary childhood. It is necessary to unseat the way that these ideas work as assumptions that ground our ways of thinking and acting in order to be able to gain critical purchase on the governance of child sexual abuse, and on the reiteration of calls of 'crisis' in this governance.

In practice, of course, assumptions are necessary. Arguably, one cannot 'do' science or perform the tasks of child protection at the same moment as holding up for question what one is doing (both may be performed by the same person, but at different moments). My purpose is not to say that assumptions are necessarily bad, since they are inevitable. However, the concern of this book is not that of devising proposals for amendments to the Children Act or issuing notes of guidance to child protection practitioners. Those who do this work do so in contexts of recurring 'crises'; specialists, the media and politicians faced with problems in child protection practice all repeat the mantra 'never again'. Foucault shows why, in the structure of our discourses and practices there is always repetition of such events.[1] Accordingly, the concern here is to interrogate the ideas and assumptions that ground the governance of child sexual abuse, to hold them up to question for the work that they do in maintaining contemporary patterns of governance. In this, Foucault's work provides a useful conceptual 'toolkit' that we can develop to reflect on the governance of child sexual abuse, and in particular on the ways in which specific forms of reasoning about the relation between public power and private autonomy, and about the relationship between legal and scientific discourses, have in constituting and maintaining existing practices of governance.

This chapter examines some of the central features of Foucault's orientation to the task of social criticism by sketching his understanding of his work in terms of a number of histories of problematisations, reflecting on his genealogical 'method' of investigation, clarifying the use made of the terms 'power', 'knowledge' and 'ethics', and formally specifying the concepts political rationalities and technologies of governance. Its aim is to establish the ground for the following chapters and to distinguish Foucault's approach from those of the writers discussed thus far. Chapter 5 elaborates these themes in relation to the history of liberalism as a rationality of government.

Problematisations

> It is true that my attitude isn't a result of the form of critique that claims to be a methodical examination in order to reject all possible solutions except for the valid one. It is more on the order of 'problematization' – which is to say, the development of a domain of acts, practices, and thoughts that seem to me to pose problems for politics.
>
> (Foucault 1984c: 384)

In an interview conducted late in his life, Foucault gives a retrospective account of his work in terms of a history of problematics (Foucault 1984c). By this he refers to the analysis of the ways in which human beings turn aspects of experience into questions to be addressed, and the range of solutions articulated in response to these questions, in the form of new forms of knowledge, political practice and subjectivity: 'the proper task of a history of thought [is] . . . to define the conditions in which human beings "problematize" what they are, what they do, and the world in which they live' (Foucault 1992: 10). As an example of this we can consider the ways in which 'child sexual abuse' has become a 'problem' for us, with the concomitant development of new forms of knowledge of what constitutes abuse and its effects, distinct practices of intervention, and novel forms of self-understanding and interpretation (see Chapter 1).

Foucault's focus on problematisations points us to several important features of his work. This work consists not of histories of particular periods, but rather of specific analyses of the ways in which, in certain circumstances, established ways of going on are called into question. For example, in the introduction to the second volume of *The History of Sexuality: The Use of Pleasure* (Foucault 1992), he characterises his investigation of the sexual practices of classical antiquity thus: 'It was a matter of analysing, not behaviours or ideas, nor societies and their "ideologies", but the *problematizations* through which being offers itself to be, necessarily, thought – and the *practices* on the basis of which these problematizations are formed' (1992: 11, emphasis in text). Foucault's concern here is not with establishing moral principles, lists of prescriptions and proscriptions, but with examining how such lists (however similar in appearance) exhibit and enact particular ways of thinking about and acting upon experience, that is how various areas of experience become objects of concern, reflection, and for the development of practices of government.

This mode of analysis works to uncover the 'historical a priori' of particular ways of problematising experience (Foucault 1994: 315). Foucault situates himself within the critical tradition established by Kant, suggesting that his work forms a critical history of the modes in which relations between subject and object are formed and modified in so far as these relations constitute a field of possible knowledge (1994: 314). He suggests that this critical history of thought concerns tracking the modes of objectivisation and subjectivisation through which the 'historical a priori of a possible experience' might be discerned:

> This objectivization and this subjectivization are not independent of one another; it is from their mutual development and their reciprocal bond that what we might call 'truth games' arise: not the discovery of true things, but the rules according to which, with respect to certain things, what a subject may say stems from the question of truth and falsehood. In short, the critical history of thought is neither a history of the acquisitions of truth nor a history of its occultations; it is the history of the emergence of truth games. It is the history of 'veridictions', understood as the forms according to which discourses capable of being deemed true or false are articulated with a domain of things: what the conditions of that emergence have been; what price has been paid for it, as it were; what effects it has had on the real; and the way in which, linking a certain type of object with certain modalities of the subject, it has constituted for a time, a space, and particular individuals, the historical a priori of a possible experience.
>
> (1994: 315)

Foucault's analyses, therefore, do not begin by attempting to establish normative principles concerning punishment, sexuality, the treatment of the mad and so on, as this would be to presuppose definitions of 'problems' which he wishes to hold up for question. Rather, Foucault's tendency is to begin with particular 'events' that act as points of transformation in relations of competing forces. An 'event' 'is not a decision, a treaty, a reign or a battle, but the reversal of a relationship of forces, the usurpation of power, the appropriation of a vocabulary turned against those who had once used it' (Foucault 1984b: 88). By examining 'events', it is possible to discern the dominant styles of reasoning through which a problem is constituted as a particular kind of problem and within which a range of solutions may be proposed.

Foucault's concern is to reproblematise given problematisations (for example, of madness, punishment and sexuality). These reproblematisations take the form of critical analyses of the ways in which, at certain times and places, specific aspects of existence become uncertain or difficult. The task is to examine the manner in which these difficulties are posed as problems, and the character of the responses given to these difficulties. Foucault's question is what makes particular ways of posing aspects of experience as problems and the diversity of responses made to these problems, which, he points out, are often contradictory, simultaneously possible. He suggests:

> the work of a history of thought would be to rediscover at the root of these solutions to the general form of problematization that has made them possible – even in their very opposition; or what has made possible the transformations of the difficulties and obstacles of a practice into a general problem for which one proposes diverse practical solutions.
>
> (1984c: 389)

A history of thought conducted as a history of problematisations is therefore 'a question of a movement of critical analysis in which one tries to see how the different solutions to a problem have been constructed; but also how these different solutions result from a specific form of problematization' (Foucault 1984c: 389). The aim is to analyse the ways in which particular forms of experience are constituted as problematic in the first place, and thus as objects of knowledge and intervention, and to examine the limits and possibilities that exist within the forms of reasoning and practice established around particular styles of problematisation.[2]

Foucault's attention to problematisations leads us to examine the grammar of styles of reasoning within which aspects of experience are raised for question. His use of the term '*dispositif*' clarifies this focus.[3] For Foucault the term *dispositif* indicates 'strategies of relations of forces supporting, and supported by, types of knowledge' (Foucault 1980c: 196). His concern is with the analysis of the (multiple) relations of discursive and non-discursive practices that constitute a 'grid of intelligibility' (Dreyfus and Rabinow 1982: 121).[4]

This mode of analysis asks us to question how aspects of experience become figured as problems, as objects of knowledge, and as sites of practical intervention.

This figuring occurs through grids of intelligibility, which involve specific styles of reasoning, evaluation and judgement. Within specific styles of reasoning, particular forms of knowledge constitute and represent objects of attention and make possible practices of intervention. The task of the analysis of problematisations is therefore to examine the forms of knowledge that constitute aspects of our experience as objects for practical intervention, to ask how our forms of reasoning are tied to the exercise of authority in relation to acting upon the problem so identified, and to assess the limits and costs of this.

If we look to how the issue of child sexual abuse has recently been problematised we can see that contemporary discourses concerning child welfare and protection condense around a number of issues and assumptions. For example, the events of Cleveland problematised existing practices of child protection, simultaneously raising questions concerning the limits of the legitimacy of public interventions into family life, the veracity and authority of expert knowledge of child sexual abuse, and the adequacy of training of the professionals involved in the detection of danger. The public inquiry into this case was called because the practice of governing this problematic had been called into question, and its deliberations and judgements demonstrate diverse forms of reasoning and proposed solutions to the problem as defined, all conducted within an established framework of understanding in which childhood is regarded as a distinctive or special phase of life (see Chapter 6). Our experience of child protection is figured in terms of the delineation of the limitations of public rights to intervene in the private ordering of families, where the legitimacy and limits of appropriate intervention are established through appeals to expertise in child development. The domain of childhood, a distinction between public and private life, and various forms of expert knowledge are simultaneously presupposed and contested in such battles.

An analysis of the governance of child sexual abuse conducted in these terms asks how contemporary discourses concerning practices of child protection variously constitute notions of childhood, the relations between public and private life, and the appropriate relations between legal and scientific authority in the governance of the practice of child protection. The aim of such a critical analysis of the governance of child sexual abuse is to reproblematise our given ways of problematising this issue, to hold up for critical inspection the ways we govern this domain.[5]

Genealogy

Foucault's 'method' for investigating and reproblematising given problematisations is a genealogical one. A significant feature of this 'method' is its capacity to open up a form of critical analysis that does not presuppose a distinction between public and private life, or the necessary relations between law and science, but rather asks us to investigate them as they are exhibited in practical discourses of governance.

Genealogy is concerned to reflect critically on apparently constitutive limits to thought and action in order to clarify which of these apparently constitutive limits are only regulative. Its aim is to unseat the natural, self-evident character of our concepts and categories, showing how things that we take as necessary have come into being through particular ways of thinking about and acting upon ourselves and others. Genealogy thus exhibits a critical attitude toward the examination of the descent of series of practices through which we have become what we are. Crucial to this is how we problematise our experience and the practices that hold in place these ways of problematising experience. By examining the ways in which we make aspects of what we are and what we do the focus of particular practices of thought and reflection, we can gain distance on how we have become what we are, assess the stakes of this, and open up possibilities for change.

Foucault conceptualises the task of genealogy variously as providing a 'historical ontology of ourselves' (Foucault 1984a: 45), a 'history of the present' (1977: 31), or a real or 'effective history' (*wirkliche Historie*) (1984b: 87). This he counterposes to traditional history, stating that, whereas a traditional approach to history studies things furthest from itself under a cloak of supposed objectivity, 'Effective history studies what is closest, but in an abrupt dispossession, so as to seize it at a distance' (1984b: 89). Foucault therefore begins with the present, in order neither to affirm nor to deny that present, but in order to interrogate how the present has come to be as it is. These rather cryptic remarks require that we look a little more closely at Foucault's scattered comments on the character of genealogy in order to flesh out an account of the orientation of his work.

Foucault's aim is to put our entrenched ways of thinking and acting into question, to render our principles of judgement up for judgement. This is done not in the service of a nihilistic denial of the values of the present, but in the service of an attempt to think critically about the limits and possibilities of that present.[6] Genealogy explores the 'self-evidences (*evidences*) [. . .] the practices we accept rest on' (1982b: 33). Its aim is 'to show that things are not as self-evident as one believed, to see that what is accepted as self-evident is no longer accepted as such' (Foucault 1988b: 155); practising criticism is, then, on this account, 'a matter of making facile gestures difficult' (1988b: 155). Those things which we take for granted in the present 'have been made, they can be unmade, as long as we know how it was that they were made' (1988a: 37).

Dean elaborates on this by contrasting genealogy both with the 'meta-histories of promise' of modernist social theory and with anti-Enlightenment despair, thereby stressing the 'de-dramatizing' effects of genealogy (1999a: 42). He suggests that 'two impulses' constitute Foucault's genealogical orientation to historical work (1999a: 44). The first impulse is a 'diagnostic' one; genealogy 'is an orientation to the present as an open set of possibilities' (1999a: 44), aiming to 'sort out what we take to be necessary and contingent in the ways we think and act in regard to the "conducting" of our lives and those of others, and to discover what problematizations of this are possible' (1999a: 44). The diagnostic value of genealogy is thus to open up the 'conditions of a renewed task of political invention' (1999a: 44). The second feature of genealogy as outlined by Dean is its anti-anachronism. 'By making explicit the immersion of its historical analyses in an experience of the present, genealogy [. . .] seeks also to limit the tendency to read the past through that experience' (1999a: 44). By examining regimes of practices '*by means of* their own terms' (1999a: 44, emphasis in text) we restore a sense of the particularity of the present and destabilise the apparent naturalness and immutability of our current conceptions and ways of acting.[7]

Dean notes Foucault's comment that in its orientation, genealogy refuses the '"blackmail" of the Enlightenment', that we must be either 'for or against' it (1999a: 42, quoting Foucault 1984a: 42; see also Osborne 1998; Schmidt 1996). Instead, Foucault's genealogies aim to reveal anew some of the significant features of our entrenched forms of reasoning about and acting in the world in order that we might be alive to and better able to judge the limits and costs of these forms of reasoning and acting and to explore possibilities for change. Ransom articulates this point with acuity when, in criticising the widespread tendency to read Foucault's studies as 'exposes on "power" as a general category' (1997: 81), he suggests that the 'critical effect of genealogy' is to transform the '"ready to hand" and thus unexamined into something that is "present to hand" and a proper subject for critical reflection' (Ransom 1997: 81). This practice of criticism is centred on turning limits into questions:

> In what is given to us as universal, necessary, obligatory, what place is occupied by whatever is singular, contingent, and the product of arbitrary constraints? The point, in brief, is to transform the critique conducted in the form of necessary limitation into a practical critique that takes the form of a possible transgression.
>
> (Foucault 1984a: 45).

Genealogy can thus be characterised as a way of gaining critical distance on the present without positing an ideal against which to measure that present (the latter would assume that one could know the contours of an appropriate ideal, and be able to step outside of one's time and place in order to legislate for it).

We can now turn to reflect on the implications of Foucault's orientation to criticism for our concern with the contemporary governance of child sexual abuse. We have noted that genealogy is concerned critically to reflect on apparently constitutive limits to thought and action that may be only regulative limits and that, through denaturalising our present assumptions, it works to offer a diagnosis of the present in terms of the limits of our forms of reasoning and acting.

Modes of reflection and action are interwoven. The ways in which we understand ourselves and others are produced through grids of intelligibility that simultaneously make it possible to know ourselves and to act, and work to constrain the horizons of this knowledge and action. Foucault's work sets up a way of thinking that takes our current conceptual frameworks and forms of practice as phenomena to be investigated in terms of the work they do, the practices they articulate, and the effects they engender. From this we can note that Foucault's suggestions change our orientation to the public/private distinction, contemporary notions of childhood and the family, and relations between law and science. Rather than assume this distinction and set of relations as constitutive features of our political landscape, as with liberal political theory and Habermas' Critical Theory, Foucault suggests that we ask how these ways of problematising our experience are held in place by various ways of thinking and acting. How do we come to conceptualise relations between families and the state and the appropriate role of law and scientific knowledge in the ways that we do? What holds these ways of thinking and acting in place? What are the effects engendered by these ways of doing things?

Contemporary distinctions between public and private life are ways of conceptualising and acting on limits to the state and other public agencies (see Chapter 2). However, such distinctions are continuously maintained and reinscribed by juridically circumscribed forms of positive knowledge in order that 'appropriate' relations between public and private can be maintained; the 'private' only remains such in so far as the norms governing the conduct of relations within this sphere are regarded as legitimate. Notions of what is legitimate vis-à-vis parent–child relationships are continually undergoing change. Similarly, we might say that law and science are both ways of conceptualising and acting upon the real, ways of grounding our reflective activity toward the world that have long histories. However, the boundaries of these endeavours, what counts as truth within them, and the objects they constitute have altered over time and their contemporary relations and effects are questions in need of investigation.

Since Foucault's approach to the history of the present neither presupposes contemporary distinctions between public and private life nor predetermines what to look for in relations between law and science, he provides a set of analytics with which we might go about looking at how the governance of child sexual abuse is organised, maintained and reconstituted through the deployment of these terms within the forms of knowledge and practice concerned with the governance of child sexual abuse. In order to provide an account of the operation of the distinction between public and private life and of the relations of law and science in the contemporary governance of child sexual abuse it is necessary to specify how these relations operate in specific contexts and practical discourses of governance; this will be the focus of Chapters 5 to 7. Prior to this, we need to specify more closely the conceptual tools that articulate Foucault's genealogical method: power, knowledge and ethics.

Power/knowledge/ethics

Foucault is concerned with the relations between ways of acting and reflecting on ourselves and others and the development of specific modes of these ways of acting and reflecting. He suggests that we conduct such analyses (the 'historical ontology' of ourselves) by addressing three axes of experience, those of knowledge (how we conceptualise and reflect on ourselves and others), power (how we have our conduct organised or organise the conduct of others), and ethics (how we organise our own conduct):

The historical ontology of ourselves [. . . will] address the questions system-
atized as follows: How are we constituted as subjects of our own knowledge?
How are we constituted as subjects who exercise or submit to power relations?
How are we constituted as moral subjects of our own actions?

(1984a: 49)

His studies of madness, delinquency and sexuality emphasise each of these
axes respectively, but he suggests that these three are 'necessary for constituting a
field of experience. [. . .] a game of truth, relations of power, and forms of relation
to oneself and to others' (Foucault 1984c: 387). It is the task of this section to clarify
Foucault's characterisation of these terms and to begin to locate how they might
provide a grid for the analysis of the governance of child sexual abuse.

We can begin by specifying Foucault's formulation of the concept power-
knowledge:

Perhaps we should abandon the belief that power makes mad and that, by
the same token, the renunciation of power is one of the conditions of
knowledge. We should admit rather that power produces knowledge [. . .] that
power and knowledge directly imply one another; that there is no power
relation without the correlative constitution of a field of knowledge, nor any
knowledge that does not presuppose and constitute at the same time power
relations.

(Foucault 1977: 27)

From the 1970s, Foucault's work takes the form of a series of genealogies of
power in particular spheres, such as the constitution of criminality and of sexuality
(Foucault 1977, 1979a). These texts examine the particular ways in which subjects
are constituted within power-knowledge or, more precisely, the ways in which
specific forms of subjectivity are constituted within particular domains of power-
knowledge. We can clarify this conception of power and knowledge as reciprocal
by noting Foucault's comments on the character of power, before relating this to
his account of truth and of ethics.

How, then, does Foucault conceptualise power? This is nowhere sketched
as such. Indeed Foucault is clear that power is not an entity, but a specific type of
relationship, 'power in the substantive sense [. . .] doesn't exist' (1980c: 198).
However, several broad features of the concept of power can be drawn from his
work. Foucault conceptualises power as capillary, relational and exercised through
social practices, productive, and linked internally to knowledge.

Pervading Foucault's work is a concern for power in its 'capillary' forms, that is
with the micro-analysis of relations of power as these occur at every level of modern
social practices. There is a concern with 'power at its extremities, in its ultimate
destinations, with those points where it becomes capillary, that is, in its more
regional and local forms and institutions' (1980a: 96). The second feature of
Foucault's conception of power is a notion of power as relational and exercised
rather than as a possession. Power is 'a mode of action on the actions of others'

which 'structure(s) the field of possible actions of others' (Foucault, 1982a: 221). Relations of power thus form 'an open more or less co-ordinated cluster of relations' (1980c: 199) in which 'power is employed and exercised through a net-like organisation' (1980a: 98).

This second feature of power, power as relational and exercised, is tied to Foucault's nominalism with regard to power 'as such' and his concern instead with its forms. He suggests that, 'Power exists only when it is put into action, even if, of course, it is integrated into a disparate field of possibilities brought to bear upon permanent structures' (1982a: 219). This explains his refusal to elaborate a 'theory' of power and insistence that we focus on the 'how' of power if we are not to presuppose its existence, origins and basic nature. Focusing on the question 'how?' is to:

> Ask oneself what contents one has in mind when using this all-embracing and reifying term; it is to suspect that an extremely complex configuration of realities is allowed to escape when one treads endlessly in the double question: What is power? and Where does power come from? The little question, What happens? although flat and empirical, once it is scrutinised is seen to avoid accusing a metaphysics or an ontology of power of being fraudulent; rather it attempts a critical investigation into the thematics of power. 'How,' not in the sense of 'How does it manifest itself?' but 'By what means is it exercised?' and 'What happens when individuals exert (as they say) power over others?'
>
> (1982a: 217)

Foucault's concern to focus on the 'how' of power leads to the third point noted above, his concern with the productivity of power. Power 'produces reality – it produces domains of objects and rituals of truth' (1977: 194). Foucault thus rejects 'juridical' or 'sovereign' conceptions of power as essentially repressive, a formulation he identifies with liberal and Marxist approaches in common (Foucault 1980b: 116). In contrast, he argues that if power were only repressive it would be fragile, whereas its strength derives from its productive role with respect to the shaping of knowledge, pleasure, discourse, and so on:

> The notion of repression is quite inadequate for capturing what is precisely the productive aspect of power. In defining the effects of power as repression, one adopts a purely juridical conception of such power, one identifies power with a law which says no, power is taken above all as carrying the force of a prohibition. Now I believe that this is a wholly negative, narrow, skeletal conception of power, one which has been curiously widespread. If power were never anything but repressive, if it never did anything but to say no, do you really think one would be brought to obey it? What makes power hold good, what makes it accepted, is simply the fact that it doesn't only weigh on us as a force that says no, but that it traverses and produces things, it induces pleasure, forms knowledge, produces discourse. It needs to be considered as a productive

network which runs through the whole social body, much more than as a negative instance whose function is repression.

(1980b: 119)

This brings us to the fourth point, Foucault's account of the internal relation of power and knowledge. For Foucault, power and knowledge are not antithetical,[8] rather power concerns 'the production of effective instruments for the formation and accumulation of knowledge' exercised through specific techniques of observation and classification and contained within particular procedures for investigation and control: 'All this means that power, when it is exercised through these subtle mechanisms, cannot but evolve, organise and put into circulation a knowledge, or rather apparatuses of knowledge' (1980a: 102).

Power and knowledge are immanently related to each other, but are not identical. Foucault makes this clear in the following statement:

> When I read – and I know it has been attributed to me – the thesis 'knowledge is power', or 'power is knowledge', I begin to laugh, since studying their *relation* is precisely my problem. If they were identical, I would not have to study them and I would be spared a lot of fatigue as a result. The very fact that I pose *the question of their relation* proves clearly that I do not identify them.
>
> (Foucault, quoted in Keenan 1987: 12, emphasis in text)

This comment brings us to Foucault's concern with truth.

From the foregoing, we can see that Foucault's concern with truth is not with the Platonic question 'What is truth?', but rather has the form of a number of examinations of how the true is constituted. That is, it is a concern with the rules governing the production of truth and falsity within specific domains of knowledge and practice. Foucault raises a series of questions about what a society makes function as true or false, how phenomena come to be constituted as objects of knowledge, how we reflect and act on these objects and the mechanisms for the production and reproduction of fields of knowledge governing those who are authorised to speak the truth. His concern is with 'the ensemble of rules according to which the true and the false are separated and specific effects of power attached to the true' (1980b: 132). Foucault puts forward two propositions regarding how we might go about studying truth:

> 'Truth' is to be understood as a system of ordered procedures for the production, regulation, distribution, circulation and operation of statements. 'Truth' is linked in a circular relation with systems of power which produce and sustain it, and to effects of power which it induces and which extend it. A 'regime' of truth.
>
> (1980b: 133)

Despite these comments, such statements have been read to suggest that Foucault 'reduces' truth to power. How are we then to understand Foucault's comment that power and knowledge are mutually related, but not identical, that 'one simply cannot say that games of truth are nothing but games of power' (Foucault 1989c: 445)?

Put positively, Foucault's concern is to 'bracket' the question 'Is this true?' in order to examine how statements come to function as true or false, that is, in order to examine the rules governing the production of truth. This is not a call to abandon the serious examination of the conditions of truth, rather the opposite. Referring to the examination of scientific discourses, Foucault suggests that his focus on examining transformations in regimes of truth is a concern with 'a modification in the rules of formation of statements which are accepted as scientifically true' (Foucault 1980b: 112). In this context, the 'games of truth' that Foucault is concerned with can be considered as rules for the formation of forms of knowledge, for what is to count as knowledge within a particular set of practices. The phrase 'games of truth' here has a specific meaning:

> The word 'game' can lead you astray: when I say 'game', I mean a set of rules by which truth is produced. It is not a game in the sense of an amusement; it is a set of procedures that lead to a certain result, which, on the basis of its principles and rules of procedure, may be considered valid or invalid, winning or losing.
>
> (Foucault 1989c: 445)

Given this account of power-knowledge, how are we to understand ethics? We can clarify this by recalling that Foucault characterises power as 'a mode of action on the actions of others' (Foucault 1982a: 221). That is, power is exercised in relation to subjects who are free. Ethics denotes a concern with practices of the self, with forms of self-elaboration. Thus Foucault's concern with ethics can be clarified as a concern with forms of reflection and action on oneself, as a practice of freedom acted upon oneself involving relations of knowledge and forms of the organisation of conduct (Foucault 1989c: 432–49).

From this outline of the axes of power, knowledge and ethics that Foucault suggests form a grid through which we can provide a historical ontology of ourselves, we can further develop the productivity of this orientation in thinking for our analysis of the governance of child sexual abuse. The previous sections of this chapter have indicated the ways in which Foucault's focus on problemati-sations guides us to an examination of how the sexual abuse of children is figured as a problem of governance defined in terms of a set of conceptions of childhood as a specific phase of life, where public powers to intervene in the private ordering of family relationships are organised through various juridically circumscribed forms of scientific evidence concerning abuse, its detection and its effects. His comments concerning genealogy suggest that, rather than presuppose this political and epistemological landscape, we hold up for question the dominant ways in which we think about and act upon child sexual abuse and ask how this landscape of governance is configured and the limits and costs it imposes on us.

Taking up Foucault's conceptualisation of the relations of power and knowledge, such that the mutual articulation of these relations produces specific '*regimes du savoir*' (Foucault 1982a: 212), we can now add that it is through particular conceptions of childhood and of parenting that our policies of child protection are articulated. This involves a number of relations of knowledge and power. It implies knowledge and power relations between parents and children in which the authority of parents is held in place by forms of truth-telling that articulate the idea that parents have 'natural' jurisdiction over children unless and until this is transgressed by 'abusive' conduct; it implies relations of knowledge and power in so far as the contours of what is to count as abusive conduct are established by general social mores and prohibitions (from religious organisations, communities and so on) and by expert discourses concerning child abuse which in turn exercise power over parents by enforcing certain standards of child-rearing and definitions of what is to count as abuse, where these forms of positive knowledge articulate juridically circumscribed practices of child protection.

Definitions of child abuse through which practice is organised change. For example, where the practice of physical punishment was once regarded as part of the formation of individuals of strong character, it is now increasingly regarded as abusive. Where incest was generally regarded as interfamilial sexual relations it is now defined as penetrative sex with a minor with whom one is in a specific legal relationship. Where child abuse once referred almost exclusively to physical abuse this definition has expanded to encompass not only sexual abuse but emotional abuse also (see Chapter 1). In each of these examples, changing knowledge of childhood and its vicissitudes is produced through and has effects of power. Research into child abuse is commissioned and conducted by various agencies; this research may then become part of the framework of knowledge for agencies of intervention and for the regulations governing their conduct. These changing relations also have an impact on our ethical life; for example, where once fathers might have bathed their children without questioning how this would be interpreted (or indeed questioning themselves about their motives), this domain of conduct is now called into question or problematised.

At this point it is worth noting that, although I have made some suggestions concerning the manner in which we might take up Foucault's account of the relations of power and knowledge to analyse the governance of child abuse, Foucault's suggestions concerning the relation of power and knowledge leave open the character of specific power knowledge relations at particular historical junctures and on particular sites; that is, the nature of the relation between power and knowledge cannot be decided in an a priori fashion, the task is to establish how this relation operates in specific contexts through empirical investigation.

Political rationalities and technologies of governance

Having provided a formal articulation of Foucault's conception of the relation between power, knowledge and ethics we can make one further set of conceptual refinements by specifying the use he makes of the term 'government', linking this with the concepts political rationalities and technologies of government. To do this, we need to return to the theme of power and develop the account specified above.

Clarifying Foucault's account of power as 'a "structure of actions" (Foucault 1980: 220) bearing on the actions of those who are free' (1996b: 97), Hindess notes that, 'it follows from this, in his [Foucault's] view, that power relationships will often be unstable and reversible' (1996b: 97). He goes on to specify the distinctive use that Foucault makes of the terms 'domination' and 'government' to refer to power relationships in which a relatively stable hierarchy of relations of force is established:

> Domination refers to conditions under which the subordinated have relatively little room for manoeuvre. Government lies between domination and those relationships of power which are reversible; it is the conduct of conduct, aiming to affect the actions of individuals by working on their conduct – that is, on the ways in which they regulate their own behaviour.
>
> (Hindess 1996b: 97, also Foucault 1989c: 447–8)

Foucault uses the term government in two ways. He uses it in a general sense to refer to the 'conduct of conduct', to the ways in which individual and collective conduct is conducted; he also uses the term government and in particular 'governmentality' to refer to a historically specific form of thinking about and exercising power in modern societies (Gordon 1991). This latter use of the term will be examined in more detail in Chapter 5. What we can do at this point is formally to specify the terms political rationalities and technologies of government. This will show how Foucault's focus on problematisation, his genealogical orientation and account of the mutual relations of power and knowledge, provide a distinctive way of approaching the governance of child sexual abuse within which we can hold up for question contemporary conceptualisations of the distinction between public and private life and of the relations between law and science.

Government, considered as the 'conduct of conduct', implies knowledge of the objects to be governed (it involves forms of positive knowledge and elements of calculation) and forms of practice through which government is organised. The term 'political rationalities' or rationalities of rule refers to the forms of reasoning and truth-telling that are used to make possible the governance of a particular domain. That is, rationalities of rule specify what is to be acted upon or on behalf of and how that which is to be acted upon is best conceived. Rose expresses this succinctly in stating that to analyse a political rationality is 'to diagnose the moral, epistemological and linguistic regularities that make it possible to think and say certain things truthfully – and hence to conceive and do certain things politically' (Rose 1999a: 275). He elaborates that political rationalities have a '*moral* form', that is they embody particular conceptions of the character of legitimate authority, its appropriate distribution and the principles according to which this should be organised; they have an '*epistemological* character', that is they involve particular conceptions of that which is to be governed; and they have a 'distinctive *idiom* or language' (Rose 1999a: 26–7, emphases in text).

The term 'technologies of government' refers to the ways in which these forms of authority and knowledge are inscribed within the practical exercise of rule. Technologies of government may be characterised as 'ways of entering reality into the calculations of government', making it 'amenable to interventions' through specific devices for the organisation of information in the form of 'written reports, drawings, pictures, numbers, charts, graphs, statistics' (Miller and Rose 1990: 168). Miller and Rose clarify the relationship between political rationalities and technologies of government in the following way:

> If political rationalities render reality into the domain of thought, these *'technologies of government'* seek to translate thought into the domain of reality, and to establish 'in the world of persons and things' spaces and devices for acting upon those entities of which they dream and scheme.
>
> (Miller and Rose 1990: 8, in Dean 1996: 49, emphasis in text)

In the governance of child sexual abuse, contemporary rationalities of rule are ones within which children are figured as special types of subjects, requiring particular care and guidance in order to develop from minority to majority; relations between families and the state are understood in terms of the limits of public power to intervene in a pre-existing naturally 'private' sphere; and where the legitimacy of public intervention is grounded in concerns for the 'best interests' of the child, as disclosed by specialised knowledge in child development. Thus we have a range of rationalities of rule articulated around the distinction between public and private life where the justification for and delimitation of the public right of intervention is predicated on the availability of expert knowledge in child development and child abuse. The forms of truth-telling that articulate the distinction between public and private in this area by providing positive knowledge of child abuse comprise paediatric medicine, psychology, psychoanalysis, psychiatry and social work. These variously constituted forms of scientific knowledge make possible the articulation of programmatic statements and policies concerning child welfare. They specify the epistemic grounds that are used to justify practices of intervention. That is, specialised forms of knowledge of child development form 'grids of intelligibility' concerning the phenomena called 'child sexual abuse' and these grids of intelligibility are central to the articulation of rationalities of rule in this area.

Contemporary rationalities of rule in the governance of child sexual abuse comprise grids of intelligibility that act as frameworks through which elements of the objects of government, in this case children and families, are codified and through which decisions are made concerning the appropriate forms and limits of intervention into family life. From this codification of knowledge of childhood and of families, child abuse risk indicators are established and different agencies of intervention organised. In the arena of child sexual abuse, technologies of government comprise child protection legislation, judicial statements, the documents of public inquiries, notes of guidance, child abuse registers, training manuals, tables of risk indicators and so on. Such technologies embody ways of reasoning about and produce and circumscribe ways of acting in the domain of child protection.

Reflecting on this, we can note that contemporary practices of child protection can be characterised as 'programmes of conduct which have both prescriptive effects regarding what is to be done (effects of "jurisdiction") and codifying effects regarding what is to be known (effects of "veridiction")' (Foucault 1991: 75). The legal powers of child protection agencies are intertwined with epistemic powers governing what is and can be known about child abuse. The analysis of the governance of child sexual abuse can be conducted by identifying the forms of problematisation, modes of reasoning and truth-telling, techniques and agencies of intervention brought to bear on this domain. This will involve the analysis of a range of mechanisms through which the task of government is thought and practised, including legal, administrative and scientific ones.

Conclusion

The importance of Foucault's orientation to social criticism for the concern to examine the governance of child sexual abuse lies in its capacity to destabilise assumptions held in place and further entrenched by other forms of social and political criticism. His work provides a productive way of looking at how the concepts public and private and the discourses of law and science are constitutive of modern political rationalities and of the ways in which child sexual abuse has recently been problematised as an issue for governance.

Where Habermas[9] provides a theoretical argument that can be applied to examine the governance of child sexual abuse, Foucault suggests an analytical approach to producing specific critical histories. Foucault asks us to examine how we constitute child sexual abuse as a governable problem and to assess the effects of this. His mode of analysis brings to the centre of attention the importance of how something is framed, and the impact this has on our capacities to deal with it. In this context, rather than presupposing a public/private distinction as antecedent to government, or providing a theoretical determination of the character of the relations between law and science in specific domains, Foucault invokes us to question how these concepts and categories are constituted through our practices of governance.

Having sketched this formal outline of Foucault's orientation to the task of social criticism through a discussion of problematisations, genealogy, power, knowledge, ethics, political rationalities and technologies of government, the next chapter moves on to establish how this is mobilised within Foucault's work around a concern to delineate the forms of power constitutive of our present, in terms of the analysis of modern political rationalities. Foucault's work provides a grid for the analysis of practices of power within our present in terms of the notions of 'biopolitics' and 'governmentality'. In order to analyse the Cleveland Inquiry and the reporting of the Orkney child abuse case, we need to establish an outline of these themes, of the ways in which they provide a set of co-ordinates for analysing the interrelations of law and science, and of the ways in which these interrelations constitute the possibility and limit of the contemporary governance of child sexual abuse. This is the concern of Chapter 5.

In conclusion, and as a preface to taking up these themes in order to analyse the problematisation of the governance of child sexual abuse in Cleveland and Orkney, we can note that for Foucault a central characteristic of modernity is the concern with right and its relation with truth. Foucault identifies this concern in the following way:

> I have been [. . .] concerned with the how of power. I have tried, that is, to relate its mechanisms to two points of reference, two limits: on the one hand, to the rules of right that provide a formal delimitation of power; on the other, to the effects of truth that this power produces and transmits, and which in their turn reproduce this power. Hence we have a triangle: power, right, truth.
>
> (1980a: 92–3)

Here Foucault signifies a concern to examine the conditions for the constitution of regimes of truth and their delimitation by rules of right; looking at the notions of biopolitics and governmentality will bring us back to our central concern with public and private, and law and science, their interrelations and modes of truth constitution.

Part II

Examining the governance of child sexual abuse

5 Governmentality and liberal political reason

This chapter returns to the work of Michel Foucault in order to develop further a set of tools for analysing Cleveland and Orkney. Chapter 4 specified Foucault's concepts of power, knowledge and ethics, and political rationalities and technologies of government in general terms. This chapter more closely examines Foucault's suggestions concerning the rationality of contemporary strategies of governance, developing the outline of the concepts of power and knowledge in the context of Foucault's specific historical analyses. This will flesh out how Foucault's work can help to elucidate the ways in which relations between public and private life are constituted and continuously redrawn through forms of juridical and veridical knowledge in practices of legal and scientific truth telling. In so doing, the chapter provides an account of how the relations between public and private, and law and science, taken for granted in much contemporary discussion concerning child sexual abuse, are constituted within a particular form of political rationality, and specifies the ways in which this works to render governable the problem of child sexual abuse.

Further examination of the interrelation of public and private and the role of law and scientific knowledge in constituting child sexual abuse as a governable problem necessitates consideration of liberalism as a political rationality. This will enable us to see how modern conceptions of the distinction between public and private life, as demarcating the boundaries between the public powers of the state and the private relations of civil society and the family, are predicated on specific relations operating between law and science that deliver forms of knowledge and practice so as to enable the operation of liberal governance. The public/private distinction, treated as foundational in other accounts, is, through the lens of this analysis, to be regarded as an effect or outcome of a set of governmental practices orchestrated through relations between law and science. In order to examine the public–private nexus more closely, this chapter considers three particular aspects of Foucault's work: namely his account of biopolitics, governmentality and of the interrelationship between law and science in securing modern forms of rule.

Following an initial discussion of biopolitics as a description of the general grammar or rationality of modern power, the chapter examines Foucault's work on 'governmentality' as a specific expression of the relations between power and knowledge in the exercise of rule developing from the eighteenth century onwards. This is the context in which liberalism appears as an extension of governance rather than as a form of the limitation of government, where this is achieved through relations between normalising forms of knowledge and the juridical framing of right. Having repositioned liberalism as a rationality of rule involving productive relations between law and science, the final section goes on to show how law and science are combined to produce specific objects and concepts that ground and articulate contemporary strategies of governance. The chapter ends by elaborating on the public inquiry as a mechanism through which the practice of governance is reflected upon, and through which relations between law and science are re-articulated where these have become problematic, thus re-establishing the possibility of governance.

Biopolitics

Foucault's account of power as relational, productive, and internally related to knowledge is elaborated in specific historical studies in *Discipline and Punish* (1977) and in *The History of Sexuality* (1979a). In these texts Foucault develops the theme of biopolitics as an expression describing a general form or rationality of modern power: 'biopower [is used] to designate what brought life and its mechanisms into the realm of explicit calculations and made knowledge power an agent of transformation of human life' (1979a: 143). Developing an account of biopolitics, the institutional sites on which it develops, and the forms of knowledge it makes possible, will demonstrate the ways in which Foucault's conception of power as productive of forms of knowledge suggests an examination of practices of power not recognised by conceptions of power as essentially repressive. Before turning to Foucault's account of the emergence of biopolitics, it is worth re-emphasising the impact of this shift of focus.

Drawing from Chapter 4, we can see how Foucault suggests that sovereign conceptions of power as repression, and the concomitant focus on the legitimacy or otherwise of power relations, deflects attention from the ways in which certain forms of truth telling confer rationality, and thus potential legitimacy, on the practice of power relations (see Gordon 2001: xxxi). Thus Foucault suggests that, 'we need to cut off the king's head' (Foucault 1980b: 121), to look beyond conceptions of power as manifestations of the state and sovereignty. The latter are insufficient since the state is not the locus of all power relations and because it always operates on the basis of other already existing power relations (Foucault 1980b: 122–3). Foucault describes the counterposition of truth and power, the assumption that these form an antinomy, as the 'Oedipus complex in our civilization' (Foucault [1973b] 2001: 17), obscuring the relation between forms of truth telling and relations of power. It is the connection between specific forms of truth telling and the operation of particular practices of power that Foucault analyses in his discussion of biopolitics.

Foucault locates the emergence of the exercise of biopolitical power over life in the period from the mid-seventeenth to the end of the eighteenth century. This was a period in which new forms of knowledge of and concerns over populations began to be developed through statistical enquiry (Hacking 1990), in which the epistemological basis of modern medicine was established (Foucault 1973a), and in which new forms of spatial arrangement, for example within the modern prison, would render individuals visible in new ways. What Foucault highlights here is the emergence of forms of knowledge-power in which individuals are conceived as members of a population. Biopower combines two axes: one centred on the body as a machine to be made useful through discipline, an 'anatamo-politics of the human body'; the second focused on the supervision and regulation of the species body, a 'biopolitics of the population'. Together these form two poles of the organisation of 'power over life' (1979a: 139).

This double focus of biopolitics is coterminous, at the level of knowledge, with the development of the individual case history documenting the details of an individual's life, and with the development of statistics of population, documenting demographic patterns.[1] Foucault argues that these individualising and totalising forms of knowledge are made possible and linked through the emergence of the human sciences and through the development of panoptic and confessional technologies that provide institutional sites for the concerns of these 'sciences of man'.

The 'panopticon' and the 'confession' are two major mechanisms that Foucault explores as technologies making possible and articulating the double concern of biopolitics. Foucault develops the theme of panopticism as a constitutive element in modern forms of power most significantly and explicitly in his study of the birth of the prison, *Discipline and Punish* (1977). In this text he charts the emergence of a new form of power, disciplinary power, in a range of techniques aimed to achieve continuous and uninterrupted surveillance of the individual and social body, in this case of the growing prison population. Within the prison, continuous surveillance is made possible by a diagram of power that takes an ideal architectural form in Bentham's blueprint for the 'Panopticon' (Foucault 1977: 200). The spatial arrangement produced by this design establishes a new form of individuality by making each action of every individual potentially visible. On the one hand, 'panoptic technology' produces individualising visibility aimed at the continuous and exhaustive observation and efficient management of individuals. On the other hand, this technology provides synoptic visibility; that is the architectural design and organisation makes possible the overview of the population and relations within it (Fraser 1989: 22). In this way panoptic technologies function to generate both individual case histories and statistical norms for the classification of populations, thus generating a space for the articulation of the mutual concern over the processes of individual life and the life of populations. Foucault suggests that panoptic technologies operate within prisons, but also more generally in the reorganisation of space generated with the development of schools, hospitals and so on. Such institutional sites operate as observatories and as laboratories. They make possible an observational and clinical knowledge of individuals and comparison of individuals against norms of conduct, health and development, and form contexts for the organisation of corrective training.

Through disciplinary techniques power operates directly on the body but with the aim not simply of subjection but of correction and training, seeking to reform the individual, producing a 'docile and useful' body (1977: 305). As a system of training, discipline works through hierarchical observation, normalising judgement and systems of sanctions and rewards. Disciplinary power represents a distinctively modern form of power. Its productivity is regarded as a result of its strategy of not repressing, but utilising the power of opposition to it in order to produce new forms of knowledge and government of the population.

Foucault suggests that the system of surveillance made possible by the panopticon is achieved not only through external control over bodies, but by an internalisation of discipline through the threat of continual observation. Ideally, within such a regime individuals come to police themselves. Thus, 'the major effect of the Panopticon: to induce in the inmate a state of conscious and permanent visibility that assures the automatic functioning of power' (1977: 201). This interiorisation forms an essential part of the functioning of discipline as a normalising and corrective practice. This theme of the internalisation of power is extended in the consideration of the mobilisation of a range of confessional technologies in the context of the emergence of biopolitics. To examine this we can focus on Foucault's account of pastoral power and on his study of the history of sexuality.

The discussion of confessional techniques in *The History of Sexuality* (1979a) can be regarded as an inflection of Foucault's concern with 'pastoral power', a theme he develops in a series of lectures and essays on the 'political rationality of the modern state' (Foucault 1988d: 161, also 1982, 1988e, [1979c] 2001). Giving an account of this helps establish how Foucault begins to link his ideas concerning the microtechniques of power and biopolitics to an explicit concern with the 'state' as a complex confluence of techniques of government.

Foucault argues that since the emergence of the modern state in Europe in the sixteenth century, a new political rationality has been developing that combines 'individualization techniques and totalization procedures' (Foucault 1982a: 213). This combination is due to the integration of the Christian pastoral into the modern state as it developed. If the state is the political form of centralising power, Foucault regards pastorship as a technique of individualizing power (Foucault 1988f: 60). The latter is traced back to the idea of the shepherd of men in early Christianity and involves the key notion that 'certain individuals, due to their religious qualities, can serve others as pastors' (1982a: 214). 'Pastoral power' has the role of constantly ensuring, sustaining and improving the lives of individuals (1988f: 67). In its early Christian ecclesiastical form this involved responsibility for each individual within the flock and ensuring individual salvation in the next world. This was achieved through personal submission or obedience (in return for sacrifice for the flock if necessary) and necessitated a particular knowledge in the form of the exploration of souls to provide knowledge of conscience and the ability to direct it. Pastoral knowledge is individualising (1988f: 68–9, 1982a: 214).

Foucault's hypothesis is that with the development of modern societies and the emergence of science, in particular the human sciences, pastoral power is separated from its religious context and generalised across the social domain. The modern state becomes a matrix of new technologies of pastoral power. In its modern form, the concerns of pastoral power are transformed so that the aim becomes salvation in this world, worldly security, wealth and well-being. The examination of conscience and practices of confession are reoriented around the integration of individuals into normality. This, it is argued, has produced an increase and diversification of the agents or officials of pastoral power, and the development of totalising and individualising knowledge of individuals through the deployment of the new techniques of power over life. Pastoral technology implemented in the exercise of state power means that 'the care for individual life is becoming at this moment [the late eighteenth century] a duty for the state' (Foucault 1988d: 147).

Foucault examines the implications of these developments for the ways that we are governed in *The History of Sexuality* (1979a). He argues that the two technologies of power developing around the individual and social bodies are joined together through the 'deployment of sexuality' (1979a: 140). In contrast to the common supposition of the 'repressive hypothesis' (1979a: 140),[2] Foucault argues that power is exercised through the production of, and incitement to, discourse about sex and sexuality. Discourses on sexuality produce new mechanisms of power by providing access to the life of the body and of the species, and subjects who understand themselves in terms of the truth of their sexual experience.

Foucault characterises modern western discourse about sex as a science of sexuality (*scientia sexualis*) as opposed to the erotic arts (*ars erotica*) developed by other civilisations (1979a: 57, 62). He argues that western society has sought to produce 'true' discourses on sex by adapting the procedures of confession and assimilating these into the rules of scientific discourse, a discourse producing the subjection of individuals through the demand that it 'tell us our truth' (1979a: 67–70).[3] Foucault argues that, since the Middle Ages, Christian confession has striven to turn sexual desire into speech (1979a: 20, 60), producing the subjugation of the confessor by virtue of the power relationship of the confessional situation (1979a: 61–2). As noted above, he suggests that from the eighteenth century the techniques of confession associated with the Christian pastoral have undergone secularisation. Discourse on sex has become a matter of 'public interest' (1979a: 23), taken from its religious context and used within a range of new disciplines that spread it more thoroughly throughout the social body. This has produced a change in the nature and status of the confessional, as discourses on sexuality have become matters for the emerging sciences of medicine, psychiatry, pedagogy and psychoanalysis (1979a: 65–7). This 'dissemination of the procedures of confession' (1979a: 63) coincided with increased concern for population, with the biological and social aspects of social reproduction, so that sex has become 'not simply condemned or tolerated but managed' (1979a: 24).

Foucault argues that, since the eighteenth century, this new 'technology of sex' (1979a: 116) has been one of the central techniques of modern power. From this period sex has been ordered in relation to 'normality' as old codes and prohibitions around sex have been reformulated in terms of the 'natural' and 'unnatural' and integrated into the modern state (1979a: 37–9). Within new administrative systems of regulation and welfare forming from this time, focused on the life and vitality of the population, concern over sexuality and the maintenance of 'normal sex' became a major strategy of government.

Foucault suggests that a central target of this concern with population and normal sex was the masturbating child. He points to the upsurge of concern about child sexuality in the eighteenth century as a new form of problematisation that directs attention toward a precise government of the conduct of children (1979a: 27–30), suggesting that this in turn produces an intensification and reform of family relations as a site invested with concerns about sex and its management. Specifically, the focus on the masturbating child as a problem is the context for the articulation of a more general concern with child-rearing. Childhood becomes something to be managed by parents responsible for the child's moral and physical supervision, and themselves subject to education and advice from experts concerning child development and the dangers of child sexuality (in the form of family medicine, psychoanalysis and popular advice offered to the privileged classes, and later through philanthropic interventions into the lives of the poor (1979a: 122)). Where parental responsibility fails to secure the child's moral and physical well-being, the family becomes a site for the direct intervention of expertise (1979a: 108–13, 1980d, 2000a: 53–4; see Rose 1999b, for a more extended discussion of these themes). Overall, Foucault points to the deployment of sexuality in four strategies developed during the nineteenth century: 'the sexualization of children, the hysterization of women, the specification of the perverted, and the regulation of populations' (1979a: 114). This text therefore suggests a confluence of concern about childhood sexuality, perversion and population, which become sites for the management of life organised through the developing practices of medicine, paediatrics, psychology and so on.

From this brief sketch, several important aspects of the productive character of biopower can be specified. First, biopower, as a concern with the individual and the species body, produces forms of scientific knowledge of individuals and populations. Second, these forms of knowledge are normalising in that they discern and document the internal regularities and irregularities of their objects and enable individuals to be measured and ranked against statistical averages. Third, the designation of phenomena along a continuum of normality and pathology produces the possibility of governing whole populations. All are to be concerned with the maximisation of life. Fourth, norms and techniques for recognising deviations from them (for example, statistically generated norms of child development) are means of appraising individual health and of conducting interventions to correct abnormalities; they open up fields of possible governance. Fifth, these normalising forms of knowledge enable the governance of phenomena in relation to their intrinsic regularities; that is, norms create rules of judgement internal to themselves, independent of philosophical or religious values (see Dean 1999a: 119) and as such make possible the claim to govern in the name of truth of that which is governed (see Rose 1999b: 75, 130, 150). We can relate this to the discussion, in Chapter 1, of child abuse as a normalising concept.

Here I noted that the increased visibility and spatial separation of childhood from the eighteenth century onwards in schools and hospitals provided the context for the development of medical and psychological knowledge of the child, and the associated ideas of normal development and its aberrations. Reflecting on this in the context of Foucault's discussion of biopower and its orchestration through panoptic and confessional techniques, we can add that, for example, schools, hospitals, social service units, children's homes and families themselves act as sites (observatories and laboratories) for the generation of normalising knowledge of child development. Such forms of knowledge are central to the contemporary investment in childhood as a specific phase of life requiring special care and attention, and more specifically to attempts to govern child sexual abuse.

Both medical and psychological knowledge of child development are premised on norms. The former uses norms of physical maturation to discern deviations and abnormalities, finding abuse in otherwise unexplained failures to achieve expected levels and patterns of growth, and in signs of the truth of abuse written on the child's body. The latter seeks to establish the patterns of mental and emotional maturation of children as a measure against which to assess and correct deviations within individuals, where the veracity of abuse is to be elicited from the child through the demand that children tell of their experience or where this is inferred from patterns of behaviour. As Rose has pointed out, the development of such technical forms of knowledge is not simply a new way of documenting a 'familiar reality'. Rather the conceptual systems of paediatric medicine and developmental psychology 'make new areas of life practicable' (Rose 1999b: 153); 'failures' of particular families become so through the normative grids of child development established within medicine and psychology. That these discourses function to provide knowledge presented as facts (truths) concerning child development is central to the justification of expert interventions into family life. These truths also structure a problem space for parents and children in general, by furnishing ideals for parents to strive towards in rearing children, and by providing norms of development that render the space of childhood an anxious one.

The productive and normalising character of medical and psychological knowledge of child development will be returned to in Chapters 6 and 7 in relation to discussion of medical and psychological evidence concerning whether the children involved in Cleveland and Orkney were being sexually abused. In these cases, a move took place from a search for the truth of abuse on the child's body through the discovery of physical signs (where the body is an object for physical medicine), to a search for the truth as something to be elicited from the child through disclosure interviews (where the child is figured as a subject capable of telling the truth of their experience). Prior to this, though, we need to give an account of how these forms of knowledge and practice have been articulated in relation to legal procedures in the governance of child sexual abuse. As was pointed out in Chapter 1, the sexually abused child is a veridically and juridically constituted subject/object; an entity both scientifically and legally conceptualised and acted upon. This brings us to a consideration of Foucault's concern with governmentality.

Governmentality, liberalism and the family

In his work *Governmentality* (1979b), Foucault develops his concern with centralising and individualising forms of power in order to reflect on 'the political rationality of the modern state' (1988d: 161). This work therefore links the concern with biopolitics as a modern form of power over life with the question of rationalities of rule as specific forms of the conduct of conduct, that is with ways in which individual and collective behaviour is orchestrated. 'Governmentality', in its most general sense, signifies a concern with the range of institutions, apparatuses and forms of knowledge that constitute, regulate and survey the political domain (Gordon 1991).

We can begin by noting that on the basis of the foregoing account of biopolitics we can reposition liberalism, providing an account of liberalism as a rationality of rule. In a perceptive analysis of liberal governance, Dean has pointed out that 'biopolitics is a necessary condition of liberalism' (1999a: 113), and that at the same time the democratisation of right within liberal political orders checks biopolitical imperatives concerning the administration and augmentation of life. What are the implications of this? As a preliminary to examining Foucault's reflections on liberalism, it is important to clarify the difference between considering liberalism as a political theory or political philosophy on the one hand, and examining liberalism as a political rationality on the other (Foucault 1988d: 161).

Chapter 2 considered liberal political theory in terms of the ways in which liberal settlements concerning the problem of political obligation deliver a modern understanding of the public/private distinction as a distinction between the public power of the state and the private relations of civil society and the family. In this context, we have seen how the child is figured both as an archetypically private being and as a subject of central public concern within strategies focused on the attainment of autonomy. Two central concerns of liberal political theory are thus, first, the question of the limits of legitimate public authority and securing the boundary of a private realm free from public interference, and second, concern with childhood as a transitory state of dependence to be made ultimately autonomous through appropriate child-rearing. Within this frame of reference, the public/private distinction is presupposed and childhood becomes a naturalised state of dependence to be rendered autonomous through liberal practices of governance.

Foucault's concern with liberalism is with liberalism considered as a critique of, and as a rationality of, rule. As Dean and Hindess have recently pointed out, to examine liberal governance is only in small part to regard the practical exercise of authority as the realisation of political and economic theories. The central questions in examining liberalism as a rationality of rule concern how, and under what authority, particular ideas are taken up and integrated into practices of government, how they are connected to particular administrative techniques and programmes of regulation (1998: 7, 17).

This concern with liberalism as a political rationality is therefore a different order of concern than that which dominates liberal political theory and Habermas's

Critical Theory.[4] The latter bodies of work focus attention on the problem of legitimation, on where to draw a line between public and private life or between system and lifeworld. In contrast, Foucault's focus is on the forms of reasoning that render liberal governance possible. Within this frame of reference the central questions are neither where to draw a line between public and private life, nor how to legitimate the exercise of power. Rather, Foucault's work exhibits a concern with how liberal practices of governance are articulated, and with the forms of knowledge and practice that underpin them. As such, this form of analysis makes it possible to interrogate how assumptions concerning the distinction between public and private life, and specific relationships between juridical and normalising forms of knowledge, make possible and constrain the contemporary governance of child sexual abuse. Liberal and Critical Theory assume a distinction between public and private life and naturalise familial relations and childhood dependence. As such, they provide an overly narrow scrutiny of the reach of liberal governance

For Foucault, liberalism emerges as a critique of the form and functioning of the territorial administrative state and its dominant modes of regulation, and is the point of establishment of a new rationality of government organised around population and with the aim of security/welfare. Foucault's essay *Governmentality* (1979b) documents a series of shifts in conceptions and practices of government from the sixteenth to the eighteenth century. With it, we can begin to disclose an account of liberalism as a rationality of rule, predicated on limits to specifically juridico-political authority, where the tasks of governance are increasingly conducted through normalising knowledge drawn from the human sciences.

Foucault suggests that the period from the mid-sixteenth to the end of the eighteenth century in Europe is one in which a general 'problematic of government' (1979b: 6) is raised. This is an effect of the intersection of two processes: the formation of territorial administrative states out of the breakdown of feudalism, this producing state centralisation, and the Reformation and Counter Reformation, this producing religious dissidence and questions concerning how individuals are to be spiritually ruled (1979b: 5–6). He locates the roots of liberalism in the critique of the forms of political rule that developed with the formation of the modern state during the sixteenth and seventeenth centuries, that is, in critiques of *raison d'état* and police. We need to examine these latter two constellations briefly, since Foucault's argument is that though these forms of governance are overcome, some of the practices that emerge with them are transformed and incorporated into modern practices of government.

Emerging from the breakdown of feudalism in Europe was an increasingly centralised form of territorial administrative state. With this developed the first crystallisation of an art of government in the form of reason of state (1979b: 14). Sixteenth- and seventeenth-century texts concerning reason of state articulated an art of government involving rational knowledge of the state, oriented toward reinforcement of the state itself; the aim being the 'state's preservation, expansion and felicity' (Foucault 1988d: 148). This was an art of government in which the state was to be governed according to 'rational principles which are intrinsic to it and which cannot be derived solely from natural or divine laws or the principles of wisdom and prudence' (1979b: 14). Foucault outlines four features of this art of government. It is continuous with other forms of power and government (in order to rule the ruler must be able to rule himself, and political rule should be modelled on family *oeconomy*); government concerns the general management of individuals in their relations with one another, it concerns the 'right disposition of things' (1979b: 10–11); government has a finality of its own, it concerns the management or 'disposing' of things 'so as to lead to a convenient end' as distinct from simple submission to sovereignty; and it comprises rule through 'knowledge of things', of the 'objectives that can and should be attained' (1979b: 14).

Foucault suggests that this art of government animated the development of the administrative apparatuses of sixteenth- and seventeenth-century territorial monarchies. In particular, from the end of the sixteenth century it fostered the development of new forms of detailed knowledge of the state in the form of statistics, alongside practices of policing which aimed at the detailed and exhaustive knowledge and regulation of territory and individuals. Statistics became indispensable to the aim of rational government, delivering precise knowledge of the state's strength in order that this might be secured and augmented within a competitive inter-state framework (Foucault [1979c] 2001: 317; see also Hacking 1990, Chapter 3). Concern with augmenting the state's strength also underpinned the seventeenth- and eighteenth-century development of practices of policing (1979b: 14, [1979c] 2001: 319). That is, increased empirical knowledge, combined with competitive inter-state relationships, had implications for the relationship between the individual and the state: 'the individual becomes pertinent for the state in so far as he can do something for the strength of the state' (1988d: 152). During the seventeenth and eighteenth centuries policing aimed at fulfilling this role of concern with the welfare and integration of individuals. Policing has a broad meaning here, referring not to a body of armed officers, but to a concern properly to administer the internal functions of the state, intervening to enhance the lives of individuals in their relations with one another and with things in order to 'supply them with a little extra life – and, by so doing, supply the state with a little extra strength' ([1979c] 2001: 319). This set of practices can thus be regarded as a kind of 'secularized pastoral' (Gordon 2001: xxvii), aiming to secure the well-being of each and all through detailed knowledge and regulation. Foucault cites Louis Turquet de Mayerne's utopian programme for a policed state (presented in 1611 to the Dutch Estates General): 'The police's true object is man' (Foucault [1979c] 2001: 319). Thus policing, understood in its seventeenth- and eighteenth-century sense, centred on the production of good order and the happiness of society; concerned 'the specific techniques by which a government in the framework of the state was able to govern people as individuals significantly useful for the world' (1988d: 154). Nor was this a governmental technology in the narrow sense: seventeenth- and eighteenth-century policing was not an exclusively state orchestrated affair. Rather it figured a general concern with order exhibited by the state in its concern with administration, and also, and more importantly than as a concern of the state in England, by popular movements concerned to secure order within their own communities (Foucault [1973] 2001: 59–68). This concern with policing as administration was spread in practical policies such as cameralism and mercantilism, and as a subject to be taught in the form of *Polizeiwissenschaft*, the science of administration ([1979c] 2001: 319–20).

Foucault details two internal limits to the development of the art of government comprised by reason of state and the mechanisms of police (in addition to the military, political and economic stresses of the seventeenth century). First, it was premised on the framework of sovereignty and operated through the provision of laws, decrees and detailed regulations. Second, it was organised around family *oeconomy* as a model for governance. He suggests that demographic expansion, increased wealth, agricultural production and the plotting of these by statistical means led to the displacement of these limits in the eighteenth century as new questions concerning the art of government opened up around the 'problem of population' (1979b: 16). That is, statistical knowledge, developed within monarchical systems of administration, gradually revealed that the population had its own regularities irreducible to the model of the family and impervious to traditional mechanisms of sovereignty. With this the notion of government was recentred:

> It was thanks to the perception of the specific problems of the population, related to the isolation of that area of reality that we call the economy, that the problem of government finally came to be thought, reflected and calculated outside of the juridical framework of sovereignty.
>
> (1979b: 16)

On Foucault's account, therefore, liberalism emerges as a critique of reason of state and police, and the limits of the models of sovereignty and family *oeconomy*, and develops as a rationality of rule around the problem of population. The emergence of knowledge of the population and its dynamics poses new ways of problematising the exercise of political rule. Statistical knowledge suggests that the population, economy and society have their own laws, natural laws of tendency, and in this context, the task of government becomes that of securing the capacity to function of these pre-existing quasi-natural relations. This implies that:

> Government not only has to deal with a territory, with a domain, and with its subjects, but that it also has to deal with a complex and independent reality that has its own laws and mechanisms of disturbance. This new reality is society. From the moment that one has to manipulate a society, one cannot consider it completely penetrable by police. One must take into account what it is. It becomes necessary to reflect upon it, upon its specific characteristics, its constants and its variables . . .
>
> (Foucault 1989a: 337)

We can clarify Foucault's account by noting the limits of classical mechanisms of sovereignty indicated by knowledge of the internal processes of populations. Rates of birth, morbidity and death, cycles of scarcity and abundance, those regularities internal to a population, do not succumb easily to the decrees of a sovereign (issuing laws is unlikely to produce a population increase, or to increase the rate of production of foodstuffs). This is part of the force of Adam Smith's critique of mercantilism ([1776] 1981 Book IV) and his argument for individual liberty as both desirable in itself and as a necessity in securing the well-being of society. In Smith's account, the beneficent effects of the 'hidden hand' of individuals engaged in free market exchange is counterpoised to the deleterious effects engendered by then existing mercantile practice. That is, the idea of a self-sustaining and autonomous sphere of commercial relations problematises the idea that governance should consist in attempts at pervasive regulation.

Foucault's account suggests that liberalism comprises a political and an epistemological revolution. First, with the idea that the economy and society have natural laws the boundary between state action and inaction becomes problematic (Foucault 1989a: 337); the boundary between governing and not governing sets up an enduring question concerning the limits and nature of government. Second, this boundary between the legitimate exercise of sovereignty and an already existing, independent and opaque reality of economy and society opens up the question 'how is government possible?' (Foucault 1989a: 337), a question that calls for technical knowledge of the self-reproducing character of society, in order that the state might secure the self-reproducing existence of society, enforcing its natural processes with mechanisms of security (for more detailed discussion of these points, see Gordon 1991; Burchell 1993).

Thus within liberalism the juridical question of the justification of sovereignty, the rules governing its use and who is entitled to use it, is joined by a 'technical problem: how can power be exercized in the best and most efficient way in society' (Foucault 1989b: 419). Posing technical problems of rule raises the question of the appropriate 'equilibrium between what is free, what has to be free, and what has to be regulated' (Foucault 1989b: 419). The relationship between freedom and regulation becomes a form of problematisation to be addressed by forms of technical knowledge and expert intervention.

This is evident in the playing out of the question of the relationship between freedom and regulation within liberal concerns across the latter half of the eighteenth century and into the nineteenth century. In particular, the 'ethical liberalism' (Bellamy 1992: 2) of the eighteenth century, the thesis of natural sympathy and the proposition that the progress of civilisation was to be achieved through sociability and commerce (of which Smith was a major proponent), broke down under the growing pressure of industrialisation, so that nineteenth-century liberals faced the task of finding ways to address the Social Question (Collini 1979; Wolin 1960). During the nineteenth century a range of scientific and administrative solutions were found to the problems attending liberal forms of government: the growth of administrative law, economics, medicine, psychology, psychiatry and sociology aimed to address the internal regularities of the social and economic domains through technical knowledge of their processes. At same time science, which had taken a form fairly undifferentiated from natural philosophy to the eighteenth century, underwent differentiation and specialisation, becoming increasingly separate from moral discourse and focused on expertise in relation to specific problem areas (Gregory and Miller 1998: 22). This development of expertise in relation to specific problems dispersed the Social Question into a series of discrete social problems calling for specific interventions (Rose 1999a: 123). In the process professional knowledge and expertise, with its claims to truth, provided the possibility of scientific and administrative solutions to ethical problems, expertise made possible the claim to be governing neutrally, in the name of the nature of the phenomena governed.

In the light of this, we might say that if within liberalism the appropriate role of the state is defined by reference to an already existing autonomous society, the role of the state being to secure its self-reproducing existence by enforcing natural processes with mechanisms of security, then the idea of a realm protected against state intrusion relies on a prior ordering and management of social existence. As Dean suggests, biopolitics is a condition of liberalism. This is so in terms both of the production of technical knowledge legitimating intervention in the name of the truths of the phenomena governed, and of certain sorts of subjects capable of manifesting autonomy. We can note here that the sorts of subjects that liberal political theory takes for granted and that Habermas privileges in discourse ethics are themselves the products of particular practices of governance. Hence Foucault's suggestion that we need to examine the modes of constitution of subjects if we are to analyse how power functions.

Foucault develops this point by suggesting that, since the eighteenth century, there has been a 'governmentalization of the state' (1979b: 20), whereby the state as a set of institutions has become one mechanism in a wider field of governance organised and articulated through a range of technical forms of knowledge of the social domain. In this, governance has been reconceived as government through particular processes opaque to sovereignty, but specifiable by particular forms of knowledge of the objects and processes to be governed. Through the governmentalisation of the state, positive sciences become practical elements in government. Foucault indicates here the manner in which a range of normalising knowledge and forms of practice articulate the possibility and limits of governance by documenting new areas of life and prescribing the manner in which they are to be governed. In this context:

> It is the tactics of government which make possible the continual definition and redefinition of what is within the competence of the State and what is not, the public versus the private, and so on; thus the State can only be understood in its survival and its limits on the basis of the general tactics of governmentality.
>
> (1979b: 21)[5]

This account therefore reproblematises liberalism's self-conception as a set of principles and structures delimiting government by aiming to show the ways in which the liberal problematic of ensuring the working of natural and quasi-natural processes it regards as independent of itself are in fact premised on particular forms of knowledge and strategies for governing these 'natural' relations.

There are two particularly important features of this account for our concern with the rationality underpinning the governance of child sexual abuse: first, the repositioning of the family with the emergence of liberal political rationalities; second, the question of the relationship between sovereign (or juridical) knowledge and practice on the one hand, and scientific (or normalising) knowledge and practice in orchestrating contemporary strategies of governance on the other. In order to begin to address these themes in more detail, let us turn to some critical questions raised about Foucault's account.

Whilst Foucault's account is helpful in centring attention on the ways in which, toward the end of the eighteenth century, governance was fundamentally rethought in the light of problems concerning the internal regularities of populations, a number of critical questions have been raised about this account as an adequate model of the dynamics producing liberal forms of governance. This bears upon the ways in which Foucault conceptualises sovereignty and the position of the family in the context of the emergence of liberalism as a rationality of rule. In particular, Hunter has argued that in Germany questions of religious toleration and sovereignty lie at the heart of how liberal governance and a detheologised politics emerged. As such, he suggests that the slow emergence of social and political liberalism in Germany were not the outcome of a 'liberal "critique of state reason" but [are best regarded as . . .] products of the statist deconfessionalisation of politics and pacification of society' (Hunter 1998: 247). This account indicates that the problem of sovereignty is not reconfigured in the way that Foucault's account suggests, and points to the need to develop a more nuanced account of the relationship between sovereignty or juridical power and extrajudicial forms of power than that he provides.[6] We will return to the issue of the relationship between sovereign or juridical and nonjuridical power within modern rationalities of governance in more detail in the next section. Before doing so we can amend Foucault's account of the emergence of liberalism by reference to the discussion of liberalism in Chapter 2.

In Chapter 2 we saw the emergence of the liberal principle of limits to the legitimate authority of the state as a response to seventeenth-century civil and religious war. Thus in seventeenth-century political writing, texts that precede the recognition of population and its internal dynamics as such, we see a conceptual separation of political society from society. This is most clearly drawn out by the contrast between Hobbes and Locke. While both regard political society as an artefact, as conventional, and develop this in criticism of the then dominant descending thesis of political authority in which familial, political, and divine rule form a continuity, for Locke human sociability pre-exists political society, it is not constituted by it (contra Hobbes). That is, in Lockean liberalism political rule is figured as a specific form of rule, distinct from other forms of rule such as that within the family, and resting on already extant social relations. This constitutes a break from the idea that society is only possible with government, where government is co-extensive with the population and territory to be governed. Rather society pre-exists government; in Lockean terms sociability pre-exists political society. Eighteenth-century concerns with population, witnessed for example in Smith's critique of mercantile practice, thus follow concerns to reposition sovereignty; they are not contemporaneous with them. Whilst Foucault's concern is to document the emergence of new practices of government from the eighteenth century, the account of how this takes place and its antecedents needs reconceptualising. In particular, this has an impact on the way in which we read Foucault's account of the repositioning of the family with the emergence of liberal rationalities of government.

Foucault suggests that with the shift of focus to the problem of population, there is a change in the position of the family. The family as the model of government (*oeconomy*) 'disappears' (Foucault 1979b: 17), being superseded by a science of government that takes the family not as the model of government, but as an internal element of population and an instrument of government directed at population:

> Prior to the emergence of population, the art of government was impossible to conceive except on the model of the family and in terms of economy conceived as the management of a family; from the moment when [. . .] population appears [. . .] the family becomes an instrument rather than a model: the privileged instrument for the government of the population and not the chimerical model for good government.
>
> (1979b: 17)

He suggests that the family, from being regarded as the model for political rule within literature on reason of state (1979b: 10), is refigured as a field of intervention for a range of new technologies aimed at securing the management of population as the ultimate end of government. He points to campaigns around mortality, marriage and vaccination, all of which have since the eighteenth century mobilised the family as an instrument for enhancing the life of the population (1979b: 17). In this new formulation the family becomes an instrument of government, providing a privileged site for the gathering of information relating to the population and as itself a point of intervention and regulation.

However, in the light of the discussion of liberalism in Chapter 2 we can ask whether the change in the conceptual space occupied by the family pointed to by Foucault is achieved with the emergence of the problem of population, or whether this shift actually begins in struggles over the foundations of legitimacy of political rule. This has implications for the way in which the relationship between liberal strategies of governance and the family are conceptualised. The delimitation of the sovereign authority of the state within liberalism is intimately connected with the conceptual repositioning of the family. In an attempt to dislocate the theological from the political, liberal writers articulate an understanding of two spaces of rule premised on different principles: a rational conventional account of a delimited sphere of political authority and a natural or naturalised account of the family. This suggests that, rather than the problem of government being figured outside the juridical framework of sovereignty (Foucault 1979b: 16), with regard to the family it works with a divided conception of sovereignty. The family is conceptualised as a separate space of rule organised around principles different from those of the state.

Thus, modifying Foucault's suggestion that the family becomes an instrument in governance, and against feminist suggestions that liberalism forgets the family (see Chapter 2), we might say that within liberalism the family is simultaneously configured as juridically private and as a locus of concern for and instrument of welfare. It retains some of the vestiges of sovereignty whilst at the same time becoming a key mechanism in the ordering of social existence. While the modern family might be regarded as a 'positive form of solution to the problems posed by a liberal definition of the state' (Donzelot 1979: 53), within liberal forms of governance the family forms a site of tension; it is at once regarded as a private juridical unit with rights and as a privileged locus of public concern regarding social welfare.[7] As such, the family is a site of perpetual ambivalence and tension for liberal political orders regarding questions of not only when to govern and when not to govern, but also how to govern well. This tension is managed through the mobilisation of expertise in science and law, for example in the field of child welfare.

This ambivalence in the position of the family, as simultaneously juridically private and as a locus for, and agent of, welfare, mirrors the more general formulation provided by Foucault concerning the modern subject as simultaneously a citizen with rights (part of a juridically constituted polity) and a subject of normalisation (part of welfare society). Foucault specifies this as 'the welfare state problem': 'the tricky adjustment between political power wielded over legal subjects and pastoral power wielded over live individuals' (Foucault 1988f: 67). This suggests a link between the biopolitical management of populations and discourses of sovereignty that remain as their justification, and leads to the next focus, the relationship between legal and scientific forms of knowledge and practice in articulating modern liberal modes of governance.

Law and science

> It was in connection with liberalism that they [problems of population] began to have the look of a challenge. In a system anxious to have the respect of legal subjects and to ensure the free enterprise of individuals, how can the 'population' phenomenon, with its specific effects and problems, be taken into account? On behalf of what, and according to what rules, can it be managed?
>
> (Foucault 2000b: 73)

In suggesting that liberalism is predicated on biopolitics, this chapter has so far sought to demonstrate that the distinction between governing and not governing, public and private, is orchestrated through normalising forms of knowledge of the social domain. However, as is indicated by the above quotation, liberal political reason also evinces a concern with 'right'. This produces a continuation of the theme of sovereignty, where this is articulated in relation to various forms of normalising knowledge that offer claims to truth rendering social life governable. Thus while liberalism signals limits to the state and vigilance in the exercise of political authority, it also links liberty and security. This, in its most general form, is the space of contemporary relations between law and science: within liberal rationalities of rule, legitimate government is juridically and veridically constituted.

Foucault characterises modern forms of governance as containing 'heterogeneity between a public right of sovereignty and a polymorphous disciplinary mechanism' (Foucault 1980a: 106). How then do relations between law and normalising forms of scientific knowledge make possible and delimit contemporary strategies of governance? We will examine this by looking at how Foucault conceptualises the relationship between law and science in specific contexts and by developing an account of the public inquiry as a mechanism of governance.

At the end of *Governmentality*, Foucault suggests that the emergence of the 'problem of population' does not signify the cessation of sovereignty, but rather is the moment when new questions concerning sovereignty emerge, when 'the problem of sovereignty is made more acute than ever' (Foucault 1979b: 19). He concludes that,

> We must [. . .] see things not in terms of the substitution for a society of sovereignty of a disciplinary society and the subsequent replacement of a disciplinary society by a governmental one; in reality we have a triangle: sovereignty–discipline–government, which has as its primary target the population and as its essential mechanism apparatuses of security.
>
> (1979b: 19)

Foucault provides several different formulations for the relations between sovereign and normalising forms of knowledge and practice. Whilst suggesting that they are counterpoised and conflicting, he also suggests a number of ways in which law is reformulated in relation to new fields of expertise. Moreover he suggests that, on a number of sites, legal mechanisms and normalising forms of knowledge combine to produce new objects for, and concepts of, governance. A detailed critical analysis of Foucault's conception of law is beyond the scope of this chapter (see Hunt and Wickham 1994). Instead we will seek to develop an account from Foucault's suggestions concerning the relationships between legal and normalising forms of knowledge in contemporary practices of governance, in order to analyse the relationship between legal and scientific knowledge and procedures in constituting child sexual abuse as a problem capable of liberal governance. This section first looks at Foucault's counterposition of law and normalising forms of knowledge. Second, it explores the ways in which he analyses the mutual articulation of law and normalising knowledge in securing governability in particular contexts. Third, it examines his suggestion that with the governmentalisation of the state law is reformulated from its classical expression as the command of the sovereign to its modern role in providing regulatory instruments, developing this through an account of the public inquiry as an instrument of government.

Foucault counterpoises sovereignty and discipline. He describes the development of disciplinary power in the seventeenth and eighteenth centuries as the development of a mechanism of power that is 'absolutely incompatible with the relations of sovereignty' (Foucault 1980a: 104). This is because, where sovereignty allows for the expression of obligations through a legal framework 'draw[ing] the line that separates the enemies of the sovereign from his obedient subjects' (1979a: 144), it does not provide for the organisation of continuous surveillance and correction. He elaborates on the difference between juridical rules derived from sovereignty and normalising forms of knowledge and practice in the following manner:

> Disciplines have their own discourse. They engender [. . .] apparatuses of knowledge (*savoir*) and a multiplicity of new domains of understanding [. . .] The disciplines may well be the carriers of a discourse that speaks of a rule, but this is not the juridical rule deriving from sovereignty, but a natural rule, a norm. The code they come to define is not that of law but of normalization. Their reference is to a theoretical horizon which of necessity has nothing in common with the edifice of right. It is human science which constitutes their domain, and clinical knowledge their jurisprudence.
>
> (1980a: 106–7)

Foucault clearly distinguishes juridical or sovereign forms of power (power as right, law and repression) from disciplinary or normalising forms of power (power as the capacity to organise, sustain and enhance life). The laws of tendency discerned by biopolitical knowledge, gained by effecting 'distributions around the norm' (1979a: 144), are distinct from law conceived simply as a juridical system of right.

However, as has already been noted, Foucault argues that the emergence of disciplinary power and normalising knowledge has not led to the disappearance of sovereign power (right). Rather he suggests that the latter has continued to provide the organising principle of legal codes that underscore discipline; sovereignty and discipline come together (1980a: 105). In a move that echoes his formulation of the 'welfare state problem' as comprising the conjunction of the city–citizen game and the shepherd–flock game within modern forms of rule, he argues that since the nineteenth century society can be:

> Characterised on the one hand, by a legislation, a discourse, an organisation based on public right, whose principle of articulation is the social body and the delegative status of each citizen; and on the other hand, by a closely linked grid of disciplinary coercions whose purpose is in fact to ensure the cohesion of this same social body.
>
> (Foucault 1980a: 106)

This suggests the operation of two distinct forms of reasoning about, and acting upon, the social domain. We can begin to elaborate how these might be articulated together by returning to *Discipline and Punish* (1977). In this text Foucault suggests that modern rationalities of rule combine 'the binary opposition of the permitted and the forbidden [with . . .] a "penality of the norm", which is irreducible in its principles and functioning to the traditional penality of the law' (1977: 183). This text clearly signals the differences between legal and scientific forms of reasoning and at the same time indicates their mutual operation in articulating modern forms of governance.

In considering discipline and the development of panoptic technologies in *Discipline and Punish*, Foucault documents a transformation in the character of punishment from public display of the power of the sovereign to the containment, supervisory and corrective practice of the prison and its timetable. With this he suggests a changed vision and mode of operation of law as it combines with forms of disciplinary and normalising knowledge. The shift in political imagination comprised by this transformation is most clearly brought out through consideration of his account of the exclusion of lepers in contrast to the ordering and surveillance of individuals in plague-stricken towns at the end of the seventeenth century. Foucault documents how the exclusion of lepers was characterised by a 'binary division'; the leper was to be 'marked' and 'rejected', 'exiled' from the community (1977: 198). The management of the plague, on the other hand, involved the operation of continuous power and administration: 'Rather than the massive, binary division between one set of people and another, it called for multiple separations, individualizing distributions, an organization in depth of surveillance and control, an intensification and a ramification of power' (1977: 198) in practices of inclusion, isolation, quarantine and detailed analysis ([1975] 1999: 41). Thus the 'exile of the leper and the arrest of the plague do not bring with them the same political dream. The first is that of a pure community, the second that of a disciplined society' (1977: 198). The latter vision, that of the disciplined society, relies upon the invention of a range of technologies of power over life and is therefore linked to the development of normalising knowledge of and control over the population.

Foucault suggests that although the practices of marginalising lepers and quarantining plague victims are distinct, they come together:

> It is the peculiarity of the nineteenth century that it applied to the space of exclusion of which the leper was the symbolic inhabitant [. . .] the technique of power proper to disciplinary partitioning. Treat 'lepers' as 'plague victims' [. . .] individualize the excluded, but use procedures of individualization to mark exclusion – this is what was operated regularly by disciplinary power from the beginning of the nineteenth century in the psychiatric asylum, the penitentiary, the reformatory, the approved school and [. . .] the hospital.
>
> (1977: 199)

Foucault goes on to suggest that such modern forms of government combine law (binary division) with normalisation (distribution and management) in an individualisation of the excluded. What produces this individualisation of the excluded? To address this, and the relationship between law and normalising forms of knowledge that it implies, we need to turn in more detail to Foucault's account of the transformation of the power to punish at the end of the eighteenth century, and to his analysis of the relationship between judicial and normalising forms of knowledge and power in securing specific practices of government. This can be elaborated by looking at how these themes are developed in 'About the concept of the 'dangerous individual' in 19th-century legal psychiatry' (Foucault 1978a) and in *Les Anormaux* (Foucault [1975] 1999).[8]

The transformation of the power to punish during the eighteenth and nineteenth centuries was a consequence of the emergence of biopolitical concerns and is associated with the interlocking of sovereignty and normalisation around the problem of population. Through this focus on population 'the social "body" ceased to be a simple juridico-political metaphor (like the one in the *Leviathan*) and became a biological reality and a field for medical intervention' (Foucault 1978a: 7). Foucault suggests, 'the doctor must therefore be the technician of this social body, and medicine a public hygiene' (1978a: 7).

We can clarify the implications of this by noting that Foucault suggests that within classical law a crime was not simply damage to the interests of others or to society, but was a crime against the sovereign: 'in the slightest crime, there is a small fragment of regicide' ([1975] 1999: 76, also [1979c] 2001). Punishment was not just retribution for a crime committed, but was centred on providing a demonstration of the power of the sovereign, 'it was the sovereign's revenge, it was the reply of his force' ([1975] 1999: 76). Within classical law, the sovereign manifestation of power through the public spectacle of punishment involved 'disequilibrium' ([1975] 1999: 77); the punishment had to be greater than the crime, and was expressed in terms of terror. Central to this economy of power was therefore not the 'law of measure' but 'the principle of excessive demonstration' ([1975] 1999: 77). Within the new technologies of punishment established at the beginning of the nineteenth century Foucault suggests a different economy of punishment emerges. This requires 'finding a unity of measure between the crime and the punishment' ([1975] 1999: 82); that is, punishment involves discerning the 'profit' or reason for the crime in order that the punishment meted out restore equilibrium to the social order. With this transformation, punishment demands a new knowledge of criminality ([1975] 1999: 83). Foucault argues that it is not the circumstances of the crime, nor the intentions of the criminal, that are the most important questions in this new economy of punishment, but 'the immanent rationality of criminal conduct, its natural intelligibility' ([1975] 1999: 83). We will return to this point below in discussing the introduction of psychiatric knowledge into the legal process; for the moment the important feature of Foucault's account is that it indicates that within a penal system concerned to supervise and correct individuals rather than simply to punish infractions, the possibility of punishment becomes dependent on establishing a particular type of knowledge of the criminal, of what makes or made him/her act as he/she did, in order to ensure that the punishment is appropriate to the crime.

Foucault claims that as punishment became a system of procedures designed to reform lawbreakers, rather than the sovereign parading of power, law required a new type of knowledge in order to function:

> The terrifying example of torture or exile by banishment could no longer suffice in a society where exercise of power implied a reasoned technology applied to individuals. The forms of punishment to which all the late eighteenth century reformers, and all the early nineteenth century legislators rallied – that is, imprisonment, forced labour, constant surveillance, partial or total isolation, moral reform – all this implies that punishment bears on the individual himself rather than on the crime, that is on what makes him a criminal, on his reasons, his motives, his inner will, his tendencies, his instincts.
>
> (1978a: 8–9)

This need to know the criminal establishes a link between the operation of law and normalising forms of knowledge within modern rationalities of rule.[9] This can be specified more closely by reference to Foucault's analysis of the entry of psychiatry into the judicial apparatus.

Commenting on the recent trial of a man accused of, and pleading guilty to, rape being asked to explain why he committed the crimes for which he was being tried, Foucault states that the 'penal machine can no longer function simply with a law, a violation and a responsible party. It needs something else, a supplementary material' (1978a: 2). The 'supplementary material' required is a type of discourse about the accused that reveals who he or she is. That is, within modern penal systems it is not sufficient to have an offence and a penalty; there is also a need to know the criminal, to provide an account of the motives for the crime, in order to organise measured and appropriate punishment and correction.[10]

Foucault argues that psychiatry stepped into the space created by the need to 'know' the individual in order both to meet out proportionate punishment and to reform him or her. Psychiatry proposes an explanation of what should be punished and offers the ability to predict danger, thus enabling 'the transfer of the point of application of the punishment, from the infraction as defined by law, to criminality visualised from a psychologico-moral perspective' ([1975] 1999: 17). With the emergence of normalising knowledge of populations and the constitution of domains of technical expertise based upon the idea of 'dangers inherent in the social body' (1978a: 7), medical experts, here psychiatrists, are specialists, that is bearers of expertise in the detection of danger. This expertise enables legal machinery to operate by providing knowledge of the phenomena to be governed and claims to truth that justify particular courses of action in specific contexts. The inadequacies of the old judicial mechanisms in dealing with criminality in the context of a penal system designed to reform law breakers therefore establishes a domain of 'medico-legal-criminality':

> Neither the 'criminality' of an individual, nor the index of his dangerousness, nor his potential or future behaviour, nor the protection of society at large

from these possible perils, none of these are, nor can they be, juridical notions in the classical sense of the term. They can be made to function in a rational way only within a technical knowledge-system, a knowledge-system capable of characterizing a criminal individual in himself and in a sense beneath his acts; a knowledge-system able to measure the index of danger present in an individual; a knowledge-system which might establish the protection necessary in the face of such a danger. Hence the idea that crime ought to be the responsibility not of judges but of experts in psychiatry, criminology, psychology, etc.

(1978a: 13–14)

Foucault argues that through the course of the nineteenth century this combination of law and psychiatry moved from its original focus on 'monstrousness' associated with the extreme crime of homicidal monomania, to the regulation and supervision of the whole population and its minor problems via the idea of risk, where the possibility of dangers inherent in the social body gives rise to the need to manage minor perversions through predictive knowledge of dangerousness (1978a: 14; also Castel 1988).

The notion of risk and the possibility of its prediction in turn locate problems within the family as sites for the intervention of psychiatry, so that the nineteenth century sees the emergence of a pathology of the field of family relations organised around the psychiatric notion of the pervert. The psychiatrist becomes the family doctor (Foucault [1975] 1999: 135–6).[11] With this:

You have a pathologisation of the relations of the intra-familial field, a pathologisation formed out of what? Precisely from the absence of these good sentiments. It is not loving one's mother, it is harming one's little brother, it is beating one's big brother, it is all of this, which now, in itself, constitutes pathological elements.

([1975] 1999: 139)[12]

Through this process, the norm of the good family is installed and psychiatry becomes 'medico-juridical': 'Between the description of social norms and rules and the medical analysis of anomalies, psychiatry will essentially be the science and the technology of the abnormal, of abnormal individuals and abnormal forms of conduct' ([1975] 1999: 151).

Therefore, whilst Foucault counterpoises law and normalising forms of knowledge, he argues that they 'interlock' ([1975] 1999: 128) in modern forms of governance; there are a range of sites on which the application of law requires normalising knowledge in order to function:

disciplinary normalisations come into ever greater conflict with the juridical systems of sovereignty: their incompatibility with each other is ever more acutely felt and apparent; *some kind of arbitrating discourse is made ever more necessary, a type of power and of knowledge that the sanctity of science would render neutral.*

(1980a: 107, emphasis added)

That is, a variety of forms of medical and quasi-medical knowledge (clinical medicine, pathology, psychiatry, psychology), claiming the sanctity of science, form a point of resolution of the conflict between sovereignty and normalisation by claiming neutrality and technical competence or expertise.[13] In this way, modern forms of governance can be said to combine strategies of sovereignty and of normalisation. We can summarise this in the following way: within liberalism as a rationality of rule, sovereignty (the right to govern) is premised on and achieved through claims to knowledge and expertise with which to govern. Expertise forms a mechanism for the positive resolution of the liberal problematic concerning when to govern, when not to govern and how to govern well.

With this account therefore Foucault indicates how, within liberal governance with its concern over governing too little versus governing too much, normalising forms of knowledge such as medicine, psychiatry and psychology have an active interface with law through a range of strategies for the regulation of the social. In liberal governmental practice, science is seen as providing facts that can be subject to legal judgement. In this way, normalising knowledge and forms of expertise render judicial mechanisms operable by offering knowledge and claims to neutrality through which law can come to act as a tactic of government. These forms of expertise today include psychological determinations of the capacity for reason, procedures for gathering evidence and so on. As such, they have come to focus not solely on the criminal, but also on the victim and the victim's 'truth'; this is an important aspect of the generalisation of this set of technologies of government.[14]

Moreover, the establishment of a medico-legal nexus in the governance of populations not only ties together law and scientific knowledge and practice, but also establishes a new set of objects and concepts. The transformations produced by the institutionalisation of the relation between juridical and normalising forms of knowledge:

> Took place not only from medicine towards law, as through the pressure of rational knowledge on older prescriptive systems; but that it also operated through a perpetual mechanism of summoning and of interacting between medical or psychological knowledge and the judicial institution. It was not the latter which yielded. *A set of objects and of concepts was born at their boundaries and from their interchanges.*
>
> (Foucault 1978a: 17, emphasis added)

Foucault points to the emergence of the 'degenerate', the 'pervert' and the more all-encompassing idea of the 'dangerous individual' as foci of medico-juridical conceptualisation and intervention from the late nineteenth century onwards. Extending this, we can add that the sexually abused child is also an idea born at the boundaries of law and medical and psychological knowledge, a simultaneously juridically and veridically constituted subject/object (see Chapter 1).

Foucault does more than to suggest that modern forms of governance combine juridical discourses of sovereignty with veridical discourses drawn from domains of scientific knowledge, bringing with them new objects for, and concepts of, governance. He also suggests that in this process law itself is reorganised. This brings us to the third element of Foucault's treatment of the relation between law and science. In the context of a discussion of disciplinary power, Foucault states:

> I do not mean to say that the law fades into the background or that the institutions of justice tend to disappear, but rather that the law operates more and more as a norm, and that the judicial institution is increasingly incorporated into a continuum of apparatuses (medical, administrative and so on) whose functions are for the most part regulatory.
>
> (1979a: 144)

Foucault claims that, in the context of new forms of knowledge of populations, law itself, from its role as the instrument of sovereignty, becomes one of a range of tactics of government (1979b: 13). He suggests that 'within the perspective of government, law is not what is important' (1979b: 13) in the sense that the importance of law and its concern with right is reorganised around concerns with the governance of populations. That is, concern with governance produces a shift in the role of law in relation to scientific knowledge and the new possibilities for governance that it opens up.[15] With the emergence of technical forms of knowledge of society and of individuals, Foucault suggests that law's role is refigured in relation to new fields of expertise. Developing this theme, Foucault's work suggests that not only do normalising forms of knowledge necessary for modern governance come into an institutionalised relation with law, but that we may see law as itself increasingly governmentalised, developing new forms in the context of the governmentalisation of the state. We can develop this theme by looking briefly at Foucault's discussion of the 'mutation within the law' (1978a: 14) that occurs with the recognition of risk as an element in legal calculation, before developing an account of the role of the public inquiry in contemporary strategies of governance.

In 'About the concept of the 'dangerous individual' in 19th-century legal psychiatry' (1978a), Foucault documents how the notion of risk entered law through the civil law development of no fault liability in the face of industrial accidents during the latter part of the nineteenth century. No fault liability made it possible to attribute responsibility on the basis of harm caused rather than via the attribution of fault and opened the way for law to be used as a regulatory instrument in the governance of risk. By eliminating fault from the system of civil liability, civil lawyers introduced the analysis of causal probability and risk to the legal system, and with it the idea that sanctions, rather than being focused on punishment, should be designed to ameliorate the effects of industrial practices and to engender the minimisation of risk by inducing actors to introduce greater security into their procedures. The effect of this was to tie legal reckoning to causal analyses in a new manner; the idea of guilt and responsibility was displaced from its central role in such legal judgements by a reorientation of the legal system around the management and reduction of risk. Law itself has become a tactic of governance in the arena of industrial accidents in so far as it provides detailed regulatory instruments oriented toward conducting the conduct of organisations so as to achieve and maintain security and minimise risk (see Castel 1991).

Foucault does not develop this concept of a 'mutation' in law very far. In the text discussed, he examines the emergence of no fault liability in relation to industrial accidents in order to highlight the importance of the change in the concept of legal responsibility that this brings, opening the way to causal analyses of risk that, he argues, are incorporated into other branches of law – enabling for example the governance of 'the criminal' on the basis of what he is rather than (or as well as) what he has done.[16] We can, however, use this as an opportunity briefly to examine the emergence of the public inquiry as an instrument of governance in the development of administrative law in England and Wales during the nineteenth century, and to indicate the ways in which contemporary inquiries bring together legal and scientific concerns in the management of public issues.

What Foucault alludes to in discussing the emergence of no fault liability in nineteenth century civil law is the growth of a more general concern with and reorganisation of practices of government in the face of the growing complexities of industrialism. Whilst inquiries, as mechanisms for generating knowledge of territory and resources, have a long history in English and continental European law (see Keeton 1960; also Foucault [1973] 2001: 45; and Wraith and Lamb 1971: 17, with regard to the Domesday survey), one can argue, adapting Foucault's terminology, that there was a governmentalisation of law around the administrative difficulties of governing enclosures of land, dealing with industrial accidents, and organising and regulating local government activity during the eighteenth and nineteenth centuries, one effect of which was to produce the modern form of the public inquiry as an instrument of government combining 'fact finding' and 'conflict resolution' (Wraith and Lamb 1971: 303).

The nineteenth century saw fundamental changes in the organisation and powers of government. Arthurs plots a steady growth of administrative forms of governance and institutions from the 1830s on, whereby central government inspectors, tribunals and inquiries replaced an extensive range of localised regulations (Arthurs 1985: 89). He suggests that as the idea of rational scientific solutions to the problems of industrialism gained ground in the nineteenth century, for example, through the ideas and activities of Bentham and Chadwick, centralised forms of control replaced local ones, and that in these forms of control there was a shift from reliance on criminal law to administrative regulation. '"Ordinary courts" and "ordinary law" were judged inappropriate for the handling of important public and private business' (1985: 129), much of which was conducted by detailed regulation produced through circulars, inquiries and requests (1985: 124–5). Arthurs points to the development of systems of inspection (in factories and workhouses) and to independent regulatory commissions (appointed to undertake and regulate the running of public works) as evidence of these developments, describing this as a period of attempts to translate public policies into reality that led to the development of a new form of 'law' (1985: 130), 'the indigenous law of the social field' (1985: 181).

Through the nineteenth century therefore one sees a growth in the use of administrative instruments to deal with the increasingly complex business of government. Administrative law can thus be seen as developing in contexts in which the mechanisms of the formal judicial system were judged 'unsuitable for the performance of particular social tasks' (Arthurs 1985: 197). The modern public inquiry system arose in this context.

The development of public inquiries toward their modern form took place through attempts to find an appropriate mechanism to regulate the enclosure of land during the nineteenth century. From the mid-eighteenth to the mid-nineteenth century, the conflicts of interest produced by enclosures were dealt with individually by private Acts of Parliament (Kemp 1985: 180). This system was an expensive and repetitive system of individual judgements. The General Enclosure Act of 1845 introduced greater uniformity into this process. In particular, it adopted the legal device of the provisional order that brought with it the requirement to hold a public inquiry. From this point applications were made to government departments (rather than to Parliament), and inquiries were conducted by inspectors appointed by the ministers concerned (Wraith and Lamb 1971: 19). Through the latter half of the nineteenth century, in relation to development of local government activity, and with respect to industrial accidents, detailed procedures concerning the conduct of public inquiries were laid down, so that Wraith and Lamb claim that by the end of this period the public inquiry approximated the form taken by a modern statutory instrument (1971: 20, also 23–6).

Public inquiries take a wide variety of forms. They arise in an ad hoc manner, being called into existence by ministers of state where there is a need to collect information prior to making a decision (for example, planning inquiries) and where tragedies have occurred and/or conflicts require resolution (for example, inquiries held after major accidents, where child protection practice has become contested and so on). The latter form, with which we are concerned, has an important role in resolving problems of governance by airing and proceduralising issues apparently at arms length from politics. Important here is their 'public' character, for inquiries are widely seen as open and objective mechanisms for establishing the facts of an issue and for producing new ideas concerning how contested public issues should be dealt with.[17] They are regularly called for by the press and by directly affected parties in contexts in which the day-to-day practices of governance are seen to have failed. By being 'public', they can be seen to be open, and through their quasi-judicial status they produce apparently objective and orderly discussion on subjects that are the cause of public alarm. They thus form one of the means by which the practice of government is reflected upon, by focusing attention on what has happened in a particular case; they are also a means through which new procedures are orchestrated, by focusing on what should be done, and on how to govern more effectively. In this way, they can have what Stephen Sedley QC calls a 'special value', in that they 'can bridge the gap between government and governed, between authority and liberty, in situations where those sides have pulled apart to an extent which could damage the body politic' (1989: 473).

The basic functions of public inquiries are veridical – collecting and ordering information to establish facts about some contested issue – and juridical – resolving conflict, establishing what should be done in a particular case, and establishing who or what was responsible for a particular series of events (Wraith and Lamb 1971). Whilst inquiries established by central government have statutory powers, being able to compel the attendance of witnesses and production of documents,[18] they are not courts of law. Rather, public inquiries mix the administrative and the judicial. They have a predominantly regulatory and administrative function, not being concerned primarily with guilt or innocence, but with ensuring the correct functioning of social institutions. Thus, where criminal and civil courts focus on alleged infractions, testing these against specific standards of proof (respectively, beyond reasonable doubt and the balance of probability), delivering individual judgements of guilt or innocence, and applying sanctions according to judgements reached, inquiries proceed on a different and more flexible basis. They do not have the limits and restrictions of a court of law. The chair, appointed by the relevant secretary of state, has wide discretion concerning who is asked to give evidence, the nature of the evidence presented, the rules concerning cross-examination of witnesses, and the overall manner in which the inquiry is conducted. Thus, while public inquiries are most often headed by lawyers, frequently judges or senior barristers, they are not bound by the usual evidentiary rules of courts and are not predicated on an adversarial formula. Instead, they are usually inquisitorial in character, being open to the elaboration of different accounts of what has taken place in a particular context, to the presentation of a wide range of expert evidence and opinion, and to discussion of usual and best practice in other contexts, with the aim of investigating and giving an account of what has happened in a particular case, and of making recommendations concerning necessary reforms to ensure best practice in the future.

Through these functions, public inquiries provide fora for the review of governmental practice, deal with publicly contested issues, provide recommendations, and restore confidence in practices of governance. In this sense, inquiries can function 'as a kind of socio-legal fire brigade', working to 'absorb and still controversy' (Sedley 1989: 477, 478), without necessarily having a major impact by directly inspiring legislative change. The recommendations of successive child abuse inquiries and associated circulars of guidance issued prior to the 1989 Children Act were important in shifting attention and resources away from child care and towards child protection conducted in a more hierarchical and defensive manner than previously well before the major legislative changes introduced by the 1989 Children Act (Parton 1985a; Hallett 1989). Thus inquiries and their recommendations can have an important impact on policy and practice even where they do not inspire legal change. As such, in their effects they bear a resemblance to the forms of administrative regulation developed during the nineteenth century.

We might therefore characterise the public inquiry as an institutional space organised to resolve problems in the governance of state–social relations through reintroducing productive and legitimate relations between legal and scientific knowledge and practice and public and private concerns, where these have become problematic. Public inquiries are mechanisms of governance that incorporate legal and scientific knowledge and forms of reasoning in order to debate publicly contested issues in a contained manner and to restore the possibility of governance. We can specify this in relation to child abuse inquiries by recalling the discussion of successive calls of 'crisis' in the governance of child sexual abuse in Chapter 1. That chapter outlined the form of calls of 'crises' of rationality in child protection as comprising the questioning of legitimacy, in which the relationship between the family and the state is at issue, and the problematisation of expertise, in which the knowledge and professional expertise of the agencies of child protection are subject to interrogation, their veracity questioned. Public inquiries, as quasi-judicial mechanisms that call upon scientific knowledge, form a central site for, and mechanism in, the attempt to negotiate relations of sovereignty and discipline. Through so doing, they can be said to manage moments of 'failure' in particular programmes of governance, providing contexts for the problematisation and reformulation of existing strategies of governance, and re-entrenching the authority to govern by airing the issues and proposing reforms to practice. In this way, they process the 'failures' of particular governmental programmes, providing an 'element of utopian duplication' (Foucault 1977: 271) by re-articulating formulae for rule.[19]

Public inquiries function as instruments or technologies of governance by recalibrating the balance between public and private interests concerning a specific issue, hearing and assessing the evidence and opinions of experts, and delivering recommendations for sound practice. They operate in the context of 'failures' of normal governmental practice to restore confidence in government by functioning as particular types of 'truth establishment' (Foucault [1973b] 2001: 45).

Foucault provides an account of the inquiry as 'a particular way of knowing' ([1973b] 2001: 40) that can help us to address this. Referring to the practice of judicial inquiries developed from the twelfth century on, he describes the emergence of the inquiry as 'a type of truth-establishment closely tied to the administrative management of the first great state form known in the west' ([1973b] 2001: 45).[20] By gathering individuals who, under oath, could give evidence of what they knew, a particular way of arriving at the truth, and thus rendering a judgement, was formed. Foucault describes the inquiry as a way of 'extending actuality, of transferring it from one time period to another and of offering it to the gaze, to knowledge, as if it were still present. This integration of the inquiry procedure, reactualizing what had transpired, making it present, tangible, immediate, and true, as if one had witnessed it, constituted a major discovery' ([1973b] 2001: 47).

The importance of the public inquiry as an instrument of governance is that it links judgements of right and judgements of truth in a flexible and yet proce-duralised manner:

> The inquiry is absolutely not a content but, rather, a form of knowledge – a
> form of knowledge situated at the junction of a type of power and a certain

number of knowledge contents [*contenus de connaisance*]. . . . The inquiry is precisely a political form – a form of power management and exercise that, through the judicial institution, became, in western culture, a way of authenticating truth, of acquiring and transmitting things that would be regarded as true. The inquiry is a form of knowledge-power.

([1973b] 2001: 51–2)

The public inquiry might thus be regarded as a crystallisation of the 'Oedipus complex' referred to in the first section of this chapter. It functions to produce authority and reinscribe the possibility of governing by providing a quasi-judicial framework for contests over scientific expertise, being seen as an arena of objectivity and disinterested judgement within which truth can win through. In operating to reform governmental practice, and to achieve an appropriate balance between public and private interests and between legal procedures and normalising forms of governance, the public inquiry operates as a polyvalent technique of government.

Conclusion

Foucault's focus on biopolitics and his account of government enables us to reposition liberalism, disclosing liberalism as a rationality of rule maintained by productive relations between law and science, where these forms of knowledge and practice create and sustain the public/private distinction by specifying objects and concepts of government. Through the lens created by Foucault's work, it becomes possible to see the public/private distinction as an effect created by governmental practice, and maintained by relations between law and science. In this context, the law–science relation articulates the public/private distinction by providing justifications for interventions premised on the truths provided by scientific discourse, where the latter are in turn framed by discourses of right. Within liberal political rationality, jurisdiction and veridiction are tied together in securing the possibility of governance. Where this relationship is threatened, for example by calls of 'crisis' in the governance of child sexual abuse, public inquiries form a site for the interrogation of existing formulae and practices of governance, and for the re-establishment of programmes of rule. Chapters 6 and 7 elaborate these themes in relation to problems in the governance of child sexual abuse exhibited in Cleveland and Orkney. The 'crises' articulated around these events offer a space in which to examine how assumptions concerning the public/private distinction and concerning the appropriate relation between law and science work by opening them to scrutiny.

Foucault's account of liberalism as a rationality of, and a set of practical technologies of, government that call upon legal and scientific forms of knowledge and practice in sustaining the possibility of governance, leaves open the question of the precise specification of the relation of law and science within any particular context thus maintaining a space within which legal and scientific knowledge and practice may be conceptualised as symbiotic, conflictual and/or mutually undermining. It is this space that renders Foucault's ideas productive in relation to an examination of the relation of science and law in recent cases of child sexual abuse as it refuses to provide a prior theoretical specification of the relation of science and law, while at the same time prioritising this relation for analysis. Foucault's work thus directs attention to the productivity of specific combinations of discourses and practices in constituting new domains of knowledge and rituals of truth. What are called for therefore are specific analyses of the ways in which knowledge and the forms of practice it articulates combine to produce particular rationalities of government and domains that are governable. It is to these that we now turn.

6 Reconstructing the liberal governance of child sexual abuse

The public inquiry into Cleveland (1987)

This chapter considers the report of the Cleveland Inquiry (Butler-Sloss:1988) in order to examine the rationality underpinning the practices involved in the governance of child sexual abuse. This inquiry, instituted following calls of 'crisis', formed the moment when policies and procedures concerning the management of child sexual abuse were first opened to intense and sustained public scrutiny in the UK. It offers an important illustration of how problems in the liberal governance of child sexual abuse are worked through 'on the ground', in particular because, to date, it has been one of the largest and most wide-ranging of inquiries into the governance of child sexual abuse in the UK context,[1] and because it has had an important effect on current governmental practice through its impact on the Children Act 1989 and in the production of guidance notes for the reform of practice (DoH 1991a).

Chapter 1 presented, in broad outline, the course of the events that took place in Cleveland in 1987. The inquiry into these events begins from the paralysis that resulted from the breakdown of normal relations in child protection. In this context, the inquiry aimed to 'ventilate the issues', to 'ascertain the facts' and to 'offer guidelines which restore some degree of confidence in the working of those agencies both for the agencies themselves and for the public, locally and nationally' (Butler-Sloss 1988: 7, 1). The report of the inquiry offers an opportunity to examine the grounds that constitute legitimate intervention in child sexual abuse, by enabling us to analyse what happens when claims to legitimacy break down. As a review of governmental processes, it provides a window through which to examine the anatomy of liberal welfare rationality as a rationality of rule, looking at how the public/private distinction is constituted and reconstituted within liberal governance, and at how particular forms of authority, grounded in law and science, configure and reconfigure child sexual abuse as a governable problem.

This chapter seeks to show how the inquiry process operates within a liberal rationality of rule to re-establish the possibility of reasonable governance where this has broken down. To do this it draws on the discussion in Chapter 5 of the relationship between liberalism as a rationality of rule and biopolitics, and on the suggestions made there concerning the public inquiry as an instrument of governance. The first section examines how, in its assumptions and suggestions, the Cleveland Inquiry mirrors and reiterates liberal understandings of the appropriate relation between families and the state, where the family is regarded as a prior and private domain and intervention justified through specific knowledge of 'harm', or risk of potential harm, to a child. From this premise, the second section examines how expertise in the governance of child sexual abuse was problematised in Cleveland. It focuses on two specific aspects of the inquiry's discussion of evidence and professional practice, those involving the use of reflex anal dilatation (RAD) and disclosure interviews in the diagnosis of sexual abuse. Having examined the status of RAD and disclosure as these are presented and managed within the inquiry, the third section looks at the institutional location of these practices, at the ways in which the report discusses these issues in terms of a problem of the provision of evidence for different purposes and the ways in which it attempts to rework the normalising and juridical aspects of practice in this area through demands for more and better knowledge, training and co-operation.[2]

Negotiating the public/private distinction: the relationship between the child, the family and the state in Cleveland

The Cleveland Inquiry simultaneously assumed and reinvoked a distinction between public and private. The report states the priority, naturalness and privacy of the family:

> There is no inherent right to remove children from their homes. The power in every case derives from specific child care and child protection legislation. Parents alone (except possibly in wardship) have inherent rights and obligations in respect of a child.
>
> (Butler-Sloss 1988: 16.8, 227)

At the same time, however, it states that, 'at the heart of this inquiry we were concerned with the best interests of the children' (ibid.: 11, 2). How does the inquiry negotiate this tension?

The assumptions contained within the report are broadly consonant with those of liberal political theory. The report presupposes a distinction between public and private life, assuming the naturalness and priority of family autonomy unless and until intervention is rendered justifiable by a breach of specific legislation. In the case of a breach, the report identifies the need for intervention into the private sphere of the family to be based on evidence drawn from indicators of harm to children's welfare, citing criteria including a 'child's proper development being avoidably prevented or neglected', its 'health being avoidably impaired or neglected or being ill-treated' or the child being 'exposed to moral danger' or 'beyond the control of parents', where such harm is disclosed through appropriate child protection practice (ibid.: 16.21, 229). The report points out that, in addition to being satisfied that one of these criteria apply, 'the court must also be of the opinion that the child or young person is in need of care or control which he [*sic*] is unlikely to receive *unless* the court makes an order' (ibid.: 16.22, 229, emphasis added),[3] this statement further underwriting the privacy of normal family relations, their priority and naturalness as compared with the artefactual character of interventions.

Embodied in the report is a clear delineation of the privacy of familial relations unless and until these are questioned, this latter possibility producing a demand for expert knowledge to determine what constitutes health and its impairment. The report therefore reflects the ambivalent position of the family within liberal welfare rationalities as simultaneously juridically private and as a potential site of normalising intervention. This ambivalence is contained by the report through an argument for balance and reasonableness, something reflected in the way the inquiry handled submissions put to it.

In their evidence to the inquiry, Drs Higgs and Wyatt, the two paediatricians involved in taking the children into care, emphasised that their primary duty was to the children. Both stated clear opinions that where there were suspicions of abuse children's interests should take precedence over family rights, and used this to justify their interventions in the cases concerned (ibid.: 8.8.2, 131; 8.9.12, 147; 8.9.42, 152). By contrast, others asserted the priority of the rights of families to privacy in such circumstances. For example, PAIN (Parents Against Injustice) expressed concern about the protection of family life and of children from what it called 'misguided' and 'overzealous' professionals (ibid.: 9.2.9, 162). In her evidence to the inquiry, the director of PAIN argued that 'to remove children on the test of the balance of probabilities was an infringement of civil liberties' (ibid.: 9.2.11, 162), adding that 'until child abuse was established, the emphasis on our society should be on the protection and preservation of family life (ibid.: 9.2.9, 162). In a similar vein, Stuart Bell MP appealed to a populist characterisation of social services departments as bureaucrats engaged in 'empire building'. Bell attempted publicly to discredit the case in statements made to the media, in which he accused social services of 'looking for child fodder' and likened the events of Cleveland to the Salem witch trials (ibid.: 9.3.28, 168; also Bell 1988; Campbell 1988).

During the inquiry, therefore, different groups asserted that priority should be given to child protection, or that precedence should be granted to family privacy. The report provides a space for the articulation of the different positions of those involved and at the same time affirms a concern for balance, measure and calm. Specifically, it positions itself through a refusal to come down on one side, criticising both positions and the events and actions that followed from them. It attempts to mediate between the positions and groups involved, reasserting the possibility of reasonable governance within the terms of liberal welfare rationality.

The report was critical of Bell for making 'intemperate and inflammatory remarks' to the media (Butler-Sloss 1988: 9.3.28, 168), and concludes that whilst there was disruption to the lives of those concerned, 'at no time was there an intention to make a fundamental attack on family life' (ibid.: 9.3.22, 165). At the same time, however, the inquiry was critical of the use of PSOs (Place of Safety Orders) in Cleveland as contravening established guidelines and producing a lack of accountability on the part of social workers and paediatricians involved. In particular, it notes that there were 'a substantial group of children in whom signs of sexual abuse had been diagnosed without there being a complaint either from the child or from a third party' (ibid.: 4.57, 61), and comments critically on the fact that firm diagnoses of sexual abuse were made in Cleveland without full social work assessment (ibid.: 8.9.48, 153). Whilst the report notes that this use of PSOs was a product of genuine concern with child abuse as an emerging problem, and of the difficulty of finding appropriate ways of recognising sexual abuse and developing adequate responses to it, it notes that the orders were used as a device in 'managing the denial' (ibid.: 37, 11) surrounding such abuse by holding children in care so that disclosure work, regarded by both paediatricians and social workers involved as the 'gold standard' (ibid.: 8.9.30, 150; also 4.92, 66; 8.9.49, 153), could take place.[4] This action is criticised as being conditioned by 'experience of physical abuse cases and the need to take steps for the immediate protection of the child concerned' (ibid.: 8.9.30, 150). The report therefore presents the concern on the part of the paediatricians to investigate potential abuse as leading to hasty action and to an invasion of parental rights (ibid.: 8.9.47–9, 153). In so doing, it emphasises the need for more broadly based professional agreement prior to making firm diagnoses and suggests that different thresholds for action may be appropriate in suspected sexual and physical abuse cases.[5]

In attempting to manage the tension between the priority of family privacy and recognition of children's interests as potentially necessitating intervention, the report mobilises both a juridical discourse of rights and a normalising discourse of interests, eliding the potential problems this entails through the idea that children's best interests are usually served by a private ordering of family relationships, and by focusing its attention on elucidating clear grounds for intervention when this is not the case. That is, the problem posed by countering children's interests with parents' rights is overcome by equating children's interests with family autonomy. Where this is not regarded as possible, the report demands that intervention be made on the basis of sure knowledge and expertise (ibid.: 13.2, 213). The inquiry thus attempts to negotiate the difficult tension between public and private spheres of life through a demand for expertise in judgement. Such expertise promises a way of managing the distinction between public and private life by providing adequate knowledge and competent practice, where this in turn provides the possibility of credible evidence able to sustain the legitimacy of intervention. In this way, the inquiry hopes for interventions that could be 'not only successful in securing and underpinning the welfare of the child, but also respectful to the rights of parents' (ibid.: 13.14, 214).

The idea of balance in the relationship between the public powers of the state and the private relations of the family is an organising theme of the report. It begins with the twin premises that families are and should be private, and that adult–child sexual contact is wrong. It then argues for reasonable, measured intervention grounded in professional knowledge and competent expertise, where this secures an appropriate boundary between public and private life. The legitimacy of interventions and the possibility of securing a balance between public and private life is based on a series of claims concerning, and imperatives to provide, physiological, psychological and social knowledge of children and families, where these forms of knowledge have to be juridically as well as veridically well founded. It suggests that what is required to achieve this is an improvement in the knowledge, procedures and training of the professionals involved in order to produce greater competence in treading the line between the welfare of the child and families' rights to privacy. The report thus focuses on reordering existing relationships so as to balance public and private; current understandings of the family as prior to and usually outside the scope of the state are accepted, and attempts are made to reground an appropriate balance between them, through improving knowledge and procedures. This acts as a set of demands to intensify already existing relationships and practices.

At this point a closer examination of questions concerning the adequacy of the knowledge and competence of the practice of those involved is central to further examination of the inquiry's attempt to re-establish the possibility of reasonable governance. The next section therefore considers how the question of appropriate boundaries between the family and the state is linked in the inquiry to the problematisation of the knowledge base and forms of practice of those involved in the Cleveland case and to demands for more and better forms of knowledge and practice within child protection.

The politics of truth: the relationship between law, medicine and psychology in Cleveland

The question of the adequacy of medical and psychological knowledge of child sexual abuse was central to the concerns of the Cleveland Inquiry. The report both questions existing, and makes calls for more and better, forms of knowledge and practice. It does this in order to ensure that the social policy objective of child protection is met, and, because knowledge and practice are adequate, parents' rights and the private sphere are not illegitimately invaded.

Chapter 5 noted that the distinction between public and private, as it is articulated within liberal rationalities of rule, relies for its viability on the existence of a series of practical forms of knowledge of that which is to be governed. The inquiry opens a space to consider the role of expertise grounded in biopolitical knowledge within liberal welfare rationality. By examining the report's discussion of the use of the sign of reflex anal dilatation (RAD) and disclosure interviews in the cases concerned we can see how the authority of the expertise of those involved is problematised, and how this threatens the terms of liberal welfare rationality, and at the same time examine the way in which the inquiry invokes expertise in the form of other professionals as privileged truth tellers and judges, thus reproducing the figure of the expert by calling on expertise from outside the case concerned. The problematisation of expertise is resolved through recourse to expertise. This is central to the ways in which the inquiry manages the problem of maintaining and reinstating the possibility of reasonable intervention in the face of 'crisis'.

Questions concerning the status of knowledge drawn from child medicine and psychology, and the competence of the practitioners involved, are focal points around which the relationship between different ideas of childhood, family and forms of knowledge and practice within the field of child protection are articulated in the course of the Cleveland Inquiry's attempt to (re)entrench a legitimate distinction between public and private life. The inquiry addresses this by asking what constitutes evidence of child sexual abuse and by interrogating whether the professionals involved were competent experts in their fields. We can state this as a concern with the expert as a figure of epistemic authority and competent judgement. This concern arises because the idea of good practice is predicated on the twin ideas of epistemologically adequate knowledge and, thus, on the expert as truth teller, and on the idea of competent judgement, where the expert is able to engage with the evidence before them in a considered and disinterested manner, and to act accordingly. In this context, the achievement of good practice requires commitment to an attitude of scientific detachment (disinterestedness) as the condition of possibility of scientific knowledge (truth), where this is combined with a capacity for dispassionate judgement (objectivity) in particular cases. It is in this way that the figure of the expert as truth teller and fair judge sustains the possibility of governing reasonably within a liberal rationality of rule, providing knowledge and the technical means through which the distinction between public and private can be legitimately managed within liberal governance.

Reflex anal dilatation (RAD)

> The sign is as follows: when the buttocks are separated, the external sphincter and then the internal sphincter open so that the observer can see through the anal canal into the rectum. The anal sphincters are controlled in part automatically, in part by learned subconscious behaviour, and in part consciously; *all in a very complex system not altogether understood by the experts.*
>
> (Butler-Sloss 1988: 11.26–7, 190, emphasis added)

Whilst the Cleveland Inquiry discussed a number of potential physical signs of child sexual abuse, controversy centred on the question of habitual anal abuse and its diagnosis using the sign of RAD (ibid.: 11.18, 188).[6] Despite the publicity surrounding its use in Cleveland, this sign is not in itself a recent medical discovery. The report elaborates a number of differing medical interpretations of its significance, ranging from its use as evidence of homosexual activity, through to interpretations of potential causes of anal dilatation specifically in children, including constipation, threadworms, fear, anxiety and medical examinations and procedures such as the use of suppositories (ibid.: 188–91). In Cleveland, reflex relaxation and anal dilatation were used by Higgs and Wyatt, along with a range of other indicators such as 'failure to thrive', as a sign indicative of anal sexual abuse (ibid.: 8.8.61, 141).

Problematising the sign: the medical dispute over the significance of RAD

> Experts differed in the weight they placed on particular signs. Public attention, directed by the media, centred on the single sign of anal dilatation. Dr Higgs and Dr Irvine were opposed in their views as to its significance.
>
> (ibid.: 11.22, 189)

The medical dispute concerning the use of RAD in Cleveland is important for our concern with the relationship between liberalism and biopolitics. In the controversy surrounding its use it is possible to see the attempt on the part of the paediatricians involved to extend the domain of medical competence in the governance of child sexual abuse, this being rendered problematic by professional disagreement. As the scientific basis of this sign as a determinate sign of sexual abuse was thrown into question by this disagreement, its evidential worth in grounding action that could be defended within a juridical framing of right was contested.

The report documents statements from both sides of the dispute, focusing on statements made by Drs Higgs, Wyatt, Irvine, and Roberts. Higgs's evidence to the Inquiry provides a clear statement of her belief that RAD is a significant sign of anal abuse:

> 'My knowledge of the possible causes of reflex relaxation and anal dilatation, particularly in conjunction with other physical findings, is that I have only seen data to present sexual abuse as a cause for that. I have certainly seen other opinions, but not any data to substantiate other opinions. You have to keep an open mind about it, as yet there is no data to support another view, so you practice your medicine with what information you have available.'
>
> (ibid.: 8.8.62, 142)

When asked, at the inquiry, to state her present view about the physical signs she said, 'I still feel that they are very relevant and, if anything, I think the further literature that I have read has strengthened that view rather than make me think that it was not a valid view' (ibid.: 8.8.64, 142). Conviction about the significance of RAD was also evident in Wyatt's comment to the inquiry that, 'In the absence of a visible stool in the anal canal, and following reflex relaxation, I know of no other cause to explain this sign other than sexual abuse' (ibid.: 8.9.12, 147).

Higgs and Wyatt's view of the significance of RAD was directly countered in statements to the inquiry by the police surgeons involved. Dr Irvine, the senior police surgeon, expressed caution about infringing family privacy on the basis of the paediatric knowledge available. 'He was concerned about the diagnosis of sexual abuse in the absence of complaint or suspicion and felt that it was a dangerous way to proceed given the current state of knowledge' (ibid.: 7.8, 102). The report also documents Dr Roberts's conviction that the sign lacked relevance and meaning, and notes her opposition to Higgs's and Wyatt's use of it as 'uncritical', leading them to make 'a firm diagnosis' on the basis of what she regarded as 'inadequate examination', and without giving appropriate consideration to 'other factors' (ibid.: 11.63, 200).

The police surgeons' view was underscored by Mr Makepeace, a Cleveland police inspector. He stated his views on the medical dispute thus:

> 'It soon became very clear that Dr Higgs is one of only three or so doctors in the country whose clinical practice and interpretation is at variance with the vast majority of medical opinion. Dr Irvine was of the view that she was frequently in error which often resulted in care proceedings against innocent families which effectively tore them apart.'
>
> (ibid.: 6.52, 95)

This statement is important because it contains a notion of competent clinical practice as grounded in consensus or majority opinion. In directly countering 'majority medical opinion' with 'error' it maintains the assumption that majority medical opinion constitutes valid knowledge and thus disqualifies claims to expertise, made by Higgs and Wyatt, which could justify rendering relations public in these cases.

Makepeace's statement accords with the judicial determination of the definition of adequate scientific evidence as that which can withstand being tested in court. Drs Higgs and Wyatt, on the other hand, were working as paediatricians concerned to offer the children they saw optimum care (ibid.: 8.8.71, 143; 8.9.12, 147). Reflecting on this, we might say that in the contest over the significance of RAD in Cleveland normalising biopolitical concerns with child welfare, the paediatricians' concern for the 'best interests of the child', came into conflict with the juridical concern with the rights of the families and children to privacy. In so far as child sexual abuse is simultaneously a medically and a legally defined object of concern, then scientifically and juridically adequate knowledge is required to sustain the legitimacy of interventions. In this case, as medical practice meets a series of legal concerns about child protection and possible criminal prosecution, what could in other circumstances remain an indeterminate indicator, an 'abnormal sign' (Higgs, in Butler-Sloss 1988: 8.8.65, 142) to be noted in ongoing medical supervision, takes on a different significance, and, in the absence of consensus amongst experts such that no clear determination of the evidential worth of RAD can be made, is seen as illegitimate. The relationship between science and law, as a relationship between biopolitical concerns with health and juridical concerns with right, breaks down.

In this context, the British Paediatric Association points out differences in the form and temporality of science and law, and the difficulties that these differences may produce. In a letter to Dr Higgs, the Association comments:

> Where medical practice has a definitive interface with the law, as with child abuse, there is a particular difficulty because laws, once established, are

rigid and inflexible and relate to accepted practice of the time. Laws are established on consensus views and do not easily accommodate evolving, developing medical practices. Once established they are likely to encode and impose the accepted practice of today and may well inhibit the development of better practice for tomorrow. The more they are kept out of medical practice the better.

(British Paediatric Association, in Butler-Sloss 1988: 302–3)

There are perhaps two important points about this letter for our concerns. First, it suggests the desirability of a radical separation of law and medicine. Second, however, and as noted by the Association itself, in writing of child abuse this letter already refers to a simultaneously medically and legally defined problem: the abused child is a focus of concern for medicine and psychology and for civil and criminal law, a site of medico-legal knowledge and practice. This combination of normalising and juridical concerns can be seen in the report's response to the use of RAD in Cleveland.

The report concluded that Higgs was a caring, hard-working doctor (Butler-Sloss 1988: 8.8.71, 143), but criticised the certainty of her position and her and Wyatt's heavy reliance on RAD as 'premature' (ibid.: 8.8.74, 143). In particular, it stated that in 'venturing into a new field' at a point when work on RAD as a significant sign of sexual abuse 'had not been widely affirmed', Higgs 'did not allow for the boundaries of present knowledge and the possibility of the unknown. In the current state of knowledge she was unwise to come to a firm conclusion rather than a strong suspicion on physical signs alone' (ibid.: 8.8.74, 143).[7] Commenting that Higgs 'lacked appreciation of the forensic element of her work, and the need to justify her conclusions at case conferences, care proceedings and/or in the criminal courts' (ibid.: 8.8.74, 143), it concurred with the judgement of other experts that 'Abnormal physical signs are rarely unequivocally diagnostic with the exception of the presence of semen or blood of a different group to that of the child' (ibid.: 11.30, 193; also 8.9.42, 152).

The assessment that the 'current state of knowledge' was insufficient on its own to justify the interventions that took place, because insufficiently well founded to withstand legal test, provides the impetus behind a demand for the development of adequately grounded knowledge through more research. This latter demand is couched in terms of the need for a clear nomenclature amongst professionals describing physical signs of sexual abuse (ibid.: 6, 247), and for more research into the occurrence of reflex relaxation and anal dilatation in a population of 'normal individuals'. The report notes with concern that, 'it is not known whether it [RAD] occurs in normal individuals, whether it occurs in certain physiological states and whether it occurs in certain diseased states' (ibid.: 11.28, 190), and advocates closer study in this area, commenting that while 'such studies would be very difficult; they may present ethical problems; yet such information would be of great value' (ibid.: 11.28, 190–1). Such a study would be useful precisely in so far as it would provide a rule of judgement, an account of normality (and therefore a normative standard) against which the significance of the sign RAD as a sign of the existence of the pathology indicated by the term 'child sexual abuse' could be more readily assessed; that is, research promises the possibility of establishing a value–fact relation, yet at the same time it is unclear on what basis, ethical or otherwise, such a study could be convened.

In the face of disagreement amongst medical professionals concerning the significance of RAD as a sign of sexual abuse, therefore, the report construes the problem as a technical one to be resolved through more expertise. The idea of the expert as a privileged truth teller is maintained even as those involved in this case are criticised: the problem of expertise is resolved through a call for more and better expertise.

Problems of competence and interestedness

As the scientific adequacy of RAD as a sign of sexual abuse was contested within the inquiry process, the paediatricians, police surgeons and social workers involved took entrenched positions and developed explicitly evaluative discourses about the issues. Examining this will show how the inquiry presents a model of expertise premised not only on epistemic authority, but also on competent judgement.

Higgs's assumption was that there was a problem and that it must be rooted out. The report comments that her view was that 'she was discovering abuse which was "there to be found"' (ibid.: 8.8.78, 144), a rather naïve empiricism that did not seem to falter through the proceedings despite Higgs's opinion, stated in the course of being asked the value of second opinions, that only in 'gross cases' can physical signs be determining (ibid.: 8.8.39, 137; also 8.8.46, 139), and despite the apparent fluctuation in the appearance of the sign in the same children in between medical examinations (ibid.: 8.8.67–8, 143).[8] The report comments on Higgs's approach to the diagnoses in terms of her lack of professionalism, her lack of the properly scientific attitude of scepticism, and her failure to recognise the fallibility of scientific knowledge:

> From her evidence she gave us a clear impression of calm certainty and unshakable conviction about the correctness of the diagnosis made by her during the entire period of the crisis. She gave little indication of any change of attitude to the approach to and management of this problem.
>
> (ibid.: 8.8.38, 137; also 8.8.75, 144)

Higgs and Wyatt saw the failure on the part of others to recognise that RAD was a sign of sexual abuse as a question of 'denial'. The report comments that they ignored others' advice and that 'their belief in the validity of the conclusions from the physical signs led them into over-confidence in the diagnosis' (ibid.: 8.8.81, 145). Moreover, it comments that Wyatt 'became emotionally involved in and committed to his diagnosis in respect of children under his care' (ibid.: 8.9.47, 153).

By comparison, Higgs's reluctance to allow police surgeons to examine the children was largely attributed to 'the outspoken and vehement opposition displayed by Dr Irvine to Dr Higgs's method of diagnosis' (ibid.: 9.3.22, 166). The report notes that Dr Roberts's 'criticisms were couched in strong and emotive language including strong personal criticism of Dr Higgs' (ibid.: 11.65, 201). It condemns Roberts's written evidence to the Inquiry in which she stated that, 'the child cannot distinguish between an assault carried out in a hospital room by a stranger (a doctor) and a similar experience elsewhere' and accused Higgs and Wyatt of 'outrageous sexual assault of children' (ibid.: 11.65, 201) in the process of examining them, as not sustained by the investigations of the Official Solicitor representing the children.

The report notes that Roberts's view was not an impartial one, but one borne through emotional involvement and association with the parents of the children concerned. Criticising Roberts, it works with and calls for notions of expertise and professionalism as detachment and moderation:

> In her evidence on anal abuse, *she appeared to become associated with the cause of the parents and was unable to provide us with the cool, detached and considered testimony the Inquiry might have expected of the expert, particularly a police surgeon.* Counsel to the Inquiry advised us in his closing submission that the evidence of Dr Roberts proved to be: 'extremely and unnecessarily critical and contentious [. . .] far from passing to planes of increasing authority and moderation it became more and more passionate in character and thus perhaps of less value . . . We will not be urging you for a moment to adopt or accept her views, because *we seek to stress throughout the vital importance of striving for middle ground, and obviously Dr Roberts does not stand on middle ground with regard to this issue.*' This assessment with which we agree is a matter of regret.
>
> (ibid.: 11.66, 201–2, emphasis added)

The report criticises all of those directly involved in the dispute, and maintains the idea of the professional scientific expert as one able to transcend the specific interests apparent in the positions of others around them, to make decisions based on the evidence, and to be impartial in their practice. This is central to the claim to competency of the professional as a figure of authority and something that is rendered problematic in Cleveland.

The centrality of detachment and of the capacity for independent judgement to professional authority is further borne out by the report's criticisms of social workers in this case. The certainty of the diagnoses provided by Higgs and Wyatt created a problem for the social workers involved concerning how to respond, given their statutory responsibilities for child protection (ibid.: 4.144, 73). The report comments that the social workers involved placed too much reliance on Higgs, noting that they thought the way to resolve the conflict was to 'suspend disbelief', and that 'often in suspending disbelief, social workers fell into the trap of suspending all critical appraisal' (ibid.: 4.145, 73).[9]

Criticisms of the competence of the SSD focused specifically on Sue Richardson as Child Abuse Consultant. The report points out her influence on other social workers, and notes that Richardson shared Higgs's 'fervent' view that 'there was a great deal of undetected sexual abuse and they were finding it' (ibid.: 8.8.77, 144). It states that whilst Richardson knew of the difference of opinion between the paediatricians and police surgeons involved, she did not warn her seniors of this fact, so that 'Mr Bishop's recollection of the message that came across was, "Incredible as it may seem, this is something that is happening in our midst and medical opinion establishes it"' (ibid.: 4.75, 63) The report elaborates this criticism of Richardson in terms of her interestedness, her failure to recognise the rights of parents, and her exclusive focus on children as an approach inappropriate to her position. In the process, it frames the proper role of professionals working in child protection as being able to balance concerns with child welfare and concerns with the rights of parents:

> She occupied a position of some considerable importance and influence in a public authority. Her position was such as to require her to weigh any advice she gave not only with the interest of children but also the rights and responsibilities of parents, the proper consideration of the use of statutory authority, the good name of Cleveland Social Services Department and the wider public interest.
>
> (ibid.: 4.187, 83)

Reflecting on this, it is possible to see how adequate knowledge and competent practice are tied together in forging responsible intervention. Within a liberal political order the claim of professionals to act on the basis of firm evidence and independent reflection is important, this underwriting the impartiality of the expert and sustaining his or her privileged status as truth teller and judge. These concerns are amplified in the inquiry's discussion of the use of disclosure interviews in the cases concerned.

Disclosure interviews: from medicine to psychology in the governance of child sexual abuse

> An essential part of the investigation of an allegation or a complaint of child sexual abuse will be an interview with the child if he or she is old enough to say what did or did not happen to them. The child telling of abuse was often referred to as 'in disclosure' and assisting the child to talk of it as 'disclosure work'. The use and potential abuse of 'disclosure work' was the subject of a considerable amount of evidence to the Inquiry.
>
> (Butler-Sloss 1988: 12.1, 204)

In Cleveland, use of disclosure interviews sharpened considerably the question of evidence and of what was to count in the adjudication of public and private relationships. Interviews conducted with the children raised further concerns about the adequacy of normalising knowledge as grounds for action to protect children, and intensified the discussion of evidence of what is 'in the best interests of the child' which, within liberal rationalities of rule, forms the justification for interventions overriding the claim of parents' to rights to privacy. By examining the inquiry's problematisation of disclosure interviews we can further explore the relationship between biopolitical forms of knowledge and liberalism in the governance of child sexual abuse.

In Cleveland disclosure interviews, originally developed as therapeutic tools for the treatment of children, were used for diagnostic purposes, as evidence of children having been sexually abused. This followed a more general extension of the use of such interviews. For example, at Great Ormond Street (GOS), where disclosure interviews were first developed in the late 1970s, their use was at first solely therapeutic. However, as GOS saw increasing numbers of children where sexual abuse was suspected rather than confirmed the techniques were adapted and developed for use in diagnosis. 'The techniques designed to help the child talk of the experiences suffered were thus in time deployed to ascertain the truth of the allegations made' (ibid.: 12.21, 206).[10]

The report asks the question 'What should an adult do when a child speaks of abuse?' (ibid.: 12.4, 204) and records the response of Dr Bentovim (from GOS) concerning the development of practices of listening to children:

> According to Dr Bentovim, until a few years ago, it was the practice for professionals to disbelieve the child. He said, 'If a child described a sexual experience, you first of all disbelieved it and it had to be proven to you, rather than you first of all taking it seriously and saying he is entitled to belief and then obviously investigating it properly and thoroughly'.
>
> (ibid.: 12.4, 204)

The report identifies two stages in disclosure work as developed at GOS: 'In the first stage the child tells the interviewer. The second stage is a process whereby the professional attempts to encourage the child who may be reluctant to tell the story' (ibid.: 12.19, 206). This second stage is called by the inquiry and the experts giving evidence to it, the 'facilitative stage'. It is over the skills of interviewers, the boundaries between open and facilitated interviews, and the question of the change in the context and purpose of disclosure interviews from wholly therapeutic purposes to their use as evidence justifying action to protect children that dispute occurred in Cleveland.

Children's evidence in Cleveland

The report notes that in Cleveland prior to 1987, sexual abuse had been identified by a complaint from a child or from an adult. There had been little use of interviews with children for diagnostic purposes. It states that, 'during 1987 there appears to have been an immediate response to a suspicion of child sexual abuse that somebody should do disclosure work with the child' (ibid.: 12.41, 208). Both the paediatricians and social workers involved regarded such interviews as the 'gold standard' in determining whether a child had been sexually abused. In particular, the report comments that for Higgs and Wyatt disclosure 'was the most important element of the fuller assessment', adding that 'Dr Higgs was considerably reinforced in her confidence in the physical signs by the "disclosures" she understood were being obtained from children in the early part of the year' (ibid.: 8.8.51, 139).

This emphasis on disclosure as the 'gold standard', combined with the increased number of referrals of suspected sexual abuse without prior complaint by the child concerned or by a third party, produced a situation in which Cleveland Social Services:

> ' . . . had very few people who did have that sort of training or experience, and so it was the practice for social workers to try and get on and do the job themselves and fulfil the need where it was seen and sort of tutor themselves in order to do it.'
>
> (Mr Duncan of Cleveland Social Services, in Butler-Sloss 1988: 4.149, 74)

The report made a number of criticisms of the interviews conducted with children in Cleveland in 1987. It states that in this case 'anxiety, the need for a solution, beliefs about "denial" and the therapeutic benefits for children of talking about abuse, the perceived need to believe the child and some learnt information about the techniques of interviewing' came together. This produced a situation in which, 'there was in many circumstances a presumption that abuse had occurred and the child was either not disclosing or denying that abuse', and in which 'those conducting the interviews seemed unaware of the extent of pressure, even coercion, in their approach'. This pressure included 'matching the pressure on the child not to tell with pressure by the interviewer on the child at the interview' (Butler-Sloss 1988: 12.42, 208). It makes specific criticisms of the fact that in Cleveland the second or 'facilitative' stage of interviewing was used 'as a routine part of the general interview, instead of a useful tool to be used sparingly by experts in special cases' (ibid.: 12.18, 206). More generally, it comments that there was 'insufficient expertise', and that the 'the outcome of interviews in Cleveland was considered to be of such importance in the confirmation of the abuse, that the conduct of the interviews became distorted by the anxieties of the interviewers' (ibid.: 12.45, 209). The report concludes that, 'some interviews we saw would not be likely to be acceptable in any court as evidence of sexual abuse' (ibid.: 12.42, 208; also 4.148, 73–4)

From these criticisms, we can see that as the purpose for which interviews were used moved from a therapeutic to a diagnostic one, normalising concerns with child welfare and with the subjective experience of the sexually abused child came into a determinate relationship with law. Following Foucault's account of the relationship between normalising forms of knowledge and legal processes, we might say that psychological and psychiatric expertise offer a way of extending the possibilities of governing child sexual abuse, by rendering subjective experiences of harm on the part of children justiciable. The development of the use of disclosure interviews for diagnostic purposes prior to 1987 can be seen as part of the extension of normalising knowledge drawn from psychology and psychiatry into the judicial apparatus (see Chapter 5). This is an important development in the forms of knowledge and practice that attempt to render child sexual abuse governable.

The move from medicine to psychology transforms the focus of the normal-ising knowledge brought to bear upon the child, from a focus on the body of the child as an object of and for investigation, to a focus on the psyche of the child as a subject of concern. Attention to what the child tells of their experience extends the realm of possible knowledge and action of the professionals involved; focusing on the child's experience, rather than just on what the body reveals, is an important way of 'extending actuality' (Foucault [1973b] 2001: 47) in the governance of child sexual abuse, where physical evidence can be very difficult to find. On the part of a biopolitical concern with child health this might be considered a proper focus. The priority of the best interests of the child must mean focusing on the child's experience and the damaging effects of abuse. However, once this set of therapeutic techniques is extended for use as part of a diagnostic process, it comes into a direct relationship with juridical concerns that require adherence to different evidentiary procedures. In such contexts, the expertise of the psychologist or psychiatrist is crucial in sustaining the relationship between the normalising concern for the best interests of the child and the juridical concern with forensically recognised evidence and with the rights of parents.

The inquiry steered a path through the problems attending the use of disclosure interviews in Cleveland by attempting to reconstruct a working relationship between the normalising discourse of the best interests of the child and the pro-cedural concern with the rights of parents. It did so by calling on experts from outside the case concerned to discuss the merits of and appropriate procedures for interviews with children.

The debate over disclosure

Bentovim's comments above describe a shift in professional ideas toward recognition of the importance of children's statements in diagnosing sexual abuse. However, disagreements remain over the merits of interviews with children, especially for evidential purposes.[11] The main focus of attention in the Cleveland Inquiry was to secure a distinction between interviews for diagnostic purposes and those conducted as part of a therapeutic programme. Attention therefore centred on the value of the second, 'facilitative' stage of interviewing as part of the diagnostic process.

Facilitative interviews are meant to encourage a reticent child to tell of their abuse. In its general discussion of sexual abuse, the report recognises 'the pressure to keep the secret' (Butler-Sloss 1988: 17, 6), commenting that 'many children who have been subject to sexual abuse are put under pressure from the perpetrator not to tell' (ibid.: 17, 6), and noting that such pressure can include threats of violence, threats that telling others will result in family break-up, or that the child will be disbelieved. It cites expert evidence to the inquiry that:

> 'There is a powerful disincentive to disclosing the fact that one has been subject to sexual abuse. The person who discloses this has fears that he may be

regarded as having permitted himself, as having collaborated in it, as having been lastingly damaged in a sexual way. He is likely to fear ridicule, humiliation, obloquy and so on.'

(Professor Sir Martin Roth, in Butler-Sloss 1988: 17, 7)

This position, suggestive of the need for practices which may involve putting pressure on the child to 'disclose' (the idea of matching pressure not to tell with a countervailing pressure to tell), had been encouraged by successive statements and recommendations regarding social work practice as centrally concerned with the child and child protection. As an example of this, the report cites the DHSS paper *Child Abuse – Working Together* (April 1986), where this suggests that, 'a child's statement that he or she is being abused should be accepted as true until proved otherwise. Children seldom lie about sexual abuse' (Butler-Sloss 1988: 12.5, 204).

This advice was countered in evidence to the inquiry by a number of experts from outside the case: 'Professor Kolvin [speaking on behalf of the Royal College of Psychiatrists] said [. . .] "a statement by the child that sexual abuse has occurred should be taken seriously, but you are prejudging the child if you say that you believe it; in other words that you believe the child entirely"' (ibid.: 12.5, 204). Others voiced strong criticisms of 'disclosure work', being concerned that such interviews closed down the interpretive possibilities available by premising interviewing on the idea of there being something to disclose:

Dr Jones said, 'a fundamental problem of the 'disclosure' approach is that it is inherent in the concept that there is *something* to disclose. The problem is highlighted by those professionals who consider that the child is either *disclosing* or '*in denial*'. The third, and crucial, alternative possibility, namely that the child has no sexual abuse to disclose, is not considered as a viable option. In the best circumstances, the possibility of no child sexual abuse becomes an extremely unlikely possibility from such "disclosure work". The premise that abuse has occurred, yet is hidden and shrouded from discovery, is inherent in the very term "disclosure work".'

(ibid.: 12.24, 206, emphasis in text)[12]

The inquiry takes this up through the observation that the interviews conducted in Cleveland were premised from the beginning on the idea that abuse had occurred but was hidden where this idea should have been introduced into the interviewing procedure at a second (therapeutic) stage, that this should be premised on 'a formulation of what is being treated' (Dr Jones, in Butler-Sloss 1988: 12.36, 208), and that in Cleveland there was inadequate training, lack of expertise and overenthusiasm. As a result some, for example Dr Zeitlin, characterised the use of disclosure techniques in Cleveland as 'having taken on "almost the character of a crusade"' (Butler-Sloss 1988: 12.31, 207).

This criticism of practice in Cleveland, but not of the fruitfulness of interviews in general, is rearticulated in submissions by the Official Solicitor, who stated, 'The topic has acquired a mystique; and good sense is not always to be seen amongst the skills which are put to work' (ibid.: 12.31, 207), a view echoed by the inquiry itself in its observation that the DHSS *Working Together* guidance was the 'present received thinking' of a number of professionals, and that this should be interpreted as an entitlement that the child's beliefs be taken seriously, rather than that they should be necessarily believed (ibid.: 12.5, 204).

Paying heed to the expert testimony received, and to the divergences in the form and temporality of juridical concerns with rights and scientific and therapeutic concerns with normality, the inquiry distinguishes the natural from the artefactual bringing forth of the truth of the child. It does so by stating that, for diagnostic purposes, 'spontaneous' disclosure (ibid.: 12.2, 204) is to be preferred, and by making a distinction between interviews used to ascertain facts and those conducted for therapeutic purposes, stating that the former should precede the latter (ibid.: 12.11, 205; 12.36, 208; 12.37, 208). In this process the juridically well founded and the 'natural', i.e. unfacilitated, disclosure of truth are articulated together.

To elaborate, the inquiry and the experts giving evidence to it steer a path through the problematics of disclosure interviews by equating the true with the natural, where the natural is nonetheless a product of expertise. Unfacilitated interviews are presented as leading to the natural emergence of truth, as bringing forth repressed knowledge present in the child. The 'facilitative' stage, as an artificial bringing forth of the experience of the child, opens up the possibility (if not done properly) of the contamination of the natural, thus undermining truth. This mirrors the inquiry's assumption of the priority and naturalness of the family as compared with interventions that require justification (see earlier in this chapter; also Chapter 2).

Here we can see that debate amongst experts from outside the immediate case concerned promises to resolve the disjunction in the form and temporality of law and science by offering greater expertise in eliciting and interpreting children's statements, and a closer specification of the procedures through which this should take place. At this point, it is possible to see that expertise plays a critical role in sustaining the relationship between normalising concerns and juridical ones in the governance of child sexual abuse. This is particularly so with regard to interviews conducted with children suspected of being sexually abused. This is because psychological and psychiatric expertise, properly established, can transform subjective experience into material suitable for law: expertise (in the veracity of children's statements, the interpretation of behaviour and so on) functions to transform personal testimony into potentially corroborative evidence. Expertise transforms the status of the child's testimony as a function of its expertise.

In Cleveland, those conducting interviews were regarded as inadequately trained and as failing to recognise the forensic aspects of their task. The extension of normalising knowledge seen in the use of disclosure interviews for diagnostic purposes in this case therefore created a problem in so far as it brought normalising knowledge drawn from a therapeutic concern with child health into a direct relation with juridical concerns without requisite expertise. Within the terms of liberal welfare rationality no grounds for intervention could come out of this process of 'disclosure'.[13]

The report's response to this is to call for experts to be capable of harnessing interview techniques in such a way that material drawn from them can be considered natural or 'spontaneous'. This operates as a demand for specific forms of practice such that normalising knowledge drawn from interviewing accords with judicial criteria for evidence gathering. Expertise is thus central to the means by which the inquiry attempts to re-establish the possibility of governing child sexual abuse.

The outcome of this discussion is a convergence amongst the experts called concerning the need for more work and training in the area. This is backed by the report and encapsulated in its statement that, 'this area of disagreement [over the limits and usefulness of facilitated interviews] *clearly has to be resolved by the professions in the light of subsequent experience*' (ibid.: 12.33, 207, emphasis added; also 12.18, 206). In the context of disclosure interviews, therefore, as in the dispute over RAD, the report invokes a vision of expertise as combining adequate knowledge and good professional practice, and calls for further discussion, research and better training to achieve this. In this way the idea of expertise, of professional knowledge and practice in interviewing children, is maintained as a means of rendering child sexual abuse governable, while the specific form of this carried out in Cleveland is criticised. This criticism emerges not only in terms of a need to recognise that different types of interview are appropriate for different purposes, but is also couched in terms of a call for greater objectivity and openness; the report states that, 'the problems related to the *interpretation* by professionals of the comments of children who were not making clear allegations against their parent' (ibid.: 12.3, 204, emphasis added).[14]

The report takes care to warn against presuppositions in interviewing children, either in the form of refusal to recognise abuse or through refusal to see that no abuse has occurred. In aiming for a balance between the two extremes of disbelief and total faith in what children say it seeks to maintain an ideal of professional practice as open and objective. Indeed, in suggesting a middle course between listening to and believing children's statements and maintaining the possibility of the innocence of parents in the face of a child's statements to the contrary, its leaves an ambiguous area that it demands be filled by the 'open-mindedness' of professionals. In so doing the report relies upon and invokes expertise in this area as the technical means through which the public/private distinction can be legitimately adjudicated. A crisis of expertise is once again resolved through recourse to expertise.

The report attempts to clarify how expertise in the interpretation and use of children's statements should be used in contexts in which normalising knowledge has a direct relationship with law. It stresses the need to accept that the child may have nothing to tell, and for professionals to approach diagnostic interviews with an open mind (ibid.: 12.25–6, 206–7). This recommendation that a child's decision not to tell should be respected demonstrates how the distinction between public and private life is contained within and managed by expertise.[15] The idea of the child 'choosing' not to tell is important in contexts of juridical concerns for civil liberties, but does little to address the biopolitical problem that children are not necessarily going to talk of sexual abuse easily, that there is often pressure to keep things 'secret', so that this position, in attempting to hold the middle ground of 'reasonableness', could be seen to legitimate and sustain privacy and silence. Professionals, following this advice, could be accused of conspiring with abusers in allowing the silence of an unresolved problem to continue. Social workers have statutory duties to protect children and so the problem remains. The report elides this issue by appealing to the judgement of experts, simultaneously invoking expertise in normalising knowledge of child health and a juridically conceived notion of privacy in order to achieve the idea of balanced or reasonable intervention.

The report goes on to endorse and rearticulate a number of points made by the expert witnesses called concerning the conduct of all interviews. It suggests the 'undesirability of calling them "disclosure" interviews, which precluded the notion that child sexual abuse might not have occurred'; that interviews should only be conducted 'by those with some training, experience and aptitude for talking with children'; and that it was necessary 'to approach each interview with an open mind', using open-ended questions 'to support and encourage the child in a free recall'. Moreover, it comments that there should be a limit to the duration and number of interviews conducted for evaluation; that the 'interview should go at the pace of the child and not of the adult'; that the setting should be 'suitable and sympathetic'; and that it is necessary to accept the child might give 'no information to support the suspicion of sexual abuse and the position will remain unclear'. It argues that interviews should be recorded; that it 'must be recognised that the use of facilitative techniques may create difficulties in subsequent court proceedings'; and that the importance of 'adequate training for all those involved in this work' should be recognised. It states that in some cases 'facilitated' interviews may be appropriate, but that this type of interview 'should be treated as a second stage', should 'only be conducted by those with special skills and specific training', and that 'the interviewer must be conscious of the limitations and strengths of the techniques employed' (ibid.: 12.34, 207–8). This set of recommendations becomes particularly important with regard to Orkney, where children were interviewed in a manner that demonstrated a series of lessons not learned from Cleveland (see Chapter 7, also Clyde 1992; Asquith 1993).

We have seen that the paralysis resulting from the breakdown of a basis in established and agreed medical and psychological knowledge throws the inquiry into a discussion of evidence. In the context of this conflict the report is keen to maintain the possibility of appropriate knowledge and practice in dealing with child sexual abuse. Within the report, therefore, the discussion of evidence is taken up through a set of criticisms of the incompetence of the professionals involved, their ill-founded certainty and interestedness, implying as a norm a model of professionalism as founded on adequate knowledge and competent practice. In this way, the report manages a 'crisis' in the governance of child sexual abuse by suggesting that the problem faced is insufficient knowledge and certainty concerning signs of sexual abuse coupled with insufficient training, coordination and considered action from professionals. The report thus combines a set of specific criticisms of individuals involved, for acting on inadequately founded knowledge, and for emotional involvement and lack of impartiality, with a demand for more and better knowledge of sexual abuse to be produced through expert knowledge systems, going on itself to suggest a range of administrative and legal changes within which professional practice may achieve a clearer focus. This review of the forms of knowledge and practice in Cleveland, and the call for more knowledge, better training and a reform of procedures, works to overcome conditions of crisis by promising to restore reasonable governance of child sexual abuse. However, it also reiterates an existing way of problematising the issues and intensifies an existing set of concerns.

Reflecting on the report's discussion of RAD and disclosure interviews, we can see that in Cleveland the relationship between law and science was destabilised, so that decisions concerning the need for intervention came to centre on medical and social work judgement, and moved away from legal analysis. Such moments of destabilisation are not surprising given that contemporary public law increasingly focuses on expecting and requiring the state to secure ultimately the children's best interests. This expectation intensifies the parental relationship between the state and the child to an extent where reliance on traditional forms of evidentiary knowledge run up against concerns to ensure that the state does not neglect its family responsibilities. Scientific and other normalising knowledge has greater claim than law to involvement in precautionary as opposed to reactive risk analysis. Whereas science is expected to predict events, law is expected to react to events and evidence. Scientific analysis thus offers a more immediate channel of communication between the state and the child, as opposed to the more distanced, less intimate, relationship fostered under legal patronage. How does the inquiry renegotiate relations between law and science in the government of child sexual abuse?

Bringing together law and science

In Cleveland, the questioning of the significance of RAD, the undecidability as to whether this constitutes physical evidence of child sexual abuse, and the corruption of 'disclosures' by improper questioning techniques, form a point at which the medico-legal alliance in child protection breaks down. The expertise of paediatricians and social workers is seen to 'fail' at the point of its intersection with the legal frameworks governing legitimate child protection practice. Lack of medical knowledge and psychological expertise makes the claim to the legitimacy of the actions unsustainable as these are tied together in mutual dependence. The claim to the legitimacy of intervention is grounded in the authority of expertise, that is, in adequate knowledge and professional competence. The inquiry takes this up through the suggestion that professionals involved in child protection should balance their concern for the best interests of the child with due recognition of legal procedures.

In particular, the report comments that 'ultimately children can only be protected on the basis of evidence that can be tested in court' (Butler-Sloss 1988:

4.145, 73). In the absence of such evidence, it suggests that the removal of the children from their families in the first place might not be considered to be in the child's best interests (ibid.: 10.32, 177). Here, therefore, juridical concerns override normalising ones, or rather these are linked, but with priority given to the former.

In this context, the report mobilises a range of discourses concerning the emotional and psychological health of children to problematise the paediatricians' and social workers' assumptions that, in sexual abuse cases, what is in the best interests of the child is immediate removal from the context of suspected abuse. The report recognises the possibility of disturbance caused by such action in itself, the possible damage created by false-positive findings, commenting that 'some of those children suffered harm after they were removed from home whatever may or may not have happened to them previously' (ibid.: 8.8.82, 145). In this move, biopolitical concerns with child welfare are brought back against the paediatricians' and social workers' actions as being not only juridically ill-founded, but also as producing diswelfare. However, the report does more than reiterate a demand that concerns with best interests be accommodated within juridical concerns with the rights of the parties involved, it suggests a further drawing together of legal and normalising knowledge and practice.

Underlying the dispute about the significance of RAD and disclosure interviews in Cleveland was the problem that different professionals involved were concerned with producing evidence for different purposes. On the one hand, the aims and responsibilities of paediatricians and social workers centre on securing the best interests of the child. For social workers child protection is a statutory duty, while for paediatricians this focus is underpinned by an ethos of care for the patient and the Hippocratic oath. On the other hand, the prime concern of police is investigation leading to the possible prosecution of an offender.[16]

The report notes that child protection requires a child-centred approach based on the balance of probabilities and the idea of the 'real possibility' of abuse having taken place for action to secure the 'best interests of the child' (ibid.: 16.45, 232),[17] whereas police, if they are to bring a prosecution, have to gather evidence proving beyond reasonable doubt both that the child has been abused and the identity of the person(s) responsible. In referring to the relationship between child protection and criminal prosecution, and to the relation of the different agencies involved in child protection, it states:

> *Those who initiate actions which will in due course require proceedings before the courts must be aware of the need to be able to prove the facts to the satisfaction of the particular court.* In the criminal jurisdiction of the Magistrates Court and the Crown Court the proceedings are not instituted for the benefit of the child but for the trial of the accused. *Our criminal law requires the highest standard of proof that the tribunal trying the defendant shall not convict unless satisfied so as to be sure of his guilt. All other proceedings are child-centred and require the court to consider the welfare of the child on the balance of probabilities.*
>
> (ibid.: 16.44–5, 232, emphasis added)

Whilst both of these concerns have legal form, they do not coexist easily; within the combination of legal and normalising forms of knowledge through which the governance of child sexual abuse is conducted the prime concern of social work is the detection of abnormality and the production and sustenance of 'normal' or 'healthy' relationships, producing what we might call an image of the disciplined society, while the prime concern of police is that of the detection of criminality and, by excluding this menace, what we might call the purification of the community.[18] The relationship between these two concerns, therapy and prosecution, is played out in Cleveland in terms of a conflict between the idea of the best interests of the child and the principles of guilt and innocence: a normalising concern with therapy versus a juridical concern with judgement. In Cleveland, therapeutic concerns and questions of guilt became entangled, as can be seen in Higgs's and Wyatt's proactive use of PSOs and the way this was experienced and articulated, for example in comments by Bell and Amphlett, as a supposition of the guilt of parents.

The report attempts a resolution of the different criteria for evidence and grounds for action of the different agencies involved through making recommendations for increased interagency cooperation and different groups' recognition of each others' tasks (ibid.: 8, 248). In addition to these suggestions for more thoroughly coordinated practice, the report also suggests that greater knowledge and under-standing of child sexual abuse as a specific object of governance is a necessary development, on the part both of police and social workers (ibid.: 1, 245). The report thus calls for the further development of this new domain of knowledge and professional practice, with the aim of consolidating effective and appropriate governance in this area.

In particular, it suggests that social workers and the medical profession need to be attentive to 'the legal implications of and their responsibility for the evidential requirements of their work' (ibid.: 9.3, 252), that 'police training needs to be developed well beyond the acquisition of knowledge in respect of the criminal offences involved' (ibid.: 9.2, 252), and that all lawyers, judges and magistrates involved in child abuse cases 'should have a greater awareness of and inform themselves about the nature of child abuse and the management of children subjected to abuse and in particular sexual abuse' (ibid.: 9.6, 252), underscoring that in 'a rapidly changing and difficult area there is a need to review and evaluate the effectiveness of the programmes arranged' (ibid.: 9.5, 252). Achieving a framework of practice for reasonable intervention into suspected child sexual abuse is therefore seen to require increased attention to juridical frameworks on the part of social workers and paediatricians, and increased recognition of normalising concerns on the part of the police and lawyers. The inquiry calls for further interrelation of law and normalising forms of knowledge in order to further the capacity of public agencies to govern child sexual abuse.

In these recommendations one can see the inquiry attempting to renegotiate and clarify the relationships between different forms of knowledge of child sexual abuse and between different practices within which these are constituted. The report attempts to rebalance and reaffirm the relationships between legal and normalising knowledge in this area, by clarifying aims, responsibilities and powers, and by suggesting more joint training and mutual cooperation. In this way, the inquiry seeks to re-establish the legitimacy of liberal welfare rationality in child protection, grounding a 'reasonable' division of public and private on notions of expertise (adequate knowledge and competent practice). Implicit in this is the projection of an imaginary ideal in which more knowledge and better cooperation would not only ensure a consensus amongst experts concerning the signs of sexual abuse, but would also reconcile agencies on the basis of an idea of 'reasonable intervention'. The projection of this ideal, in which the governance of child sexual abuse is cast as a technical problem therefore admitting of a technical solution, underpins the activity of the inquiry and provides it with its *raison d'être*.

The report does little seriously to challenge the differences of purpose of the different agencies involved in the governance of child sexual abuse other than to suggest more joint training and interagency cooperation. Therefore, the report's statement that in difficult cases a case conference must weigh up the evidence 'in the best interests of the child' (ibid.: 216) leaves unresolved the problems faced by different agencies that have fundamentally different aims, responsibilities and powers.

The inquiry provides a space for the articulation of different grounds for action and forms of practice in the governance of child sexual abuse. It attempts to negotiate different demands, and to maintain a position of independent judgement on the issues. This leaves the report in an ambivalent position, so that at some moments its focus is child welfare and at others the issue of the civil liberties of parents. In statements such as the advice to 'listen to but not necessarily believe' a child's disclosure, the report attempts to hold on to both of these concerns at once, and to steer a course between the two which harmonises the demand for welfare and for justice. More frequently, it moves between accepting that the priority of the best interests principle may necessitate intervention, and a concern with the severity of sexual abuse as a civil and criminal act where this potentially implies breaking up families and also possible criminal prosecution. In attempting to juggle these concerns, the inquiry deploys both a conception of law as an instrument of governance and a classic juristic concern with the judgement of guilt and innocence. This problematic demonstrates and is produced by the doubling of normalising and juridical discourses within the domain of child welfare. In the first instance attention is focused on the welfare aspects of child protection. Once this is contextualised within civil and criminal law proceedings it raises the possibility of an invasion of the (otherwise natural) privacy of the family, the breaking up of this unit, and/or the attempted prosecution of those accused. The inquiry identifies this problem of welfare versus prosecution and attempts to stake out some middle ground through suggesting the possibility of an open search ('listen but do not believe') leading to truth, neither elaborating this nor paying great attention to the institutional location of these differences but instead removing the issue from its own remit into a terrain of expert debate and further research,[19] thereby projecting the ideal of expert consensus and cooperation securing legitimacy in the governance of child sexual abuse.

In summary, different forms of practice in the governance of child sexual abuse work with different aims and require different standards of evidence. These differences may become a problem for legal intervention and adjudication where one set of practices, for example social work concerns with ensuring child protection, conflicts with or leads to action without regard to other concerns, for example, concern for the civil liberties of parents, or police concern to act toward the prosecution of offenders, but requiring evidence that can be sustained 'beyond reasonable doubt' to do so. It is possible to see such problems arising in Cleveland in the way in which social workers took out PSOs in relation to certain children (based on suspicion of abuse, an action within the established use of PSOs), and then used these to deny parents access while disclosure interviews took place (an action outside the established use of PSOs). This was interpreted as an infringement of the rights of parents, as a question of their civil liberties, and also made it difficult for the police to continue to work toward prosecutions. Similarly, concerns raised about material drawn from disclosure interviews centred on their possible contamination as evidence in both civil and criminal cases, something that would not pose such a sharp problem if disclosure were set solely within the range of practices of therapy. That is, concern over what is to count as evidence is precipitated by the attempt to combine a juridical discourse of rights and liberties and a normalising discourse of welfare and interests in order legally to adjudicate public/private relations and at the same time to achieve the protection of children. In this context we find the inquiry attempting to adjudicate between different aims and resolve problems through suggestions for interagency cooperation and training. Each aspect of this process combines law and normalising knowledge, showing how within child protection these different forms of knowledge and practice are intertwined in the production of a regulated domain of the family.

Conclusion: the inquiry as an instrument of governance

This chapter has examined the ways in which the Cleveland Inquiry operated to reposition the forms of knowledge and practice that govern the relationship between public and private spheres in the management of child sexual abuse. By exploring the ways in which the public/private distinction is assumed and reinvoked by the report, tracing its discussion of evidence, and of the question of grounds for action, we have demonstrated the ways in which, within liberal welfare rationalities, the practice of child protection is predicated on ideas of the naturally private family and on credible expertise, where the latter combines adequate knowledge and competent practice producing and sustaining reasonable intervention. The task of the inquiry, its *raison d'être* as the place where existing knowledge and practice is reviewed and assessed, is to reground and rearticulate formulae for rule.

The Cleveland Inquiry both implicitly and explicitly assumes a division of public and private spheres organised in relation to knowledge of that which is to be governed or regulated versus that which is to be left alone. This idea is used to mount an argument for balance between parents' rights and children's interests, so that it becomes an organising theme of the report and a central way in which the inquiry process manages the tension involved in recognising the importance of the privacy of the family, whilst still maintaining the legitimacy of regulatory intervention where this is seen to fail. In other words, the report attempts to import 'reasonableness' into the area by reinstating the boundaries of public and private relationships through a call for more knowledgeable and measured intervention.

From this we can see that the public/private distinction operates within the constitution and management of child sexual abuse as a site of ambivalence, tension and struggle. Rather than characterising this as a 'contradiction' which liberal reason can 'iron out', I wish to suggest that this ambivalence is constitutive of the rationality of liberal welfarism and is continuously reinvoked by contemporary discourses and practices of child welfare. Within contemporary discussions of child sexual abuse the public/private distinction is both assumed as natural, given and real, and reinvoked as something culturally constituted, artefactual and in need of legitimation. This can be seen in the Cleveland Inquiry's discussion, where this both assumes and re-institutes the public/private distinction and calls for more knowledge, training and interagency cooperation on which the possibility of the 'correct balance' between privacy and intervention is predicated.

This ambivalence is articulated in terms of a discourse of 'reasonable intervention' as both the norm of child protection practice and as an achievement. The idea of 'reasonable intervention' based on expertise elides the distinction between the naturally given and politically problematic and managed. The public inquiry is a site on which the elision of this double nature of the public/private distinction becomes clear and is refigured. It is an important mechanism through which liberal governance reflects on itself and is thus a site on which we can interrogate liberal reason.

That reasonable intervention is predicated on expertise (where the latter combines adequate knowledge and competent practice) is reasserted by the report in its attempt to re-establish the relations between juridical and normalising forms of knowledge and practice in the governance of child sexual abuse. The inquiry examines what went wrong in the normal practice of child protection in Cleveland in 1987 and at the same time is part of the 'normal' reiteration of these relationships, the perpetual negotiation of boundaries that is accompanied by an intensification of knowledge claims and demands. The inquiry raises the issue of what constitutes knowledge of child sexual abuse through its discussion of RAD and disclosure, draws on expert evidence to elaborate the issues, then turns questions concerning evidence over to the terrain of further expert debate by demanding more research into the area, closer definitions, the study of 'normal' populations and so on. The bulk of the report then focuses on providing recommendations concerning training, interagency cooperation, management guidelines and procedures, with the view that this can produce a better balance between privacy and intervention. The inquiry, therefore, as a mechanism for maintaining and reinstating authority, balance and cohesion, forms a means of restoring legitimate practice where this has been rendered problematic.

This is achieved through a series of criticisms of the inadequate knowledge and incompetent (unprofessional) practice of those involved in this specific case, while the report at the same time holds open the possibility of adequate knowledge and competent practice. As such, it engages in a form of problematisation that reiterates the constituent tensions of the rationality of which it is a part. The report, in airing the issues, providing guidelines, and suggesting increased training and research locates the problems occurring in Cleveland as remediable through more knowledge and better practice. It therefore represents an exercise in maintaining authority through crisis by appearing to have dealt with the problems immediately thrown up, while at the same time calling for the production of increased knowledge in the area with the view that this is the answer to improving practice.

By demanding more knowledge and better practice, the inquiry seeks to re-establish the possibility of legitimate governance in respect of the problem of child sexual abuse. The events of Cleveland problematised the relationship between the family and the state and the forms of knowledge and practice sustaining the 'normal' relationship between public and private spheres. The inquiry and report following it both resolve the immediate concerns in seeming to deal with the 'crisis' and at the same time reproduce and further entrench the tensions constitutive of liberal welfare rationality. The inquiry holds open a space for government to reflect upon itself, re-establishing the grounds of the public/private distinction and the boundaries of 'reasonable intervention' by demanding more knowledge and an intensification of procedures in maintaining the conditions of a public/private distinction regulated by expertise in the governance of child sexual abuse. From this analysis it is possible to regard liberal welfare rationality as a perpetual exercise in 'crisis' management, reinvoking the rationality that produces crises as elements of its own solutions. The mechanism of the inquiry acts to intensify this rationality by maintaining the possibility of its imagined ideal despite continuing evidence to the contrary; in this way, the inquiry can be said to be a polyvalent tool of the political rationality of liberal welfarism.

7 Rearticulating the liberal governance of child sexual abuse

The press and Orkney (1991)

> As I read the [Orkney] report I had a weary realisation that in the approach to and management of the nine children, this might be described as 'Cleveland Revisited'.
>
> (Butler-Sloss 1993: 53)

Chapter 6 raised a number of concerns about the liberal governance of child sexual abuse through an examination of the Cleveland Inquiry. This chapter addresses the ways in which questions concerning the boundaries of legitimate public intervention, and the possibility of adequate knowledge of child sexual abuse, are refracted into the popular political imagination by focusing on the press coverage of the Orkney case.[1] This case offers a particularly useful illustration of the way in which tensions in the liberal governance of child protection are portrayed by the press. The case was widely perceived to stem from a series of lessons not learned from Cleveland, so that it offers an opportunity to examine how a 'failure' of governance leads to the intensification of attempts to govern, and it further demonstrates tensions in the relationship between the extension of normalising concerns with the best interests of the child and juridical concerns with the rights of parents and of the family to privacy.

As in Chapter 6, this chapter draws on the discussion of the relationship between liberalism and biopolitics and the role of the public inquiry discussed in Chapter 5, this time aiming to demonstrate the embedded character of the ambivalences constitutive of liberal welfare rationality within a broader public discussion. In particular, it reflects upon the ways in which the press actively constitute a public space within which the possibility of governing reasonably is reiterated at the same time as the specific interventions in Orkney are criticised. The press mobilise juridical and normalising discourses to discuss the appropriate relation between families and the state, to criticise the credibility of the evidence and the competence of the professionals involved in the case, and to present a critical discussion of the public inquiry as a mechanism for restoring authority in the governance of child sexual abuse.

Chapter 1 presented a broad outline of the events of Orkney 1991. The first section of this chapter examines the press depiction of the relationship between public and private spheres, looking at representations of the family, community and social work intervention. It explores the ways in which press reporting sustains the idea of a liberal governance of families, where this comprises neither too little nor too much intervention, but reasonable governance. The second section takes up the press discussion of evidence, examining how the press define evidence, develop discussions of evidence discrediting the case in question, and appeal both to popular wisdom or 'common sense' and to expertise in the adjudication of what is credible. The third section moves on to look at the ways in which the press regard law as a source of authority and at press demands for a public judicial inquiry into the case amid calls for better knowledge and practice, with regard both to the governance of child sexual abuse generally and also with regard to demands for justice for those persons immediately involved in Orkney. It examines how the inquiry instituted was reported during and after its course, exploring how this inquiry was criticised on a number of counts, while the idea of the public judicial inquiry as a privileged route to truth and justice is actively maintained and rearticulated by the press.

The press coverage referred to is from *The Times*, the *Sunday Times*, the *Daily Mail*, the *Mail on Sunday*, and *The Scotsman* from February 1991 to October 1992, the period of the events and ensuing inquiry. No attempt has been made to carry out a comprehensive analysis of all British newspapers for the period.[2] Rather, using a cross-section of press reporting the chapter analyses portrayals of the relation between families and the state, the adequacy of social work knowledge, the role of law and of the inquiry in this area. The aim is to raise for question the extent to which the press provide critical distance on our forms of governance and the extent to which they rearticulate and further entrench these forms of governance, and thus to examine the ways in which the tensions constitutive of liberal welfare rationality are entrenched in popular as well as governmental discourse.

Examining different newspapers, a number of general distinctions are apparent. For example, while the *Daily Mail* consciously takes the position of advocate for the families concerned, *The Scotsman* aims toward a position of disinterestedness, itself examining 'the press' (2.4.91), seeking the middle ground, and developing the complexity of some of the issues raised by the events. One general point to note here is that there is little mention of 'ritual' or 'satanic' abuse by *The Scotsman*, unlike the coverage in the *Daily Mail* and *The Times*. *The Scotsman* uses the third person to describe what other papers are saying.[3]

The 'ritualistic' and possible 'satanic' element of cases such as Orkney has both made them *causes célèbre* and has formed a substantial part of the widespread discrediting of them. With regard to the Orkney case, reporters introduced references to the alleged abuse being 'ritualistic' or 'satanic'; as inquiry chairperson Lord Clyde commented, 'they were not labels which the Social Work Department considered relevant to the case' (Clyde 1992: 12.38, 210; also 15.10, 268). In fact, looking more closely at the issues involved, the judicial procedures and epistemic assumptions used by professionals to guide practice here were little different from those employed in Cleveland. While the workers involved in Orkney were concerned about the possible existence of what they termed 'organised' abuse (ibid.: 15.8, 267), they sought and gained place of safety orders (PSOs) to detain children in care, ensured that medical examinations of the children were conducted, and combined these with interviews with the children. The public inquiry was critical of certain failures of organisation and information sharing amongst professionals; lack of information, advice and support to parents; of the placements of some of the children whilst in care; and of the expertise with which interviews with the children were conducted and recorded (ibid.: 216–62). It was also critical of the media coverage of the events for exacerbating the relationship between the Social Work Department (SWD) and the local community, for adding pressure to the social workers involved, and for the impact of the publication of the substance of the allegations on the feasibility of any continuation of the cases on the part of the SWD (ibid.: 210–14).

Therefore, while in the UK in the early 1990s, 'ritual' or 'satanic' abuse was regarded as a new form of abuse within some of the professional literature and by the press (Boyd 1991; Sinason 1994; but see La Fontaine 1994),[4] the possibility of such abuse has raised similar issues to debates concerning child sexual abuse more generally: questions of the limits and legitimacy of public intervention, and of evidence elicited to support such intervention, have been central. The pertinence of looking at Orkney, and in particular at the press discussion of the case, is to be found in the reiteration of the themes that dominated Cleveland and in the character of some of the statements made by the children and the claims and assumptions of social workers, these being regarded by the press as incredible and credulous, respectively. The discrediting of the credibility of evidence in this case served to problematise the adequacy of knowledge and competence of child protection practice, that is, it problematised claims to expertise. The breakdown of the possible legitimacy of the professional intervention into family relationships in this case thus throws critical light on professional procedures used to elicit and to deal with child sexual abuse more generally, bringing the question of how particular constellations of knowledge of child sexual abuse come to be regarded as legitimate or illegitimate to the centre of investigation.[5]

The public/private distinction in Orkney: family versus the state in press reports

This section considers the press depiction of the families, community and social workers in Orkney. It focuses on the ways in which the press present a distinction between public and private life and in particular the legitimacy of intervention, in the context of the rights of the parents and families to privacy. There are several major strands running through press reporting of this issue. The notion of the families involved as natural, orthodox in religious belief and middle-class, that is, 'normal'; the community as rural, pure (crime-free) and supportive of family life; social work intervention as overzealous, unprofessional, law-breaking and also morally unwise and harmful.

Family and community

In line with the assumptions of liberal political order, the press present the families and the community as strong, morally sound and natural contexts for action. The parents are reported to be middle-class, articulate, orthodox in religious belief, and as wanting the best for their children, for which they had come to Orkney. This as a place becomes a symbol of the 'good life', reports stressing the lack of crime and sense of community on the islands. Orkney is depicted as a place apart, to which the families had come to escape modern society in order to bring up their children. 'They settled on Orkney to bring up their children away from the worst influences of modern life' (*The Times* 6.4.91). This withdrawal from urban life is presented not as an escape into wild nature, but into civilised simplicity, an escape from the lack of civility within the modern world.

The purity of this existence is stressed. Orkney is represented as a 'close-knit rural community [. . .] where people rely on trust and crime is virtually unknown' (*The Times* 3.3.91). This community is represented as a '*God-fearing* community of farmers and fishermen', whose life 'centres on neighbourliness, self-sufficiency and sermons at the Kirk', '*shaken*' by 'rumours of *satanic ceremonies and devil-worship*' (*The Times* 3.3.91, emphasis added; also *The Times* 4.3.91, *The Scotsman* 27.3.91, 3).

In contrast to the Clyde Inquiry's assessment that the manner in which the children were removed was reasonable (Clyde 1992: 14.2, 240), the press present police and social work intervention into this pure, godly, crime free community as '*chilling*' (*The Times* 3.3.91, emphasis added), having the character of a military operation, seen here in an article that evokes memories of a nation defending itself against war:

> *It was timed with military precision.* Before dawn had broken over the bleak but beautiful winter landscape of South Ronaldsay, a *convoy* of police and social workers left the Orkney Islands capital of Kirkwall. Only one road led to the four families who had been branded guilty of child sexual abuse. It was the Churchill barriers, a series of concrete causeways built during the war to deter German U-boats. There were no such defences for the parents as they chivvied their children into readiness for the school bus. The fists hit the doors of their *scattered houses at 7 o'clock on that fateful February morning last year. There was resistance, but these were gentle people trying to live their version of the good life, away from the rat race in England. Their persecutors,* mainly flown in from the mainland, with flashlamps and bewildering 'place of safety' orders, *were uncompromising.* When one 13 year old locked herself in a bathroom, police broke down the door with a crowbar.
>
> (*Daily Mail* 28.10.92, 9, emphasis added)

This is described elsewhere as 'an SAS style operation' (Dr Helen Martini, quoted in *The Scotsman* 16.3.91, 3).

The intervention of police and social workers in this case is presented as the shattering of innocence, the '*bureaucratic rape of a community*' and also 'the individual, spiritual and intellectual *rape of the families involved, with the removal of items from their home, from their sanctuaries against the world* (Dr Peter Driver, resident of Orkney and friend of the families involved, quoted in *The Scotsman* 4.3.91, 3, emphasis added). The metaphor of rape used here is an inversion of what the social workers and police involved thought may have happened to the children; used in this way this image suggests rather the innocence of the families and community destroyed by intervention.

Against this the unity of the community is stressed. *The Times* notes that the community was 'shocked', finding the allegations 'ludicrous in a distressing way. Many parents said they wondered what would happen to them if they were to criticise publicly the social work department' (*The Times* 4.3.91). This theme is re-echoed in reports on Orkney over the period, 'No-one on Orkney's most southerly island could believe that the families [. . .] were capable of such crimes' (*The Times* 4.4.91). *The Scotsman* reports on the significance of the unity of the community in supporting the parents, stating that 'in a community where "white settlers" are often regarded unfavourably [. . .] all – incomer and Orcadian, young and old – are united in expressing their rage' (*The Scotsman* 4.3.91, 3). The reporting of this case is thus very similar to that of public tragedies such as recent ferry boat disasters, floods, famines and so on, suggesting the complete innocence and absolute distress of the families involved.

In addition to giving support, the community threatened action against the authorities; one resident is reported stating that, 'if the authorities attempt to seize another child, they will face civil disobedience'. Some spoke of blocking roads' (*The Times* 11.3.91). In the context of such threats, *The Scotsman* points out, in passing, that the police and social work joint action to take the children into care was 'perfectly legal' (4.3.91, 3). It suggests that the calls for civil disobedience were borne from 'a desire for action fuelled by impotence in the face of the authorities' (*The Scotsman* 4.3.91, 3).

From the foregoing we can see that the press depict the reaction of the parents and community to the removal of the children in Habermasian terms, as a lifeworld response to colonisation by bureaucracy. The press first present a portrait of the families and community as natural, and as part of the family of God, and then counterpoise this with the uncaring, insensitive bureaucracy of state intervention: 'The parents have not been allowed to see or speak to their children since they were *seized* from their beds in a dawn raid last Wednesday' (*The Times* 6.3.91, emphasis added). The apparent common sense of the parents is thus pitched against the conduct of child protection workers, where the latter are seen to combine a lack of common sense with a capacity directly to infringe rights. The press reports constitute a clear distinction between the natural, harmonious life and morality of the community and the unthinking action of state-sponsored officials. *The Times* then moves to support an ideal of the natural family by jarring readers' emotions; it reports that families 'claimed they were physically restrained from kissing their children goodbye' (*The Times* 3.3.91).

A vivid image of the priority of the natural family emerges from the press reporting; the families involved are also presented as representative of the normal family. Ideas and ideals of the 'normal family', 'motherhood' and 'fatherhood' emerge in a number of reports. The *Daily Mail* publishes a mother's diary entry under the heading 'The Day They Took Away Our Children'; it includes an account of the mother's anguish and the idea of 'stranger danger' (with which we are implicitly asked to identify):

> We are just a normal family. We used to tell the kids not to talk to strangers, and yet we had to help pack them into a car to an unknown destination where they would be separated from each other, for God knows how long, [. . .] And I'm their mother, for God's sake.
>
> (*Daily Mail* 6.4.91, 6)

The normality of those involved is further emphasised by the idea that this 'could be any child, it could be any family' (one of the parents involved, quoted in *The Scotsman* 6.3.91, 1).

Mothers are presented as providing a natural source of warmth and love, but also common sense and standards of discipline in child-rearing to be measured against the potential harm of thoughtless or trendy social workers. One mother is reported as asking 'if social workers would ensure her children did not watch television while in care. The family did not have one at home, and she was worried it might corrupt them' (*The Times* 3.3.91, also *The Scotsman* 3.12.91, 4). Importantly, the term 'mother' is most often used as the point of reference in such paragraphs; in relation to abuse allegations the term 'parent' or 'family' is more commonly invoked.

Fathers are represented as defending their families. In this context the press representation of Sheriff Kelbie is important; dominating reports of his role in the children being returned are accounts of him as an ethical individual and a family man (*Daily Mail* 6.4.91, 6). *The Scotsman* carries an article profiling Kelbie entitled 'The Sheriff: The man who campaigned for a more caring world'. This describes him as a 'family man', and includes details about his having previously run as an SNP candidate, his championing of public transport and ecological concerns, and his 'humanitarian principles'. Finally, a member of the Scottish Congregational College is quoted describing him as 'a thinking Christian whose concerns are not just domestic or private but who cares about the whole created world and the way things are organised' (*The Scotsman* 5.4.91, 2). Reports at this stage do not question whether his actions were wise or within the law, they assume this and depict his actions as commonsensical.

Concerns that the intervention represents an attack on the 'normal family' within articles specifically focused on the Orkney parents are reinforced by more general speculative journalism suggesting that concern about child sexual abuse is part of a vendetta against men and the family. A 'lifestyle' article in *The Scotsman* entitled 'Assault on the Heart of the Family' asserts that 'the increase in child sexual abuse has provoked a public outcry. But [. . .] the backlash against men in general has gone much too far'. This piece voices concern about what it calls the 'increasingly anti-male tone of the debate', which it links with feminists not wanting equality with but domination over men; this, it is suggested, is producing an 'erosion of the family and of fatherhood' (*The Scotsman* 21.3.91, 13).[6]

Reports often present the issues raised by the removal of the children directly as questions of parental rights against the state. One mother is quoted stating ' We have less rights than a convicted prisoner' (*The Times* 2.3.91). At the panel hearing again a mother is quoted, 'It is appalling that an agency like the social work department can have *total control* over our lives in Britain. We are not going to give up' (*The Times* 6.3.91, emphasis added). A view reiterated with comments such as 'These social workers are worse than Saddam Hussein' (one of the mothers involved, quoted in *The Scotsman* 5.3.91, 6). The idea that social workers wield unlimited power is further reinforced by a *Mail on Sunday* 'Comment: An Appalling Abuse of Power', which talks of 'the dangers of giving social workers *almost untrammelled power* to remove from their homes children suspected of being sexually abused', stating that 'it remains a disgrace to a country like ours which takes pride in its long tradition of personal freedom that social workers can with so little justification still trample on such rights with such ease' (*Mail on Sunday* 8.3.91, 6 emphasis added).

The rights of families as the seat of natural morality and authority are thus counterposed 'against what is seen as insensitive, bureaucratic interference' (*The Times* 6.4.91). Such reports work with a naturalised distinction between public and private, with the innocent family legitimately outside governmental control and supervision. The focus of reporting is almost wholly on the parents 'rights', not on them as potential abusers or on children's 'rights'; that is, little concern is given to the gravity of the allegations if they are to be proved correct. In this case, links are continuously made with the Cleveland case, regarded as a case in which parents were 'wrongly accused' (*Daily Mail* 4.3.91, 13; *The Scotsman* 15.3.91, 12), thus ignoring doubts over whether and to what extent abuse did happen in Cleveland (Butler-Sloss 1988; Campbell 1988).

Other reports regard the Orkney events as a question of 'system abuse'; this idea is detailed in a number of ways that suggest that the intervention is not just an interference in the privacy of the families involved and a 'shattering' of the community, but also that it is inevitably destructive of childhood. For example, harm caused by intervention itself is presented in a mother's statement that her little boy returned 'a very disturbed, sad little boy with distress written all over his face' (*The Scotsman* 3.12.91, 4). Another report is headed 'Crime lessons of Orkney boy taken into "care": I learned about drugs says teenager as social workers consider appeal' (*Daily Mail* 6.4.91, 6). The process of being examined and interviewed is itself reported as abusive and corrupting of innocence. In another inversion of the allegations, the press report that 'Phil Green, a senior Strathclyde social worker, told the Inquiry [. . .] that the youngsters would inevitably have been "sexualised" by the manner in which they had been dealt with during their five weeks in care' (*The Scotsman* 14.1.92, 7).

Experts' statements are frequently used to emphasise the potential abusiveness of the intervention itself; for example, psychiatrist Dr John Powell is reported in *The Scotsman* stating that, 'one boy said he felt "mentally abused" by the social

workers and police officers who had interviewed him' (*The Scotsman* 28.1.92, 1).
Elsewhere the inaugural lecture of a professor of law, Alistair Bissett-Johnson,
who, *The Scotsman* notes, has 'taught family law for 30 years and redrafted child
protection laws in two Canadian provinces', is quoted suggesting that Orkney is 'a
form of legal abuse of children regardless of whether sexual abuse occurred or not'
(*The Scotsman* 5.5.92, 7.) These representations of the abuse inflicted by the care
system itself raise questions concerning the appropriate boundaries of reasonable
intervention and strengthen the idea that 'danger to life' should be the only basis
for intervention.

Social work and the state

Press reporting provides ample images of natural families and of a God-fearing
community, rallying together in support of the rights of parents. In contrast, the
social work and police joint action is depicted as being interfering, out of touch,
crusading and illegitimate, as has been signalled already in the imagery used in
passages quoted above. In descriptions of 'dawn raids' as 'chilling' or frightening
intrusions (*The Times* 3.3.91), concerned to 'snatch' children from their
(unsuspecting) families (*The Times* 10.3.91), the evidence-gathering motive for the
timing and approach of such actions is scarcely mentioned, making them appear
vindictive. This mode of reporting then implicitly takes the view of parents in seeing
this as a 'witch-hunt' and conspiracy (*The Times* 4.3.91).

Notably, though the removal of the children from their families was a joint
action on the part of police and social workers, the press are virtually silent about
the role of the police and direct their attention to the social workers involved
(see also Clyde 1992: 12.56, 214). In a number of reports social workers are
represented as overzealous and vindictive, or just downright uncaring. This moves
from descriptions of Paul Lee, director of social work in Orkney at the time, as a
'bureaucrat' to the more venomous depiction of Sue Millar, one of the social
workers most closely involved, as a 'simpering', 'sniggering' figure.

The Times comments that Paul Lee 'is a soft-spoken and experienced bureaucrat
given to answering questions at great length and in social worker jargon' (*The
Times* 1.9.91). Note how the claim to expertise on the part of social workers is
dispelled by the word 'jargon' here. Lee is described by one mother as 'aggressive,
cold, detached and lacking any emotion' (*Daily Mail* 28.10.92, 9). In contrast
with the Cleveland Inquiry's criticism of the emotional involvement of the
professionals concerned, therefore, the press express frustration with the appearance of professional disinterestedness. At the same time, accounts emphasising the
supposedly vindictive character of social work action are most pronounced in the
witch-like depiction of Sue Millar. For example, in a statement that directly
counters her apparent lack of care with mothers' anxiety, *The Times* reports that
she is 'accused by parents of laughing at their plight during last week's panel
meeting. 'Every word she utters is an insinuation', said one parent. Another said,
'She has a *smirk* which makes every *mother* want to strangle her' (*The Times* 10.3.91,
emphasis added).

Social workers are identified as self-interested, acting overcautiously with respect to their statutory duties for child protection, and thus failing to recognise the rights and interests of the families involved: 'Defensive' social work is analogous to 'defensive medicine' in America. It means professionals taking the action least likely to lead to accusations of negligence, despite the harm which might thereby be done to others' (*The Times* 4.4.91). This claim privileges the need felt by social workers not to risk leaving children in contexts where they may be abused following castigation in cases where children have died whilst under social work supervision as an explanation of what is regarded as over-hasty action and the flouting of guidelines, leading to professional incompetence. The report both signals the difficulties for social workers working in child protection in judging potential risks and at the same time suggests that with greater expertise social workers could manage the tension between acting on grounds of concern for child welfare and not unduly threatening the liberties of parents. It suggests the need for better guidelines and more professionalism on the part of social workers in deciding what constitutes appropriate action. This is in accord with the ideals of liberal governance in child protection, where legitimate social work equals measured intervention, governing neither too little nor too much, but governing reasonably.

The defensiveness and credulity of the social workers in this case is not regarded as innocent. Rather it is articulated by the press as an issue of rights of parents against the political motivation of social work in preserving its own interests. This extends to the suggestion that social work is comprised of socialists, feminists and technocrats aiming to destroy the family. The *Mail on Sunday* view of this as an abuse of 'untrammelled power' has already been noted, suggesting that social work intervention is illegitimate and politically motivated to destroy the family, as has the manner in which the press treat Sue Millar as a 'wicked witch' figure. In this battle, others are also seen as being biased in favour of the state and social work intervention and therefore, by implication, anti-family. For example, Gordon Sloan, interim reporter to the children's panel, is described as 'refus[ing] to let Island children, *snatched* from their homes in dawn raids, return to their parents.' The paper emphasises that 'Sloan's critics accuse him of bias' (*The Times* 2.6.91, emphasis added). It is important to note the grouping of 'parents and children' as a constituency of interest here, this reiterating the ideal of the normal family. Sloan is described as 'abrasive', and the paper reports one mother stating, 'he is an Inquisitor' (*The Times* 2.6.91). Sloan is also depicted as 'a tyrant of a little man' (*Daily Mail* 28.10.92, 9).

This combination of self-interest, credulousness and political motivation is regarded as having produced a severe lack of professionalism. A vivid account of the abuse allegations that led the Orkney workers to depart from the guidelines issued following the Cleveland Inquiry is reported in an account focusing on Paul Lee's dilemma concerning the appropriate course of action in the cases concerned. This suggests a lack of professionalism on Lee's part, and counters the report cited earlier where he appears as an unemotional bureaucrat:

> Out of the mouths of children aged seven, eight and nine came a story that was rich in detail and the free use of explicit sexual language. All three had been held in separate locations for extended periods, yet their accounts matched in timings, names, places and events. To Paul Lee, the story was so powerful and vivid that he made a series of decisions that appeared to flout practically every guideline handed down by the Cleveland Report into child abuse in Britain. [. . . at the Inquiry] he continued to maintain that he had no choice but to send a small army of police and social workers, under cover of darkness, to take nine children from their homes and fly them to the Scottish mainland.
>
> (*The Times* 1.9.91)

Charges of incompetence extend from accounts of some of the social workers not having read the Cleveland Report in its entirety (*The Times* 1.9.91), to claims of religious extremism having infiltrated the Orkney SWD. The press, in describing the allegations, uses the terms 'ritual' and 'satanic' abuse regularly. In some reports, the press construct this as a contest between the authority and orthodoxy of the religious beliefs of the families and community on the one hand, and the evangelism assumed of both social work and satanic practices on the other. In such accounts social workers are depicted as religious zealots, with a corresponding belief in 'satanic' abuse and a desire to 'find' it and stamp it out.

The press report that the SWD refused to tell them where the first allegations of 'ritual' abuse came from 'but inquiries by the Sunday Times Scotland have established how ideas similar to those which helped create the Rochdale ritual abuse scandal first came to Orkney' (*The Times* 17.3.91). *The Times* locates this with 'Maureen Davies, a *fundamentalist Christian* and *self-appointed 'expert'* on ritual and satanic abuse' (*The Times* 17.3.91, emphasis added). The press suggest that religious extremism influenced the SWD. One of the parents commenting on Charlie Fraser, one of the social workers involved, is quoted thus: '*He is desperately anti-Satan*. I tried to appeal to him on a Christian level but I got absolutely nowhere' (*The Times* 10.3.91, emphasis added; also *The Times* 17.3.91). Elsewhere Fraser is reported defending himself against the claim of being obsessed with Satan, stating that he is simply 'a committed Christian' (*The Scotsman* 14.9.91, 7).

Reports on Orkney followed in the wake of Justice Douglas Brown's decision that the statements of the Rochdale children concerning their involvement in satanic rituals were fantasy. *The Times* reports that, 'lawyers acting for the parents of the South Ronaldsay children say their plight is identical to that of the Rochdale parents whom Brown said were victims of *obsessive and mistaken* social workers' (*The Times* 10.3.91, emphasis added). The *Daily Mail* states that, 'social workers seem *possessed* by the notion of satanic rings' (*Daily Mail* 5.4.91, emphasis added). This produces an image of the social workers as '*infected* with a quasi-religious zeal' (*The Times* 5.4.91, emphasis added), as on a crusade and concerned with fantasy not reality.

The credulousness of social workers is contrasted with a statement by Dr Martini, an Orkney GP, in a manner that acts to question whether the social workers involved displayed the sceptical attitude necessary to expert authority: 'One claim I've heard is that 4,000 babies a year are sacrificed in the UK' [. . .] 'but there's no proof of any of these things – which to my scientific background smacks a little bit of something odd' (*The Scotsman* 14.3.91, 3). This scientific discrediting is coupled with a contrast between Orkney Christian Fellowship and the Church of Scotland. The latter is publicly critical of the removal of the children and re-echoes the theme of rights, criticising the SWD for 'presuming that accused parents were guilty until proven innocent' (*The Times* 1.4.91). Thus, we find the religious 'zeal' of social work and the Orkney Christian Fellowship contrasted with the 'reasonableness' of the Church of Scotland and the families. Note also how the 'welfare of the child' has disappeared from this, strictly rights-based, juridical approach.

Having articulated the impossibility of the 'ritual' abuse claims, the press use this to assert the incompetence and illegality of social work practice. This is taken up through the questioning of the knowledge base and competence of the profession of social work. This is most boldly stated in an article by Professor David Marsland in the *Daily Mail* entitled, 'Sack the Lot and Start Again, after the latest shameful indictment of our arrogant, incompetent social workers'. Having outlined the events of Orkney, Marsland suggests we should celebrate the return of the nine children involved, and goes on to state that, 'since 1973 there have been something between forty and fifty child care inquiries implicating some kind of failing in social services or social workers – *disaster*'. He adds, 'I believe that the social worker was always a disastrous idea', describing the development of professional social work as a move 'from amateurs with common sense and not too much power to "experts" with unbridled powers and heads filled with zealous ideology'. Describing social work training as '*for the most part [. . .] absurdly impractical, extraordinarily woolly and dangerously ideological*', he suggests that the 'profession takes itself far too seriously and has allowed itself to become hijacked by extreme left-wing politics'. Suggesting that a great deal of social work is 'simply common sense' and 'human kindness', he nonetheless goes on the describe 'the heart of the problem we now have to face. This country needs a trained, competent cadre of carers'. Stating that he has recommended 'radical changes at government level', he concludes with the assertion that 'for the sake of all those broken-hearted families, we must get rid of the social worker and think again' (*Daily Mail* 5.4.91, 6, emphasis in text). In this comment we see a direct attack on the claims to knowledge and expertise of social workers (as well as an attack on the structure and organisation of social work), whilst at the same time we are offered 'common sense' and an (unspecified) alternative form of training as a route forward.

The reporting of the social work action thus contains a curious mixture of criticism of the alleged political and religious fervour of the Department. Unreasonable social work practice is contrasted with the 'normality' and 'reasonableness' of the families involved, with their orthodox religious and political beliefs, such that disbelief in the social workers concerns and acceptance of the demand to protect 'family rights' to privacy become the only reasonable option.

More oblique criticisms of the contemporary practice of social work are presented elsewhere, in a report entitled 'Let the Children Speak':

The best interests of the child means what someone else thinks is best for the child. In the 17th century, for instance, the Scottish Privy Council took away children from Scott of Raeburn and his wife because they were 'infected with the error of Quakerism'. [. . .] The paradigm has changed and *what is in the best interests of children today is presided over by a 'church' of psychiatrists, psychologists, paediatricians, social work child care specialists, and other experts.* Children's panel members are 'ordinary' members of the community in which they live, and judges are also 'lay' to the extent that they are not experts on children, only on the law.

(*The Scotsman* 4.4.91, 11, emphasis added)

This report is interesting as it points up historically changing conceptions of childhood, child abuse and children's best interests, and makes a call for a egal-democratic model of decision-making in child care cases, as opposed to one grounded in expert judgement. Implicitly, it assumes that 'lay' decision-making in such cases would give children more 'voice'. In this instance the law is depicted as substantially outside the domain of normalising forms of professional knowledge and as able to combine common sense and openness with which to arbitrate. Law both stands outside the tangle of normalising forms of knowledge and practice in child protection and at the same time judges these by acting as a provider of standards. In this way, legal processes are presented as less problematic as forms of knowledge and practice than the normalising concerns of social work claims to expertise.

In the context of the questioning of professional knowledge, the issue becomes one of rights and liberties in which it is possible to see different sections of the press taking different stands. *The Mail* self-consciously presents itself as an advocate for the parents, projecting a populist discourse of the rights of parents against what it regards as the bogus claims to knowledge of social work, and utilising alternative expert knowledge and opinion (for example, in the article by Marsland quoted above) to bolster its position. In contrast, *The Scotsman* projects an ideal of balance and attempts to recognise the complexity and difficulty of the issues raised by Orkney for the task of child protection. Social work is regarded much more as part of the fabric of modern society and this paper does not engage in the denunciation of its claims to knowledge in the same way as *The Mail*, instead framing its criticisms in terms of a need for greater accountability, calm and due process (*The Scotsman* 2.4.91, 11).

Reporting on the issue of the appropriate relation between families and the state then reverts to the theme of (il)legality. In an article 'Angry Crowd Marches on Social Work Department', *The Times* describes how the crowd 'accused his staff of stealing their children and *illegally interrogating* them' (*The Times* 5.4.91, emphasis added). This report also presents Kelbie's statement that the 'procedures were so fatally flawed as to be incompetent' (*The Times* 5.4.91), thus reaffirming the illegality of the actions. The report goes on to state that a full review of procedures will be carried out. In so doing, it locates the problems encountered in Orkney as a failure to follow established procedures, without specifically addressing the question of the evidence on which the allegations are based.

The emotive character of the debate around children's and families' 'rights' against the state is exhibited in the statement, 'Seized children not allowed to take toys or spare clothes', which heads an article elaborating on the perceived inhumanity of social work practice in terms of the rights of the children involved, without noting the problems faced by the social workers in attempting to develop procedures to deal with what they regarded as a new form of child abuse, including evidential problems involved here. In this case the SWD's apparently unreasonable action is contrasted with the campaign by PAIN in support of the families, the latter group being reported as agents of justice (*The Times* 10.3.91).

In contrast to the call for family 'rights' from the parents, PAIN, the press and so on, the professional social work response to the affair is to argue for organisational review, more knowledge, and improved training. For example, the British Association of Social Work (BASW) general secretary, David Jones, is reported calling for training in the techniques of interviewing children. He suggests that social workers 'are not on the streets waiting to pounce but they have to react when they hear a distressing or disturbing story from a child' (*The Times* 5.4.91). Jones goes on to state the need for community responsibility to define clear lines to determine when social workers should act, suggesting that the identification of an appropriate boundary between supervision and privacy is a political question. He thus appeals to democratic rather than professional control of law and policy-making. However, he emphasises that legislation itself can never resolve the dilemma faced by a social worker in the context of a child making allegations against their own parents, indicating that this must rely on professional judgement, (*The Times* 5.4.91).

Evocative images of the distinction between public and private life, and questions concerning the legitimacy of intervention, are raised by the press, issues which this section has attempted to address by examining how the press participate in the construction of a discourse in which some behaviours are rendered literally 'unbelievable' and others 'natural' and 'just'. Intervention in this case is characterised by press reports as unreasonable; social work intervention is not accorded legitimacy. The relationship between the family and the state is inscribed in press reports in a structurally similar way to the way that Habermas theorises the relationship between the lifeworld and the system, where the latter interferes with and renders pathological the authentic pre-existing social relations characteristic of the former. In looking at these press reports therefore, we begin to see how press discussion has a role in constituting and reaffirming the conditions and limits of legitimacy of professional intervention.

Legal procedures, scientific method and the truth of abuse

Within the liberal governance of child protection, claims to legitimate intervention into family relations are sustained by appeals to expertise. The authority of expertise is grounded in claims to adequate knowledge and competent practice that together provide the conditions for the production of credible evidence. This in turn sustains the possibility of governing reasonably by providing legitimacy to interventions and maintaining a balance between privacy and intervention. This section focuses on press discussions of the credibility of evidence in Orkney, demonstrating the interrelation of claims to knowledge and appropriate practice with the forging of a legitimate public/private distinction.

Of particular interest here is to explore how the idea of reasonableness examined earlier in terms of the boundary between privacy and intervention is reproduced in the discussion of evidence in the idea of credibility. Press discussions of evidence appeal to two distinct criteria of justification or models of credibility; on the one hand, such discussions mobilise a juridical conception of credibility, and on the other hand they mobilise a veridical conception of credibility. The former identifies evidence as credible if it has been produced through following the correct legal and administrative procedures. The latter identifies evidence as credible if it has been constituted either by following recognised scientific methods or by appealing to scientific knowledge that is already established. Examining the theme of evidence brings into focus the ways in which the press both display and reproduce the relations between the juridical and veridical threads of liberal welfare rationality. As we shall see, this dual mode of discussion of credibility inflects not only the press discussion of social work and police action, but also its discussion of the Clyde Inquiry.

In order to illustrate how the relation between the juridical and the veridical is reproduced in discussions of what counts as credible evidence, this section is divided into a number of subsections. The first subsection focuses on the ways in which the press deploy a wholly procedural notion of credibility in undermining the legitimacy of the actions taken by the SWD. A second strategy employed within the press reports forms the focus of the second subsection. Here, press reports operate with a restricted notion of epistemically credible evidence, that of the 'hard' science of physical medicine, and identify the lack of medical signs in this case with a lack of evidence *tout court*. The third subsection, which discusses press reporting of interviews with the children, examines how both juridical and veridical notions of credibility are deployed by the press in undermining the claim to competence and therefore legitimate expertise made by the SWD. It focuses on how both of these notions of credibility are used and woven together in the articulation of both common sense and expert criticisms of the interviews conducted in Orkney. Finally, the fourth subsection shows how the press criticism of the SWD, far from precluding the idea of good (i.e. justifiable) practice, both presupposes and articulates this possibility through a call for more and better procedural guidelines, more knowledge, and improved training. This will also show how the press imagine an ideal of expertise grounded in common sense.

Social work procedures

The social workers' statutory duties to protect children, combined with difficult allegations and the imperative toward accepting the truth of the child, produced a number of ways of operating on the part of professionals that were subsequently to be questioned on the basis of procedural irregularities. In press reports, failure to follow accepted procedures regarding the need for investigations in the community, consultation with other professionals, and so on, are represented as the first stage in the production of 'incredible' evidence by the SWD; that is, procedural irregularities in taking the children into care automatically generated grounds for questioning the credibility of the entire action.

On the first day of the inquiry, the press report how the original allegations (by the 'W' children), allegations that lead to the removal of the nine children at the centre of the controversy, emerged:

> After interviews with an official of the Royal Scottish Society for the Prevention of Cruelty to Children, *the three children gave corroborative evidence that sexual, penetrative abuse had taken place involving the four families children, parents and Mr McKenzie.* [. . .] B, Mrs Millar said, had made the disclosures to Ms McLean after placing a chair against the interview room door. The corroborative statements by the three W children were all made on the same day.
>
> (*The Times* 8.8.91, emphasis added)

The veracity of these original accounts is not the focus of press attention, and they are reported with little controversy.

Controversy begins once action is taken on the basis of the 'W' children's allegations. The press focus attention on social work procedures in taking the children into care, noting with concern 'deliberate departures from the guidelines on child sexual abuse' (*The Times* 1.9.91), for example that wider expertise, from the local GP, the district nurse, or from child psychologists, had not been called upon and that more general inquiries had not taken place. This is placed in the context of the social workers' rationale that organised abuse was a new form of abuse producing distinct problems for attempts to ensure the welfare of children, and in particular that the SWD 'was worried that an organised network of child abuse was in operation on the island, and we did not know in effect who knew or who did not know' (Lee, quoted in *The Times* 1.9.91).

What were the various stages of social work action that were regarded by the press and others as producing incredible evidence? Professional knowledge of organised abuse and of how to deal with such allegations was limited (La Fontaine 1994). This led to secrecy on the part of the social workers that was later frowned upon. There were two basic reasons for secrecy: first, police concern with evidence and the possibility of criminal prosecution; second, social work concern over the possibility of an organised abuse network. The press focus on what they term the 'ritual' nature of the allegations leading to the overriding of guidelines:

> Paul Lee yesterday all but acknowledged that guidelines aimed at protecting parental rights were ignored as the inquiry pressed ahead. 'We felt that was

the way it had to be. We feel we did the appropriate thing in the circumstances. We have a responsibility to children in care,' he added.

(*The Times* 10.3.91)

Reluctance to take further investigatory steps prior to removal of the children was grounded upon a need to maintain confidentiality and to avoid accidental disclosure of news about the SWD's suspicions to (unknown) potential ringleaders (*The Times* 30.8.91; *The Scotsman* 7.9.91, 4).

The inquiry's questioning of procedures gave the press the opportunity to provide some vivid accounts of the professional knowledge base and competence of social work, and to subject this to critical question. For example, the press report how the 'ritual' nature of the allegations led social workers to refuse children's requests to take toys in a series of reports that characterise the developing knowledge of social workers concerning organised abuse as problematic:

> Mrs Millar went on to say that there were worries about any belongings the parents might try to give the children. They stemmed from toy turtle presents that were sent to Mrs W's children, already in care, at Christmas, and which, social workers felt, might have had sexual connotations. 'We then knew from the three corroborative statements that the children had been dressed in turtle suits when they were taken to be abused', she said.
>
> (*The Times* 9.10.91)

Asked, at the inquiry, if these were not just popular toys, Mrs Millar is reported stating:

> 'We didn't fully understand at that stage what might be meant but we were concerned in the context of some very strange correspondence'. She told of a letter containing an explicit drawing of a child behind a tree which suggested the child was the 'biggest and the best'. She said that MW, aged eight, had described her brothers in terms of the size of their penises.
>
> (*The Times* 9.10.91)

The rationale for this line of social work action is presented in terms of certain items acting as 'inhibitors', leading to fear over presents sent to the children 'that had connections with abuse and that might intimidate a child into not talking about what had happened' (report on Mrs Millar's statements to the inquiry, *The Times* 10.10.91). However, in the same newspaper on a different day this action is reported less sympathetically under the heading 'Seized children not allowed to take toys or spare clothes' (*The Times* 29.8.91).

In the context of work on the tactics of organised abuse networks, the idea that blocks in the form of specific objects or words may be used by abusers to maintain the silence of their victims appears to gain some credibility (Boyd 1991). Such toys could be a threat to the children and to social work action to prevent abuse. If organised abuse was happening on Orkney it was very important for social workers to guard against such 'triggers' being given to children. However, these ideas concerning the tactics of organised abuse networks also point to the possible explosion of things that can be regarded as dangerous and the almost infinite possibility of the reinterpretation of 'everyday' objects to fit the idea that satanic or other rituals are being practised. In this context, social workers' assumptions appear illiberal (and thus unjustified) in the context of the juridical rationality of liberalism. Within press discussions this issue becomes one of children's welfare and rights.

Along with the initial removal of the children, a number of articles were taken from homes as potentially linked to or used in abusive practices. This is reported in a manner that suggests the credulity of the police and social workers, where this is contrasted with the common sense of readers and the parents involved. In this, readers are implicitly asked to identify with the parents, through the list of ordinary ornaments regarded by professionals as potentially significant: 'we' all have at least some of these, or know people who do, how then can they be other than innocuous? Note the following report:

> Police are examining items removed from the houses in last week's raids. They include a Nepalese sculpture of a couple making love, lifejackets, a leather cowboy hat, plastic Halloween masks, books of erotic poetry, a relaxation tape and an envelope a 12-year-old boy used to collect a 20p piece from 'the tooth fairy' every time he lost a tooth. The boy's father had sketched a cartoon of the devil, complete with his son's toothy grin, on the envelopes. Yesterday he insisted it was a piece of harmless fun.
>
> (*The Times* 3.3.91)

In contrast, the social workers involved described their actions in removing the children as 'simply a question of getting to the truth' (a social worker at the hearing of the children's panel, quoted in *The Times* 6.3.91), and as a question of securing a safe environment for the children, emphasising that child protection is a responsibility provided by legal statute (*The Times* 6.9.91; *The Scotsman* 6.9.91, 1). Against the charge that they were 'fishing' in taking the nine children, the SWD stressed that the 'W' children's statements were made separately and therefore must be true (*The Times* 30.8.91), thus ignoring the active role of the interviewer in the interviewing process and assuming that interviewers simply receive the truth of the child, unmediated by professional discourses and preconceived ideas.

The press therefore document an important process whereby allegations of organised abuse were becoming a locus for the articulation of a new area of knowledge and practice for social workers and psychologists. Reports provide a space for consideration of this new set of issues, but voice concern that action should be regulated and rendered publicly accountable, that normalising knowledge should be regulated by and incorporated into appropriate legal and administrative frameworks. The press therefore maintain a procedural notion of evidence in the face of social work attempts to constitute new practices based on normalising social work knowledge. The social work action, in departing from established guidelines, is taken up by the press as a question of the infringement of civil liberties and, as we will see later, the press conception of children as capable of being manipulated leads to an identification of social work action in this case as the incarceration of children until they agreed with the social work account.

Contrasting approaches to these questions of justice and truth presented in the press clearly highlight the dilemma bound up in the form of political rationality involved here as a problem of the politics of truth. Social workers in this case appealed to justification based on allegations of what they believed to be an emerging form of abuse and therefore their need as professionals to adapt or breach existing procedures in order to cope with new problems in the task of child protection. However, this emphasis on truth as veridiction is regarded by the press as threatening civil liberties, where such liberties are grounded in the idea that good practice implies following established procedures. Press reports thus demonstrate the difficulties of the normalising practices of social work in the context of juridical discourses of rights. The combination of concerns for rights and for welfare produces two related problems. First, a problem of truth: How are truths to be established, according to which procedural guidelines (necessary to guard against the infringement of civil liberties)? Second, a problem of action: How 'sure' do social workers or other agents of welfare have to be to take action (where is the line between protection and unlawful pretrial punishment)?

The position of social work in this reporting demonstrates the interrelation of juridical and veridical criteria of credible evidence in the constitution of notions of the child and of child abuse as 'governable'. Social workers deploy scientific and social scientific notions of childhood and child development but also have statutory responsibilities for the protection of children. This dilemma is only mentioned in passing by the press, but (as was suggested in the analysis of the Cleveland Report) this role produces tensions. Social workers have a legal duty to protect children which brings with it an emphasis on finding abuse and an associated potential threat to the privacy of families.

The initial actions to remove the children are reported on the whole as reasoned, if not justifiable, actions given fears of organised abuse. Once the press move on to discuss the evidence produced from the children whilst in care the tone of reporting becomes more critical, taking up a range of criticisms of the procedures used to interview the children, and suggesting that social work action, in addition to being procedurally deficient, was epistemically wrong-headed and productive of incredible evidence. The press then voice a series of demands for more knowledge and training, while focusing their criticism of the Orkney case on the procedural contraventions involved in the social workers' actions, countering this with a claim of rights to privacy.

Medical signs

When the press turn to examine the nature of the possible evidence in the cases, attention shifts from the procedural deficiencies of the social work action in removing the children to a question of the lack of credible corroborative signs of abuse once the children have been taken. The first stage in this shift is the reporting of the lack of medical signs of abuse found on the children, signs that are equated in some reports with evidence per se: 'The nine Orkney children, who were seized by social workers last month after allegations of ritual sexual abuse, *were neither physically nor sexually abused*, according to *medical evidence* produced at a children's hearing yesterday' (*The Times* 26.3.91, emphasis added). The QC for one of the families is reported stating that, 'Medical examinations have revealed that there is no physical evidence consistent with physical or sexual abuse. There is a *total lack of evidence*' (*The Times* 26.3.91, emphasis added).

The idea that physical medicine provides the only potentially credible source of evidence is reiterated in a number of reports. For example, the headline 'Orkney children showed no signs of sexual abuse' is followed by the suggestion that an absence of medical signs is equivalent to there being 'no signs of abuse', this being posited against Lee's assertion, in line with best practice following Cleveland, that medical examinations do not necessarily reveal evidence of sexual abuse (*The Times* 4.9.91). In this, therefore, the press take the same view as the lawyers representing the families involved, equating evidence firmly with medical evidence and leaving the SWD to question whether the lack of medical evidence is final.

The authority and common sense of medical judgement is further emphasised by reports of social services' failure to ask the children's GP about them. The common sense approach of the doctor and of asking his opinion about the cases is contrasted with the actions of social work in an article headed 'GP ignored in Orkney case'. This reports the doctor's opinion that 'all the children were in good health', that he 'could see no evidence that they had been involved in any such activities', and registers his concern that 'the children could suffer trauma by being separated from their parents' (*The Times* 12.3.91). This piece thus ignores social workers' explanations of their secrecy, and presents an image of the family doctor as an important source of expertise overlooked in Orkney.

Instead of accepting the lack of medical evidence as final, the SWD was moved to question whether this must necessarily mean that nothing happened to the children. Gordon Sloan is quoted stating that, 'while the medical evidence did not show signs of physical or sexual abuse, they did not indicate whether the children had taken part in "simulated sexual intercourse" or had been subjected to "moral danger"' (*The Times* 26.3.91). This report, using quotation marks to suggest spuriousness, counters reliance on the 'hard' science of medicine with social workers' reliance on evidence from children's statements in interviews. This was to cause many problems later in the case due to the mishandling of interviews, taken up by the press as the blurring of fact and fantasy due to a combined lack of common sense and of expertise on the part of social workers.

In some aspects of press reporting, therefore, lack of medical evidence already makes social work action problematic and potentially illegitimate. That is, some press reports appeal to knowledge drawn from physical medicine to constitute epistemically adequate evidence in an exclusionary manner. When press discussion turns to the interviews conducted with the children, this problematisation of the social work case becomes more pronounced and specified, but it is already implicit in the prioritising of physical medicine.

Interviews with the children

For the social workers involved, working in the context of a lack of physical signs of abuse, interviews with the children became central to the search for evidence. When the nine children taken into care began to 'disclose' abuse, press attention turned to the adequacy of interviews. Press reports of interviews conducted with the children raise both procedural and epistemic concerns about credibility in discussions that move between 'common sense' appeals for the need for sensible practice and reports of experts' judgements concerning the SWD's practices in this instance. Press discussion of interviews therefore brings together concerns over the juridical and veridical criteria for the construction of credible evidence. Some reports focus primarily on problems concerning the epistemic criteria for the production of credible evidence and raise concerns over inadequately scientific methods; the closed character of interviewing, the use of leading questions, and so on. Other reports focus primarily on problems concerning juridical or procedural criteria of credibility, and raise concerns over the correct documentation of interviews, the people present and so on. These are articulated in reports partly as a set of lay or common sense criticisms and partly as a set of expert criticisms, but both are run together as the press discuss the interviews conducted with the children. The mutual articulation of these themes in the discussion of interviews within the press provides a site on which we can observe these two criteria of credibility, the procedural/juridical and the epistemic/veridical, in the production (or attempted production) of the abused child as a subject for medico-legal intervention.

The press present vivid images of the closed character of the interviewing of children in this case. One boy is reported saying 'social workers kept asking me about my being involved in sex with other families. I kept telling them it was not true. They wouldn't believe me' (*Daily Mail* 6.4.91, 6). This is presented as a form of continuous pressure applied to the children:

> The BBC obtained part of a transcript of a seven-year-old girl in the case being interviewed by a social worker. Asked who has abused her, the child replies: 'Nobody, why do you have to tell me all this every day?'
>
> (*Daily Mail* 28.10.92, 9)[7]

This is reiterated in other newspapers with headings such as: 'Why did they keep putting words in my mouth?' (*The Scotsman* 6.4.91, 3, also *The Scotsman* 18.12.91, 5).

Press reports focus on interviewers' use of leading questions, coaching and bribery. This is specified particularly evocatively in an article entitled 'How the Orkney abuse probe was flawed', in which *The Times* identifies and elaborates a number of problems concerning the questioning of the children whilst in care. The article begins in the following manner:

> 'Can you draw the ring, because I'm not very good at drawing?' The

questioner was trying to get an 11-year-old Orkney boy to draw a scene from dancing rituals in which he was supposed to have taken part.

(The Times 7.4.91)

It goes on to detail flaws in the interview techniques, stating that the children 'were *interrogated* by RSSPCC experts, accompanied by Northern Constabulary Officers, *searching for evidence of ritual sexual abuse*', concluding that 'the twenty-two tapes and seventy-two sets of transcripts and interview notes reveal dramatically how evidence was twisted and the rules ignored' (*The Times* 7.4.91, emphasis added).

While reports such as the one above present the interviewers' actions as part of a conscious ploy, other reports produce a strong sense of the interviewers as credulous and as failing to listen to what the children were saying to them. This is presented clearly in a report headed 'Orkney child's lie claim "a test"', in which 'the social worker who first heard the Orkney sex abuse allegations' is described to have 'shrugged off' a remark by one of the children that the story was 'all a lie' (*The Scotsman* 5.2.92, 8). This 'denial' of children's 'denials' engaged in by interviewers is presented as an ironic refusal to believe the children by social workers and police. *The Scotsman* reports a statement by the parents that, 'Our children have been particularly distressed by this refusal to believe them' (*The Scotsman* 9.4.91, 3).

The interviewers are frequently presented as lacking a sufficiently sceptical, scientific approach to their task, as assuming that abuse had taken place. In answering a question concerning her response to the statement from a child that the allegations were a lie, Liz McLean is quoted thus: '"The child said one thing, and that child looked another. My experience has been that, very often, a child's words are saying one thing and her feeling is saying something else"' (*The Scotsman* 12.2.92, 7). The press comment on this approach as indicative of social workers' 'desire for a definitive disclosure'; commenting on transcripts of interviews *The Times* states that 'other transcripts were littered with perfunctory comments by interviewers thwarted in their desire for a definitive disclosure. One reads, *'He has not said anything yet and will have to be given time to disclose'* (*The Times* 7.4.91, emphasis added).

In contrast, social workers and psychologists are presented arguing that disbelief represents a 'backlash' against the reality of sexual abuse which social workers must fight (*The Scotsman* 12.4.91, 4), and stating that disbelief in organised and sexual abuse allegations now is the same as that surrounding physical abuse in the 1950s (*The Scotsman* 19.1.91, 6). This position is reinforced by statements that children never lie when making such allegations and that social workers can detect a child's need to tell. The following statement from a social worker involved demonstrates this position:

> 'I was not told that the children were about to disclose, but when I met MW I could see this as self-evident. She reminded me of a steam kettle about to come to the boil. She was talking to everyone she wanted to about the abuse

she had suffered. Her teachers did not want to probe and this lack of interest had the effect of closing her down.'

(*The Scotsman* 10.12.91, 4)

In this context, a report of a statement from a social work journal concerning 'satanic ritual abuse' that 'even if what children are saying is untrue, it is clear they believe it to be true, so something dreadful must have happened to them' (*Daily Mail* 8.3.91, 1) takes on a new meaning as the press present some of the ways in which social workers' beliefs and actions may play a role in constituting the truth of the child.[8]

Some reports detail criticisms of the interviews carried out in Orkney from other experts in the field. The press therefore provide a space for the expert policing of expertise through appeal to what might be called expert common sense. The critical mood of other experts is summed up by Dr Judith Trowell, a consultant psychiatrist specialising in work with abused children at the Tavistock Clinic, and a prominent witness to the Orkney Inquiry. She is reported, in an article focusing on her common sense as an expert, stating that one RSSPCC session was 'A superb example of how not to do an interview. She said 'children were interviewed excessively, asked leading questions and often pressured by interviewers' (*The Times* 29.3.91). *The Scotsman*, reporting Trowell's comment to the Clyde Inquiry that 'she would like to take the audiotape of the interview to show students how such sessions should not be conducted' (*The Scotsman* 18.3.92, 4), goes on to detail her evidence in a report that demonstrates the interrelation of psychology (as a normalising form of knowledge gained through scientific methods) and legal (juridical) processes around child sexual abuse:

> Of the interviewing as a whole, Dr Trowell said, 'The poor quality of the interview techniques makes it difficult to assess the information. Some of the children are cause for concern but there is no way these concerns can be clarified from the material presented.' She also criticised the refusal to respect the wishes of some of the children not to return to the interview centres. 'These children were apparently asked to consent to be interviewed. However, at times their wish not to attend was overruled. This must have been very confusing for the children'.

(*The Scotsman* 18.3.92, 4)

This statement combines ideas of expertise, the need for training, concern with the forensic value of interviews, and concern with the welfare of the child; it presents an ideal image of expertise (see also *The Times* 7.4.91; Clyde 1992: 252–61, 309–16).

In the context of expert criticisms, the press remain sceptical about the possibility of organised abuse in Orkney and focus their concerns on the question of justice or injustice to the parents:

> While the decision to declare a child at risk and remove it from its family 'just in case' may not legally imply guilt on the part of the adults, that is how

distressed an indignant parents are bound to react. They feel they have to prove their innocence. Possible injustice to the parents is compounded. Not having been formally accused, they cannot be formally acquitted.

(*The Times* 4.4.91)

Here we see the dilemma of parental rights versus child protection emerge sharply within the question of what evidence can be legitimately used to take children from their families. The press collapse social workers' suspicions into allegations of guilt on the part of the parents; it is then assumed that family rights are being abused as children's statements must be counted as unreliable, this inevitably leading to the implication that the rights of the families to privacy have been wronged, the terms of the discussion having produced this dualism.

A division between fact and fantasy operates within the press reports of interviews with the children, the suggestion is that this particular case is one of fantasy induced by social work questions, leaving the question of the possible existence of organised abuse to one side. This then becomes linked to questions of good and bad procedures and practice through which the gathering of credible evidence can be achieved, linking the juridical/procedural and veridical/epistemic.

The press present the social workers' belief in the children's statements, and their actions following from this, as an abuse of power. Yet not to act on suspicion of abuse would be, for a social worker charged with responsibilities for child protection, to fail to fulfil a statutory duty. Furthermore, there were at the time few guidelines available with respect to suspected organised abuse, the knowledge here was just being constituted. These contradictory impulses and 'gaps' in knowledge, reflected in the press accounts of the cases, demonstrate contemporary problems in the relation between juridical and veridical discourses that constitute child protection. This is presented by the press in terms of social workers' credulity, belief in children's statements and flouting of guidelines. The disqualification of the interviewers' actions within press reports provides continued cogency and support to legal or procedural notions of truth as providing the ultimate grounds of legitimate authority and normativity. Examining these reports thus demonstrates part of the process by which conditions of credibility or truth are constituted within our political rationality, and the ways in which following guidelines is linked immanently to the possibility of procuring credible evidence.

Returning their readers to a focus on judicial authority, the press report Sheriff Kelbie's criticisms. These criticisms led to the immediate release of the children; they included the flouting of guidelines concerning children's attendance at panel hearings and also '"repeated coaching" that may well have tainted anything that might have been repeated in a court' (Kelbie in *The Times* 5.4.91). The paper reports Kelbie's view that 'the children, far from being taken to places of safety, were separated from one another and cross-examined to break their resolve and get them to admit to having been abused' (*The Times* 5.4.91).

The possibility of good practice

> Dr Driver, who recently retired from an academic career of international renown in the field of psychology, believes the incompetence of social work interview techniques is to blame for the current crisis – and that the community will never again trust that department without radical reforms. 'Cleveland showed that scientifically, the anal dilation tests were totally useless in cases of sexual abuse', he said. 'And psychologically, when you're dealing with the mind, you're dealing with the most complex entity in the universe'.
>
> (*The Scotsman* 4.3.91, 3)

The press play an active role in the elaboration of the possibility of new and better procedures for eliciting evidence of child sexual abuse. In attempting to envision a model of legitimate or reasonable practice, press discussions mobilise both the common sense of parents and lawyers and the expertise of other professionals within social work and psychology to demand that interviewers follow juridically and veridically appropriate criteria for the constitution of evidence. The possibility of good practice is suggested within press reports through appeal to a combination of common sense and more expertise; this is articulated through a demand for better procedures, more knowledge and improved training. We will examine the development of this idea of good practice within press reporting, establishing how the 'common sense' demand for 'facts' voiced by parents and politicians is given authority through reports of experts' statements concerning appropriate scientific methods. We will then focus on the press articulation of the need for more knowledge and training. In this, reports emphasise that social workers operate at the boundaries of current knowledge in this area. From this portrayal comes a demand for specialist teams, more guidelines, research and training, in order that a better balance between privacy and intervention might be achieved.

The possibility of good practice in the management of child sexual abuse emerges in the context of criticisms of the professionalism and skill of those involved in Orkney. Press reports present this through detailing a series of criticisms of the interviews carried out in Orkney provided by other experts in the field. The press therefore provide a space for the expert policing of expertise, with reports appealing to an idea of expertise couched in common sense in opposition to the credulous assumptions of the professionals involved in this case. Press reports of experts' statements concerning the interviews conducted in Orkney have already been noted. This specific focus on experts' criticisms of methods employed in Orkney is combined with the development of a more general image of what counts as professional, scientific practice. This moves from common sense notions of facts to experts' statements about scientific or open ways of working.

The demand for action to be based on 'facts' is presented as an issue of common sense versus bogus social work hypotheses. For example, several papers report a statement by Virginia Bottomley, Health Minister at the time, that 'Social workers, police and health agencies must look for *facts not fantasy*. They should be looking for *bruises and beatings rather than ghosts and ghoulies'* (*Daily Mail* 11.4.91, emphasis added; see also *The Scotsman* 11.4.91).

The focus of these reports is not to disqualify all action, but to renegotiate the boundaries of legitimate professional intervention through procedural change accompanied by greater professionalism and scientific scepticism on the part of social workers. This is demonstrated in the following report, where the need for action to be based on facts is considered in terms of the need for an attitude of suspicion rather than gullibility on the part of social workers:

> [Social workers] training dictates that if there is any evidence of abuse, then the first requirement is to remove a child under possible threat, from the source of abuse. There is nothing wrong with that [. . .] *provided the evidence is real.* But over the years, in Cleveland, in Rochdale and now in Orkney, social workers have brought an increasingly rigid approach to that most delicate of areas. They are too readily persuaded that talk of ritual abuse, even satanic rites, has some grounding in fact when evidence consistently suggests the contrary. Denials only increase their suspicion. *They search for stray signs that it has happened, even steer children in interviews toward these conclusions instead of starting from a position of fundamental scepticism.*
>
> (*The Scotsman* 5.4.91, 12, emphasis added)

There is an irony here, in so far as the social workers in the Orkney case were not working with the idea that the cases involved 'ritual' abuse, but rather with the possibility of organised abuse, something *The Scotsman* is keen to point out in criticising other newspapers' coverage of the case.

The properly sceptical attitude of professionals is forcefully elaborated in a report in which Dr Martini expressed her scepticism over the existence of 'ritual' abuse; she stated that while children had 'wonderful imaginations that normally ought to be encouraged' [. . .] 'she questioned basing the actions of 3 weeks ago merely on their statements' (*The Scotsman* 21.3.91, 1). This statement combines Martini's authority as a doctor with her common sense as a member of the community. Other expert statements further reinforce the common sense concern with facts. Reporting on a conference on child witnesses being held in Dundee, *The Scotsman* quotes an American professor: 'Professor Stephen Ceci said investigators should try to disprove their own notions, instead of trying to find the answers to support them. [. . .] *"Interviewers who have only one hunch are looking for trouble"'* (*The Scotsman* 11.4.91, 3, emphasis added).

The concern with lack of expertise guiding professional practice in this case brings a demand for more guidelines, knowledge and training in the area of sexual and organised abuse. The process through which the press discredit current practice and yet use this criticism to mount a demand for better forms of practice through more knowledge and training can be seen if we examine several different stages in the following report. This begins with scepticism toward the social work claim of the possibility of organised abuse, suggesting that this idea is the work of fundamentalist Christians engaged in the process of manufacturing belief:

Allegations of ritual or satanic abuse started to appear in Britain relatively recently. They have been traced to efforts by *fundamentalist Christian groups*, inspired from across the Atlantic, to *convince the social work fraternity that such things happened and that they should look for evidence.* The promoters of the idea of satanic abuse argue, as one would suspect, from fundamentals. The devil, they say, is active in the world, attacking what is pure and holy. *What could be more innocent than family life and the love of parents for their children? So the devil enslaves the parents and obliges them to corrupt their children and even to assault them sexually.*

(*The Times* 11.3.91, emphasis added)

This is intended to be ironic, yet its parody of the arguments of those who are convinced of the existence of satanism replicates elements of the press' own depiction of social work action. In these reports the family and community are depicted by the press as pure and invaded (see first section of this chapter). This disqualification of the possibility of organised abuse is followed by demands for scepticism on the part of social workers:

It is almost incredible that such wild ideas could have been swallowed by professional social workers, who by their experience are supposed to be wise in the world's ways and by training, properly sceptical. But the notorious Cleveland case demonstrated (though allegations of ritual abuse were absent there) that when social workers and child psychiatrists are confronted by evidence of sexual and emotional irregularity within families, they are in uncharted and frightening territory.

(*The Times* 11.3.91)

The report is therefore critical of the social workers involved and at the same time suggests a properly sceptical approach as appropriate. It ends with a demand for more knowledge and appropriate training in order that social workers may act in a more measured way:

Evidence is often of the most subtle and nuanced kind, easy to misinterpret, all the more so if the emotional relationships within the family are already a little disturbed. *Theories which make sense of strange behaviour are always alluring. Under pressure not to leave vulnerable children in households dangerous to their wellbeing, social workers are tempted to play for safety; and then to justify what they have done by turning suspicion into fact.*

(*The Times* 11.3.91, emphasis added)

In this context, the press focus on social work knowledge as deficient but remediable, as at a 'very early stage' with respect to sexual and organised abuse (*The Scotsman* 24.3.92, 4). The image of a developing knowledge base and expertise is further reinforced in a statement by Mary Hartnoll, Secretary of the Association of Directors of Social Work, on publication of the report of the Orkney Inquiry. She is quoted stating that 'social workers were frequently being asked to work at the boundaries of existing knowledge' and calling for 3-year training for social workers (*The Scotsman* 26.10.92, 3). An editorial in the *Daily Mail* concurs, 'the answer is plain – more training' (*Daily Mail* 26.3.92, 14).

The criticism of currently available evidence and expertise developed through press reporting of the Orkney case is thus accompanied by calls for improved guidelines, knowledge and training. This second aspect of reporting forms an organisational and administrative response in which the press remain ambivalent over the potential reality of organised abuse. There are therefore two discernable moments within press reports concerning evidence of organised sexual abuse: that of disbelief and discrediting of the case at hand, and that of abstention from judgement as to the potential reality of such abuse due to insufficient knowledge. The press point to the failures of evidence in this specific case, the lack of medical evidence and problems with the interview techniques used. This is the discrediting moment. Press reports then become an arena in which the imperative to closer knowledge of the potential reality of organised abuse is vocalised; in this second aspect of the reporting the press join the demand for guidelines, a broad inquiry and further academic study of the area.

The Times reports a government announcement of an academic study into the nature and extent of organised and ritual abuse. Here, the press (and the government) raise issues of the correct legal and scientific grounds for evidence of organised sexual abuse as technical problems to be overcome: 'Bottomley's decision follows criticism by police of social work teams for the way they have made allegations of satanic or ritual abuse when police inquiries have failed to produce any evidence' (*The Times* 10.3.91). The aim of this study is to give social workers and police a 'more informed picture of why abused children make such claims and whether there is any substance to them' (*The Times* 10.3.91). Later, several papers report the announcement of a set of Department of Health guidelines for social workers that is to include a section on organised abuse. *The Times* reports Virginia Bottomley stating, 'In the guidelines we are stressing the importance of taking a cool, clear look, of calling in experts, of seeking advice and of ensuring that social workers follow sound professional principles' (*The Times* 8.6.91).

The press also suggest that a balance between parents' rights and child protection can be achieved through greater specialisation. A piece entitled 'Call for specialised teams on child abuse' reports on a study commissioned after Cleveland that 'stresses the need for a multidisciplinary investigation with full interagency cooperation where abuse is believed to have occurred' (*The Scotsman* 11.4.91, 3). In such reports, solutions to the problems of managing difficult child protection cases are regarded as something to be achieved through further specialist training combined with interagency working, training being a site on which the practical renegotiation of procedures and methods can take place.

In expressing concerns over Orkney as combining problems of inadequate procedures and faulty epistemic assumptions, the press implicitly accept that the governance of child sexual and organised abuse is a technical problem that can be solved; that is, they accept the politics of expertise on which liberal welfare rationality is predicated and advance a model of public accountability through expertise grounded in common sense. Thus, the press open a space for the expression of concern over sexual and organised or 'ritual' abuse as features of a public agenda, recognise that the relationship between parental rights and children's interests may need to be renegotiated, and play an important role in calling for this task to be undertaken, but within the existing problematisation of this as an issue of parents' rights versus child protection, and where legitimate intervention is grounded in expertise. Within liberal welfare rationality, claims to credible evidence achieved through expertise in the provision of adequate knowledge and competent practice sustain the legitimacy of public interventions into private families. The press reporting of Orkney both demonstrates the importance of this interrelation of adequate knowledge and competent practice in forging of a legitimate public/private distinction and shows how press reports play an active role in constituting the credible through their discussion of evidence.

The press coverage of Orkney both problematises the claim of expertise on which liberal welfare rationality is predicated, by criticising those involved in the immediate case concerned, and reproduces the centrality of the figure of the expert by providing a model of public accountability as the regulation of expertise through expertise and by invoking both 'common sense' and other experts as privileged truthtellers and judges of the evidence concerned. Therefore, while the press are critical of the evidential basis for action in Orkney, these reports are also part of the entrenchment and elaboration of the possibility of the legitimacy of 'reasonable' government within child protection, themselves leading calls for the production of more knowledge of dangerousness and better practices of child protection, and calling for inquiries into specific cases to ascertain facts.

Two distinct notions of justification or grounds of credibility operate within the press reporting of the Orkney case. Reports oscillate between a (populist) discrediting of the social work action predicated on a procedural notion of truth (were the actions procedurally adequate, 'within the law'?) and ambivalence toward the social work position predicated on an epistemic notion of truth. In one case, failure to follow procedures acts to render all evidence invalid. In the other, inadequately followed procedures mean that evidence becomes untrustworthy and the question of 'what really happened?' difficult to clarify. The press discussion moves between focusing on problems of procedure and on the supposed truth or otherwise of the allegations and has a tendency to collapse the latter into the former. However, as we shall see in the next section the press are dissatisfied with the exclusively procedural focus of the inquiry that followed Orkney and demand that 'the truth' emerge in order that the guilt or innocence of those involved be clarified.

The distinction between a procedural or juridical notion of evidence and an epistemic or veridical notion of evidence displayed within the press reports reveals the ways in which the tension between the juridical individual and normalised subject constitutive of modern political rationalities is underscored by a doubling of the forms of knowledge available with which to regulate these forms of subjectivity. Procedural notions of evidence appeal to the idea of the juridical individual and private family, truths constituted through the sciences of child welfare map on to and articulate the idea of the normal subject and family as sites of public concern for welfare and security. This tension between the juridical constitution of rights and the veridical constitution of normalising forms of knowledge is managed through expertise, where this combines adequate knowledge and competent practice thus providing the possibility of credible evidence capable of sustaining and reinventing a distinction between public authority and family privacy. Expertise binds together procedural adequacy and appropriate scientific methods in gathering information to produce the conditions of a simultaneously normalising and juridical political order. The press play an active role in articulating the conditions of this political order through calling for adequate procedures, more knowledge and improved training.

In summary, the press report evidence and concerns over evidential inadequacies in two different ways. In one strand of reporting there is a clear-cut discrediting of the claims of abuse, while in another set of reports there is a more agnostic discussion that suggests that claims of organised or 'ritual' abuse may be believed, but not on the evidential basis available in Orkney. This latter strand leads to calls for greater knowledge guiding clearer practice in the area. The second moment here, therefore, suggests that the Orkney case suffered due to procedural and epistemic flaws with regard to the production of credible evidence, thus moving away from a refusal to accept organised abuse as a possibility. Questions of evidence thus form shifting ground on which press reports attempt to invoke and articulate a new set of relations between legal and normalising practices in child protection. That is, press reporting is an important site for the incitement of a reworking of the relationships of legal and normalising forms of knowledge through which liberal welfare rationality is constituted and within which it is assumed greater knowledge, understanding and ability to predict behaviour can rationally 'solve' the problems encountered in negotiating the boundary between parents' rights and children's interests.

Imagining the inquiry: the press and the ideal of liberal governance

We have seen that press reporting contains an ambivalence between on one hand regarding legally grounded procedures as authoritative in determining truth (truth as procedure) and on the other hand counterpoising truth and procedure (procedural adequacy versus 'what really happened'). This ambivalence can be seen in the press reporting of the inquiry into the Orkney case, something both demanded by the press and then criticised for its inadequate, because strictly procedural, terms of reference.

This section first examines how the press present a generalised image of law as a site of authority. Second, it looks at press demands for a public inquiry into the events and at the way in which the inquiry is regarded as an objective mechanism for resolving controversy, reconciling the demands of justice and of welfare. Press criticisms of the inquiry instituted form the third focus. This is followed by a look at press demands for another form of inquiry, one that is more wide-ranging and that can address not only procedural concerns but the question of the potential truth of the allegations. In showing how the press demand a renegotiation of procedures and demand to know 'what really happened' in Orkney (in order both that justice for the parents be achieved and that child welfare be secured), this section aims to demonstrate how press reporting acts to reinvoke and further entrench the simultaneously juridical and normalising features of liberal welfare rationality; in demanding a wider remit for the inquiry the press demand a closer interrelation of these aspects to re-establish legitimacy in the governance of child sexual abuse.

Law as a neutral arbiter

In the last section we saw how, once medical evidence proved negative, the press focused on procedural and epistemic problems with the interviews undertaken with the children. In some reports, the absence of legally binding evidence is taken to imply that nothing happened; law is taken as the final arbiter of the truth of the cases and forensically valid evidence is constructed as the only acceptable standard for action. This standard is in turn taken as objective, an image of law as the neutral arbiter of the facts of the case being created within reports. This then acts to reinforce the public/private distinction, where intervention should be based on 'hard' evidence, and where, in the absence of such evidence, unmolested privacy remains the natural and desirable state of the family. A central question thus concerns how law is constituted as a site of authority by the press: how does law gain a prominent position in the determination of the form and limits of what can reasonably be said and done?

The press invoke the power of law even in the language used in reports. For example, in statements that parents accused the staff of the SWD 'of stealing their children and *illegally interrogating* them' (*The Times* 5.4.91, emphasis added). Prior to the decision to return the children to their families one parent is reported stating that the case is 'in the hands of the Lord – and the law' (*The Scotsman* 7.3.91, 1). This passage simultaneously suggests the helplessness of the parents and the idea of law as the final arbiter, as an authority to be compared with divine authority.[9]

An ideal of law as a neutral and objective adjudicator emerges clearly in reporting on Sheriff Kelbie's dismissal of the cases. One report, entitled 'The judgement' quotes Kelbie's statement that certain actions taken by the SWD were '*totally illegal*' (a reference to the failure to allow a 15-year-old boy to attend the children's panel hearing) and that the actions had '*no legal authority*' (*The Scotsman* 5.4.91, 2, emphasis added; also *The Times* 5.4.91).

When Kelbie's decision to dismiss the cases before they could reach a proof hearing is itself criticised, this criticism is launched from the position of the authority of law, through arguments that Kelbie was outside the law in dismissing the allegations before having heard all the evidence, thereby creating a 'procedural morass' (*The Scotsman* 4.6.91, 7). Reporting on this judgement, the press frame law as the paramount arena of legitimacy and truth. This emerges clearly in the following editorial, entitled 'When law loses to emotion':

After months of uncertainty, Lord Hope and his colleagues in the Court of Session have cut through the sentiment of the allegations of child abuse in Orkney to *re-establish law's central position*. In page after page of their judgement [. . .] *disciplined rationality* is the dominant feature. They do not question the Sheriff's sincerity but are forced to conclude, eventually, that he was not entitled to dismiss the applications which were the subject of the hearing before him, as incompetent.

(*The Scotsman* 13.6.91, 12, emphasis added)

Commenting that, 'it was his duty to conduct the proceedings within the law', *The Times* cites Lord Hope's judgement that Kelbie had 'breached the elementary rules of natural justice' (*The Times* 13.6.91). In this instance, therefore, the press report on the legal regulation of law.

The importance of the authority of law to the framing of appropriate procedures for securing child welfare is further established in reports discussing the general issues raised by the Orkney case for the Scottish child protection system. Several reports link the authority of law with its capacity to function as a tactic of governance. This is seen, for example, in statements that concerns for welfare must be framed within legal process in order to 'ensure a better balance of justice where allegations of child abuse are concerned' (*The Scotsman* 26.3.91, 14). Accompanying the notion that law provides privileged procedures for the determination of truth and justice is therefore the idea of the courtroom as a site for the balancing of interests, as a place of welfare not simply of justice, or of welfare as justice: 'Lord Hope said that the court had to balance the interests of the children and the parents' (*The Times* 27.3.91).

Further evidence of the law's role as a source of authority and as a tactic of government is provided in a report entitled 'Law review could have avoided tragedy' (*The Times* 10.3.91). This suggests that procedural changes could make child protection practice work smoothly. Calling for a reformulation of procedures, it sustains the idea of legal truth as necessary and even intensifies its importance in suggesting that legally enforceable supervised access between parents and children could remove 'unnecessary drama' from child protection proceedings. Importantly, this report articulates the welfare functions of law in suggesting that legal provisions could function to secure supervised normalisation.

The demand for a public inquiry

Dr Helen Martini (leader of the South Ronaldsay Parents Action Committee) said, 'one has to have faith in the judicial system. When the children are returned we want a public judicial inquiry to change the law and the guidelines.'

(*Daily Mail* 3.4.91, 5)

The press played an important role in the expression of demands for a public judicial inquiry into the events of Orkney 1991. Reports stress the popular support for an inquiry, emphasise that the judicial form of an inquiry would provide a route to clarity, and sustain the idea that an inquiry could operate as a tool with which to effect a rebalancing of the relationship between concerns for the welfare of children and for justice for parents.

Reports stress that all sides in the dispute over Orkney placed hope in the inquiry. While a headline in *The Times* comments that 'Parents called for a judicial public inquiry' (*The Times* 8.3.91) to clear their names, other reports focus on the SWD hope that a public inquiry will sustain their case, the situation having become too prejudiced by media coverage to continue under normal arrangements (*The Scotsman* 5.6.91, 3).

Much reporting suggests that the quasi-judicial form of an inquiry would be able simultaneously to represent concerns for justice for the parents and for welfare for the children and the community. This is particularly the case in the reporting of a statement by Rev. Ronald Ferguson, an Orkney minister not directly involved in the allegations. He is quoted saying that, 'There has to be justice. Until the truth is told in public, and until justice is seen to be done, there can be no healing' (*The Scotsman* 24.5.91, 9). In this, an inquiry is represented as a means of achieving truth and vindication, as a means of catharsis for all involved.

The Scotsman takes up these combined themes of justice and welfare in a 'comment' that presents the forthcoming inquiry as a constructive tool for the reinscription of relationships between child welfare and due process. It states:

> The inquiry now urgently required must confront several things. It must question first and foremost the training and attitudes brought to it by social work departments. It must examine the children's hearing system with a view to giving the Reporter both the knowledge and standing to allow firm and early intervention on behalf of the children. It must insist that the Social Work (Scotland) Act is reformed in the light of this latest case to bring a cool and objective eye to bear on what may be a fraught and controversial case. And, finally, it should give more weight to the views of children themselves. They are neither simply statistics, casework material nor material to be moulded by the social work system. They are real people, they are victims, and they are, correctly handled, the best witnesses. They should take the centre stage. They deserve our protection. It is they whose interests must now truly be represented.
>
> (*The Scotsman* 5.4.91, 12)

Here, the inquiry is seen as a mechanism for the rebalancing of relations between juridical and normalising concerns, providing a framework for a better combination of practices of child welfare and law, or rather, of child welfare through law. The press therefore back the demand for a public inquiry and, in view of the complex issues of justice for parents and the welfare of children involved, stress the need for the remit of the inquiry that is instituted to be drawn broadly (*The Scotsman* 13.6.91, 12).

Finally, at the beginning of the inquiry, the press present Clyde's statement that, 'The inquiry was not a litigation between opposing parties but an *objective inquiry into what happened*' whose 'primary purpose was to *ascertain the facts and find solutions by issuing recommendations for the future*' (*The Times* 27.8.91, emphasis added). This is heralded as an investigation into 'what really happened on Orkney' (*The Scotsman* 23.8.91, 9). At this stage the inquiry is regarded by all as the principal route to objectivity.

Press dissatisfaction with the Clyde Inquiry

> The three words 'ritual child abuse' became a litany for newspaper editorial writers worldwide. What is it? Did it ever really happen? And had it happened on South Ronaldsay? A year on, no one knows the answer to the last question. Few expect that anyone ever will.
>
> (*The Scotsman* 26.2.92, 10)

> Despite 131 days of evidence and estimated pounds 6M in costs, nobody is any the wiser.
>
> (*The Times* 29.3.92)

Once the Clyde Inquiry had been announced and was underway, the press reporting became more critical. Criticisms of the inquiry that was instituted were tied to press demands to know 'what really happened' and for a final vindication of the parents. In these reports, the inquiry's focus on procedures is therefore directly countered with demands for the truth concerning what happened. One paper points out that after much of the inquiry 'nobody in Scotland is any the wiser about whether or not there was *any truth* in the allegations' (*The Times* 1.3.92, emphasis added).[10]

Press criticisms focused on the cost of the inquiry and the limitations placed upon its remit (*The Scotsman* 9.1.92, 6). In particular, *The Times* describes the inquiry as a 'Jarndyce and Jarndyce saga', suggests that it has been 'seriously flawed' from its inception, and questions whether it is 'value for money' if 'the central problem of whether or not ritual abuse of children took place in a quarry will remain unresolved' (*The Times* 1.3.92, emphasis added). The limited remit of the inquiry, its focus on procedures rather than on guilt and innocence, is thus taken as a central problem. As we shall see shortly, this points in two possible directions: scepticism regarding the value of the inquiry as a process, or a demand for a broader remit and more powers to be given to inquiries. More immediately, it leads the press to reiterate a concern for 'common sense' (*The Times* 1.3.92).

The Scotsman focuses its criticism on the cost of the inquiry, stating that, 'in tabloid press language, "you" can scarcely hear the evidence for the sound of legal tills being rung up' (*The Scotsman* 7.12.91, 5). Other reports are more critical of the form and response of the inquiry, demanding that the inquiry report should reflect the trauma of the events and also demanding legal change:

> The report on the Orkney child abuse case is a deeply unsatisfactory end to the affair. [. . .] The report does offer a catalogue of criticisms of social

workers, the police and RSSPCC. But these criticisms are expressed in the detached manner of corrections to a poor school essay. *The dry woody tome does not reflect the sheer horror of what the social workers and others did to the children and their parents.* [. . .] The Orkney case has conjured up an image of power-mad social workers taking children from their parents in a dawn raid on the basis of wholly inadequate information. It is an image borne out by this report. *Parents require legislation which makes such actions impossible.* Of course, in extreme cases, social workers must be able to apply for the removal of children. *But the safeguards must be cast-iron.* Better procedures for social workers or better training are not good enough. What are needed are restrictions of the power of social workers to traumatise innocent families. *By law.*

(*Daily Mail* 28.10.92, 6, emphasis added)

This report therefore directly counters law as an authority with the 'flimsy' safeguard provided by more and better training. It also displays the interested position of the paper, highlighting what it calls the 'horror' of the events and regarding the dispassionate response of the inquiry as inadequate to this. The cathartic potential of the inquiry is clearly regarded by this paper as a possibility unrealised.

In the course of these reports, the press continue to express concern over both parents' rights and children's welfare. One report, headed 'Orkney parents fight on over "slur"' (*Daily Mail* 28.10.92, 1), documents that the parents are taking a case for compensation to the European Court (though it points out that this will not deliver a decision of guilt or innocence). Other stories focus on the children involved and suggest the limits of the legal and administrative processes that regulate child protection practice in securing child welfare:

> Lastly, what of the children? After the last expenses cheque is paid out, and the final bottle of Côte de Beaune washes down the last cheese-stuffed Orkney steak, after the six million has been accounted for, who pays the price for what happened to those children at the hands of social workers? And what, the nagging doubt will always remain, some social workers think may still be happening to some of them today, at the hands of those they know, love and ought to be able to trust?

(*The Scotsman* 26.3.92, 15)

At this stage, a report in *The Scotsman* provides a different image of Orkney than that provided in earlier press discussions. In so doing, it re-opens concerns over the possible existence of child sexual abuse on the Islands. Asking whether 'the idyllic "it doesn't happen here" image can any longer be sustained' the paper comments that 'since a change of Reporter last year, evidence has mounted that child abuse in general, including sexual abuse, is far from a rarity on the islands' (*The Scotsman* 21.5.92, 13). This report can be read in at least two ways: one suggesting that if there were sexual abuse going on on the Islands then the rest of community would have known about it; the other appealing to or resurrecting the myth of the rural community within which incestuous abuse is a common occurrence.

With the demand for truth unsatisfied, other reports return to a position of scepticism concerning the allegations. This return to or continuance of disbelief is demonstrated in a *Times* report concerning further allegations of organised abuse on the islands in 1992. Reporting on a stake out of a quarry, the paper comments that

> *No paedophiles turned up. But then South Ronaldsay is hardly a paradise for undercover operations.* Strangers stick out a mile and one police officer was clearly visible noting the number plates of passing cars. But then, as one local also pointed out, *how on earth could a paedophile ring hold a sex abuse session in a quarry full of water? Police refused to comment on exactly what they were expecting, the RSSPCC insisted their information was reliable, and the Orkney inquiry fizzled out.*
>
> (*The Times* 29.3.92, emphasis added)

The reporting at this stage reaches a return to the appeal of common sense with a local councillor reported as demanding 'an apology from the social work department and some sackings' (*The Times* 29.3.92).

The demand for another form of inquiry

Press criticisms of the Clyde Inquiry included issues of cost and the failure to address the truth of the allegations. We have seen that in some aspects of the press reporting this leads to a sceptical position, to the 'common sense' discrediting of the whole case. However, in other reports problems identified with the Clyde Inquiry lead to a demand for another form of inquiry. In the latter and more muted aspect of reporting the press restate the idea of the inquiry as an important means of managing the tensions between public and private and between the juridical and normalising threads of liberal welfare rationality.

Contained within the criticisms of the limited remit of the Clyde Inquiry is a demand for a more wide-ranging inquiry. Identifying limits on the remit as a problem, several reports demand an inquiry into the truth or otherwise of the allegations: 'the safety of children, not reconciliation at any price, is of greatest importance. So what matters most is simple: the truth. Did sexual abuse take place or not? If so, against whom and by whom?' (*The Scotsman* 21.5.92, 13). Another report quotes Rev. McKenzie stating that 'There should be another inquiry to see if it really did happen. It is six million pounds down the drain' (*The Scotsman* 26.10.92, 3).[11]

Concern with a range of issues of child welfare leads, in some reports, to attention to what is to happen in future, to ensuring that the events of Orkney cannot recur. This focus provides for a more positive assessment of the Clyde Inquiry as important in importing reason and balance into the discussion and in providing positive recommendations:

The most important thing about Lord Clyde's painstaking and thorough inquiry into the Orkney child abuse case is not what it says but what it causes to happen. The sort of cool-headed analysis which it has brought to compiling the report needs now to be applied to the consideration of how best to ensure that the traumatic events on South Ronaldsay cannot recur. [. . .] *What must crucially emerge is a regime of regulation and practice that strikes a balance between the two imperatives which came into conflict in Orkney: the rights of parents and the interests of children where abuse is suspected.* [. . .] Lord Clyde's report would appear to offer a wise basis for reform in this regard. [. . .] *No-one could reasonably argue with his call for better training of those required to assess children's own accounts of their experiences, for improved communication between agencies, and for observance to be paid to keeping an open mind when interviewing children.* Nor does he ask too much in expecting officials to assemble a cogent case in seeking authority to remove children from their homes, or in calling for a better appeals procedure for parents in such circumstances. [. . .] *Knowledge, forethought and compassion are hard principles with which to argue, and they underpin many of the 194 recommendations.* [. . .] Scapegoats help no one. *Learning, and implementing, the lessons is the only way to draw solid good from a distressing episode.* [. . .] Many of the report's conclusions echo those reached after the Cleveland case, suggesting lessons inadequately applied.

(*The Scotsman* 26.10.92, 12, emphasis added)

This discussion has discerned two modes of press response to the public inquiry headed by Lord Clyde into the events of Orkney 1991. One response forms a critical attack on both the cost and limited remit of the inquiry, which did not address the truth or otherwise of the allegations, focusing instead solely on procedures. The other response recognises the inquiry as important precisely in so far as, rather than focus on establishing guilt or innocence, it centred attention on developing a framework to achieve a better balance between welfare and rights in the governance of child sexual abuse. In these responses we can see the press move between veridical and juridical concerns, between a demand for the truth of the 'real events' (Scott 1988) and a concern with providing better procedures for future negotiations of the relationship between families and the state.

In these discussions, law retains its position as a site of authority and neutrality; it remains relatively unquestioned. On the other hand, the inquiry is the focus of intense press scrutiny as the site on which juridical forms of truth telling are seen openly to call upon and question scientific and normalising forms of truth telling. This suggests that legal discourse is regarded by the press as less problematic than scientific discourse, that law is regarded as lay or common sense in contrast to the expertise involved in scientific discussion. The legal framing and articulation of scientific ideas in child welfare is therefore stressed and the inquiry seen by some reports as an important site on which these relations can be better balanced for the future.

Conclusion: the press and liberal welfarism

This chapter has demonstrated the entrenched character of the ambivalences of liberal welfarism in the press imagination. Questions of the appropriate relationships between public and private life and between juridical and normalising concerns are popular, as well as governmental ideas. The press, in constituting a public space within which the possibility of governing reasonably is reiterated even as specific interventions are criticised, play an important role in constituting and rearticulating the authority of regulated practices of intervention into the family.

We have seen that within press reporting the assumption and reiteration of a public/private distinction is expressed through the representation of the community of Orkney and the families involved as the seat of natural authority, morality, purity and common sense, against the overzealousness of state social work intervention. In this case, therefore, the press depict social work intervention as unreasonable, jeopardising the claim to legitimate concern made by the SWD.

Press reporting sustains an ideal of liberal governance, governing neither too little nor too much but governing reasonably, by interrogating the evidential credibility sustaining the actions in this case. This is framed in the reporting of the case as an absence of credible evidence that could have sustained the legitimacy of the actions taken. In this, the press mobilise a procedural conception of evidential credibility to problematise the practices of intervention, and an epistemic conception of evidential credibility to discuss the scientific credibility or otherwise of evidence gathered. The SWD are criticised both for their failure to conform to legal procedures and for inadequately scientific practice in a discussion centring on the use of interviews in the case. In adjudicating the credible, press reports appeal both to common sense notions of reasonableness and to expertise from outside the case concerned to suggest the possibility of good practice in child protection. In this way, criticism acts also as the basis for the press to re-establish the possibility of reasonable intervention via expertise grounded in common sense.

The press demand more knowledge of sexual and organised or 'ritual' abuse, more guidelines, improved training, and a clearer legal framework for intervention into family relations. In this way, reports seek to balance juridical concerns with rights and normalising concerns for child welfare. The public inquiry is regarded as an appropriate site for this renegotiation; the institution of the inquiry is seen to provide the possibility of combining concerns for welfare and for justice through relating the common sense authority of law to expertise in the sciences of child welfare. The press thus call for an inquiry into the events.

The Clyde Inquiry, established to investigate the Orkney events, is criticised by the press for its exclusive focus on the procedural inadequacies of the interventions. However, this criticism, rather than leading to the wholesale denunciation of the inquiry as a mechanism of government, instead produces a demand for a more wide-ranging inquiry able to combine discussion of how practice could be improved for the future with a focus on the truth or otherwise of the allegations in the specific cases concerned. In this process, therefore, the idea of the inquiry as a tool of government is sustained and reinvoked. The importance of the inquiry as a mechanism for the reformulation of governmental practices and as a space of reflection for liberal governance is further emphasised by criticisms that lessons learned inadequately from the Cleveland Inquiry have led to the Orkney events; the implication of this criticism is that liberal governance should be more reflexive, and that this could prevent 'errors' in the management of child abuse cases. The press regard the mechanism of the inquiry as central to this process of reflection.

Conclusion

This book began by noting a tension within contemporary social and political discourse, between the imperative to protect children and the presupposition that the family is and should be private. This tension sets up a problem space for contemporary forms of governance, a space this book has attempted to address by examining the ways in which child sexual abuse is rendered governable, and by exploring what happens when such governance is called into question.

The preceding chapters have been concerned with two principal questions. First, to examine some of the analytic tools with which we might interrogate how child sexual abuse has been constituted as a problem amenable to governance, and explore the intractable problems to which this constitution of the problem gives rise. Second, to provide a substantive analysis of the ways in which recent problems in the governance of child sexual abuse have been addressed, elucidating what this reveals about our forms of political reasoning and their effects. In conclusion, I want to return to some of the main arguments of the book, to reflect on how the analyses of Parts I and II inform one another.

The governance of child sexual abuse raises questions of legitimacy concerning the appropriate boundary between public and private life, and questions of expertise, of the knowledge and professionalism of agencies of intervention. I have suggested that calls of 'crisis' in such governance have taken the form of questions concerning the legitimacy of relations between the family and the state, and questions concerning expertise, interrogations of the knowledge base and professionalism of agencies of intervention. Tensions between the family and the state are managed on the premise that expertise represents a neutral vehicle for discerning reality, so that governance can be achieved in the name of the nature of childhood itself. In the normal practice of child protection, the idea that knowledge produced by experts has nonpolitical status bridges the problem of public intervention into the private sphere.

This book has discussed a number of different ways of theorising the public/private distinction and the relation between law and science. Beginning with liberal political theory, the limitations of assuming a public/private distinction and justifying intervention on the basis of criteria of harm were outlined. Attempts to govern child sexual abuse currently occur within the forms of self-understanding established within liberal political thought and practice. A distinction between the public powers of the state and the privacy of normal family relations is assumed, and attention is focused on where to draw the boundary between public and private, using particular designations of harm drawn from medicine and psychology. Liberalism, through its simultaneous adherence to a public/private distinction on the one hand, and concern with harm on the other, provides the basic problematic within which child sexual abuse is currently thought about and acted upon as an issue for governance. Liberal presuppositions establish the space in which problems in the governance of child sexual abuse are subject to endless reiteration: 'crises' in this area of child protection are followed by inquiries that diagnose problems occurring in specific cases and issue guidance resetting the terms of engagement for public agencies, only to be followed by further crises and other inquiries recommending further adjustments to formulae for public intervention into private familial relations. It is in this way that 'failures' of governance become loci for reflection on and for the reiteration of practices of governance.

Habermas's work helps us to reframe our understanding of the public/private distinction in a manner that sheds light upon the dynamics of conflict between families and the state. His analysis of contemporary state–society relations suggests that problems attending state intervention into the family are the result of forms of legal and administrative regulation that are inadequately grounded in discursive processes, and of expert discourses that are self-perpetuating. However, his suggestion that these problems could be overcome through the institutionalisation of democratic control over expertise simply offers to finesse the forms of governance that we have already, perhaps helping to avert conditions of 'crisis' by more fully articulating expert understandings of children's well-being to a broader public. A distinction between public and private remains pivotal to his account, as does a distinctively modern conception of childhood. In these crucial respects, Habermas's argument reiterates the constituent tensions of liberalism, at best helping to refine an existing problematisation of the issues.

From this discussion it was argued that the concerns of this book required a form of analysis that would neither presuppose nor seek to destroy the distinction between public and private life, but which would show how these relations came about and the rationality and intractable problems of child protection which they constitute and maintain. Foucault's ideas suggest a productive way of looking at how contemporary understandings of the relationship between public and private are grounded in and articulated through legal and scientific knowledge and practice. Examining Foucault's analysis of liberalism as a rationality of rule enables us to reconceptualise the public/private distinction and the relation between law and science, assumed and reiterated within liberal political thought and by Habermas, showing how these concepts are constituted and maintained by particular practices of governance.

Modern liberalism, as a rationality of rule, exhibits both a concern with right and a concern with the norms delivered through biopolitical knowledge. As such it produces a problematisation of the governance of child sexual abuse as one that must be conducted within the terms of the limits of the powers of public agencies in relation to the private family, where justification for intervention must in turn be grounded in an effective relationship between legal determinations of right (effects of jurisdiction), and scientific determinations of health and normality (effects of veridiction). Some of the tensions entailed by this are played out in the Cleveland Inquiry's attempt to renegotiate rule following crisis, and in the press coverage of Orkney, where the press produce a demand for more of what they criticise.

The accounts of Cleveland and Orkney presented here have used Foucault's suggestions concerning the analysis of a problematisation. In particular, they examine the ways in which assumptions concerning the relationship between public and private life, and the interrelation of legal mechanisms with scientific knowledge and practice, constitute child sexual abuse in a governable form, and scrutinise the role of the inquiry and press in rearticulating rule and refracting this into the public imagination.

The Cleveland Inquiry acted as a mechanism for the rearticulation of authority through crisis. It worked with the assumption of a distinction between public and private, regrounding the legitimacy of interventions into the usually private space of the family through a critical examination and refashioning of expertise. It assumed and reinvoked a distinction between public and private life, and was a site for and an instrument in the repositioning of the forms of knowledge and practice through which child sexual abuse is rendered governable.

The inquiry managed the distinction between public and private by attempting to rearticulate effective relations between law and science in terms of the professional practice of child protection. Within modern liberalism as a rationality of rule, sovereignty, the right to govern, is premised on claims to and demands for knowledge with which to govern. The inquiry aimed to restore confidence in the governance of child sexual abuse by securing a better balance between the family and the state, and by calling for more knowledge and better training to underpin action on the part of professionals. This involved the inquiry in negotiating the tension between a juridical discourse of rights predicated on a division between the public and the private, and a normalising discourse of best interests predicated on knowledge drawn from paediatric medicine and psychology. The inquiry provided a procedural resolution of the problems identified in Cleveland by suggesting closer delimitation of the powers of experts, and by calling for more knowledge and better expertise in order that its ideal of 'reasonable' (i.e. measured or proportionate), intervention be accomplished. Reflecting on this we might say that the public inquiry operates as a site for governmental reflection and is a mode of resetting rules for the conduct of conduct. The public inquiry acts as a polyvalent technique in the governance of child sexual abuse through its capacity to reestablish relations between public and private and to reorient legal and normalising practices in child protection, where these have broken down.

The themes elaborated in the Cleveland Inquiry's discussion are also central to the popular political imagination. Analysis of press discussions of Orkney demonstrates the embedded character of the tensions constitutive of liberalism as a rationality of rule. The press constitute a public space in and through which the idea of the naturalness and priority of the family is sustained, and within which greater expertise in the governance of social life is called for. The press, whilst critical of intervention in Orkney, reiterated a demand for 'reasonable' governance; the 'failure' of governance in this instance became a demand for more knowledge and expertise in intervention, in order better to balance attention to the rights of parents and to the protection of children. To this end, the press criticised the Clyde Inquiry, but in the context of a demand for another form of inquiry.

This interrogation of the public inquiry and the press as sites for and instruments in rearticulating formulae for rule demonstrates ways in which failures of governance become points for its intensification. Problems encountered in attempts to govern child sexual abuse are turned back into further attempts to achieve effective governance, so that a cycle of 'crisis' is something of an endemic feature of the ways in which we try to think about and act upon child sexual abuse.

How then do the conceptual arguments of Part I of this book, and the substantive analysis of Part II, inform one another? I would like to reflect on this by returning to the forms of engagement with contemporary problems in the governance of child sexual abuse that emerge from Habermas's and Foucault's work. Habermas presents a vivid account of the dynamics of state intervention into the family as an example of the system colonisation of the lifeworld, or, in his later formulation of this issue, as the extension of ill-founded administrative procedures into the lifeworld of subjects who are rendered passive by being denied an effective voice in decisions that affect them. This account does much to pinpoint conflicts between the families and state-sponsored professionals in the cases of Cleveland and Orkney; we can regard the actions of the paediatricians and social workers involved in these two cases as that of professionals 'colonising' the lifeworld by overstepping the limits of previous practice in their attempts to intervene with new diagnostic tools in an emerging problem for governance. Habermas's diagnosis of the problem appears to accord with the reaction of PAIN and the parents to intervention in these two cases. The pertinence of this analysis is added to when we compare Higgs's assertion that she was finding abuse that was 'there to be found' (see Chapter 6) with Habermas's comment that a fact can never, in and of itself, ground a value (see Chapter 3). As was noted in Chapter 1, conceptions of normality and abnormality are empirically *and* normatively derived.

Following from this, Habermas's account of the tendency of modern administrative welfare states to produce a technocratic reduction of both evaluative questions and empirical ones is useful in highlighting some of the problems that arose in Cleveland and Orkney. These cases can be regarded as instances in which the 'technocratic' reduction of the fact/value distinction, to which Habermas points in his discussion of the role of expertise in the operation of contemporary liberal democratic welfare states, pointedly 'fails'. That is, Cleveland and Orkney can be seen as cases in which the technocratic management of social problems through which normal practice in child protection is maintained broke down, and with it the capacity to govern. In the light of our discussion of Cleveland and Orkney, therefore, Habermas's diagnosis of the problems attending public interventions into the family has some weight. What happens if we take up Habermas's suggestions for the resolution of these problems?

At this point it is useful to compare the Cleveland Inquiry's negotiation of expertise with the suggestion, made by Habermas, that democratic delimitation of the power of experts would resolve the ambivalences attending the welfare state by tying expert intervention directly to discursively sanctioned courses of action. We can note that the inquiry's demand for impartiality on the part of experts, and its criticism of the proactive stance of those involved, is consonant with Habermas's argument that experts should implement the law but not make it. However, whilst both the inquiry and Habermas suggest that the power of experts should be bound by rules of accountability, the inquiry asserts the need for such power to be rendered accountable to judicially constituted authority, while Habermas points to a need to bind both expert power and judicial determinations directly to democratically sanctioned norms.

The inquiry demands consensus amongst experts concerning the scientific adequacy and significance of RAD, and concerning the appropriate procedures for interviews with children, before these can be used to determine diagnoses of child sexual abuse. It works with the 'best interests' principle and moving designations of 'harm', where both are couched within a juridical framing of right. Now, in so far as the 'best interests' principle is enshrined in law we already have a ground of value for intervention into suspected cases of child sexual abuse, though not one that has been discursively constituted in Habermas's sense. Where in this context the inquiry calls for expert consensus, for better-founded 'facts', implying that well-founded knowledge appropriately deployed could ground legitimate action on the part of experts, for Habermas this is insufficient. This looks crucial. For Habermas, while well-founded knowledge is important, one cannot derive a value from a fact; values, and the actions to be taken on the basis of valuations, require discursive justification. Therefore discerning appropriate grounds for legitimate intervention cannot be achieved solely through expert agreement; from Habermas's point of view this is insufficient with regard to both the justification and the application of norms. Habermas solution would be a democratic injection into the formulation and application of laws. I want to suggest that this would not overcome the normalising power of expertise, but that it might articulate normalising forms of knowledge and power more fully into everyday assumptions and practices. This may prevent or forestall 'crises', but is within the juridical and normalising premises of existing rationalities of governance, it is not an alternative to them and is not the overcoming of normalising power.

We can explore this by comparing Foucault's and Habermas's respective analyses of the problems attending the welfare state. Both of these writers point to a juridical order being transformed by processes of administrative regulation and suggest that this poses problems. Foucault suggests that this problem has the character of an attempt to combine the city–citizen game and the shepherd–flock game within modern rationalities of rule, and that this constitutes an aporia: asking for law, or a polity comprised of juridical equals, and for order, or a society aimed at securing the well-being of its members through pastoral supervision, is similar to asking for 'lemon and milk' in one's tea (Foucault [1978b] 2001: 435–8). Habermas is more optimistic. He suggests that the problems produced by the administrative management of the population within welfare states can be put right by further democratisation of the justification and application of such management. Suggesting that the dilemmas of contemporary welfare states comprise a 'dialectic of empowerment and tutelage', he comments that:

> Built into the very status of citizenship in welfare-state democracies is the tension between a formal extension of private and civic autonomy, on the one hand, and a 'normalization', in Foucault's sense, that fosters the passive enjoyment of paternally dispensed rights, on the other.
>
> (1996: 79)

However, he goes on to suggest that 'it would be rash to describe this structure as itself *dilemmatic*' (1996: 415, emphasis in text) because 'the peculiarly ambivalent effects' of the welfare state are the product of the inadequate institutionalisation of the democratic genesis of law (1996: 42, 188). On Habermas's account, therefore, the normalising aspects of the welfare state lose their coercive power in so far as they are discursively grounded. But this eclipses the distinction between juridification and normalisation such that legitimate law is theorised as banishing power.

Foucault's argument concerning the simultaneously juridical and normalising character of modern political rationalities is not simply an argument about active versus passively dispensed rights, it is about the power of normalising judgement per se. When Habermas asserts that we can 'strip such power of its violent substance by rationalizing it' (1996: 42, 188), this eclipses the tension between law and normalisation to which Foucault points. Seen from the premises of Foucault's account of these relations, Habermas's suggestions are likely to tie individuals more thoroughly to scientific descriptions of normality and abnormality; this is not the elimination of normalising power but the refinement and finessing of this through discourse, it is a proposal that promises to democratise rather than to eliminate normalising power.[1]

To elaborate, Habermas asks for a discursive justification and application of programmes of regulatory intervention on the basis that facts cannot ground values. He proposes that the discursive justification and application of law would overcome the normalising power of expertise – but it would not. Rather, Habermas's suggestions are limiting of normalising power only in the specific and restricted sense of tying the operation of such power to democratic mechanisms. Democratising the processes through which criteria of harm and determinations of intervention are applied might refine the correspondence between expert knowledge and the subjects to which it is applied, but it would not overcome normalising power, rather it would be likely to extend it by more closely linking law to the regulatory supervision of the population.

Whilst Habermas's proposals go further than the Cleveland Inquiry by suggesting that expert interventions must be directly grounded in deliberative democratic mechanisms in order to be legitimate, both Habermas and the inquiry reiterate the terms of contemporary rationalities of rule and propose further normalisation. Both presuppose a distinction between public and private life, and assume models of childhood drawn from medicine and psychology. Both presuppose the attributes of subjects brought into being by specific practices of governance. Whilst Habermas advocates direct participation of the governed in formulating the rules governing them, this simply refines what we have got; involving the governed in their own government is central to the ways in which liberalism operates as a rationality of rule (see Rose 1996).

Habermas's suggestions thus operate within the horizon of liberalism as a rationality of rule. Recalling comments in Chapter 4, that such developments can have an important impact on ethical life, one might wonder whether this would make for even more anxious child-rearing. One might also note that Habermas's proposals promise further to de-ethicalise expertise. The ethical ground of expert cultures is to be evacuated such that expertise is ideally figured as an a-ethical enterprise that consists simply in the application of norms decided elsewhere. Habermas's suggestions bring him curiously close to being the voice of liberal administrative reason.

Perhaps it is symptomatic of liberalism that it attempts to turn tragedies into problems; a crisis of expertise guarantees a demand for more expertise in a process through which liberalism cuts itself off from the past and has always to look forward. This urge to the future is borne out nowhere more clearly than in relation to children. Yet in this technical understanding of problems the capacity for ethical debate is foreclosed by a prior determination that there should be a solution. Habermas alights on this problem, but does not escape it. This determination to hunt for solutions produces an endless reiteration of problems in which the constituent tensions of liberalism are further worked over. Perhaps at least this way of governing crises enables us to resist the notion that the problem is anything to do with more deep-seated cultural and political mores?

How should we attempt to address child sexual abuse as an issue of public concern? The purpose of this book has been to attempt to think critically about the presuppositions we make in coming to this question, and to examine the forms of knowledge and practice that we have available to deal with it. Given our assumptions about childhood, fraught with tensions though they are, we need to attempt to govern child sexual abuse. But the means we have for doing so are highly imperfect, and are likely to remain so. That this is so flows directly from the combination of juridical and normalising discourses that runs through our culture: we wish for the privacy and autonomy of families, we demand child protection and welfare, and we want determinations of guilt and innocence, all at the same time.

This book has purposefully not set out to provide proposals for the future governance of child sexual abuse, nor has it provided normative standards against which to assess particular practices of governance in this area. Rather the task has been the more modest one of attempting to hold up to question the ways in which we are governed, and to examine the limits and problems that this entails. This book has not addressed the question what we should do, but rather has engaged in a prior task of examining the tools with which we come to this question.

The reiteration of calls of 'crisis' in the governance of child sexual abuse attests to the need for this task. If we do not examine our forms of reasoning for the ways these act upon and constrain us, we are set on a course along which 'crises' in child protection are to be reiterated indefinitely. Critical reflection on the ways in which conditions of 'crisis' are already woven into our ways of conceptualising and acting upon 'the problem', whilst not delivering proposals for change (which in any case cannot properly be the task of one individual), may at least open up the possibility of doing things differently. Engaging in such reflection might provide a sounder basis on which to develop a response to the question as to how we should attempt to address child sexual abuse as an issue of public concern.

> Political technologies advance by taking what is essentially a political problem, removing it from the realm of political discourse, and recasting it in the neutral language of science. Once this is accomplished the problems have become technical ones for specialists to debate. In fact, the language of reform is, from the outset, an essential component of these political technologies. Bio-power spread under the banner of making people healthy and protecting them. When there was resistance, or failure to achieve its stated aims, this was construed as further proof of the need to reinforce and extend the power of the experts. A technical matrix was established. By definition, there ought to be a way of solving any technical problem. Once this matrix was established, the spread of bio-power was assured, for there was nothing else to appeal to; any other standards could be shown to be abnormal or to present merely technical problems. We are promised normalisation and happiness through science and law. When they fail, this only justifies more of the same.
>
> (Dreyfus and Rabinow 1982: 196)

Notes

1 Child sexual abuse as a problem of governance

1 This part of my discussion is greatly indebted to the work of Ian Hacking (1991a, 1994, 1999).
2 Hacking (1991b, 1999) discusses the ways in which concepts produce new possibilities for experience in terms of the 'looping effects of human kinds'.
3 Of course, this does not necessarily imply that action is effective in securing child protection, as documented by Laming (2003).
4 In addition to these cases, there have been a number of inquiries into allegations of maltreatment of children in residential care homes, most notably in Staffordshire (1989, the 'Pindown' affair, Levy and Kahan 1991), Gwent (1992, Williams and McCreadie 1992), Leicestershire (1991, Kirkwood 1993), and North Wales (1996, Waterhouse 2000). For an account of these cases, see Wolmar (2000). 'Institutional abuse' raises many similar issues to those taken up in this book, including a further iteration of the question whether public intervention produces more harm than good. These cases have not been focused upon here, as my concern is to examine the relationship between public intervention and the apparently private space of the family. More recently, events in Portsmouth in 2000, where the community of the Paulsgrove estate turned on alleged paedophiles in their midst, raised further questions concerning appropriate forms of public intervention to secure child protection that fall beyond the scope of this book (see Ashenden 2002; Bell 2002).
5 See Butler-Sloss (1988, Chapter 10) for an outline of legal processes and provisions current at the time, many of which have now been replaced by the Children Act 1989.
6 For more detailed discussion of the events and focus on some of the themes not elaborated here, see Asquith (1993), Bell (1988), Butler-Sloss (1988: 14–21), Campbell (1988).
7 The Children Act 1989 was ground-breaking in UK childcare law, replacing patchy statutory coverage and nineteenth century common law jurisprudence.
8 The children involved were five girls and four boys aged 8 to 15.
9 In La Fontaine's study 'specialists' were defined as 'Groups and individuals who claim particular knowledge of satanic abuse'; such 'specialists' had been involved in 62 per cent of the detailed cases of alleged ritual abuse studied (La Fontaine 1994: 20).
10 The Rochdale case involved seventeen children taken into care on the basis of social workers' beliefs that they had been ritually abused during satanic practices. The hearing following this case pin-pointed a number of procedural errors that indicated a failure to follow guidelines issued following the Cleveland Inquiry, including failure to video interviews correctly, or to take contemporaneous notes.
11 In January 1987, Mr 'W' was convicted and imprisoned for offences of physical abuse. In March 1987 this was supplemented by a list of charges of sexual abuse, for which he was in prison during 1991, when the Orkney events occurred.

12 There was a specific concern for evidence behind the separation of the children for their period in care. This involved the idea that if the children were kept separate from each other and away from their parents they would not be able to suggest things to each other, and parents would not be able to use pressure to prevent children telling of any abuse that may have occurred. However, separation did not address how the process of questioning itself can lead to the constitution of similarities in children's stories.

13 Colwell died, aged 7, through physical abuse at the hands of her stepfather. She had been returned to the care of her mother and stepfather after spending several years in the care of her aunt. Prior to her death concerns about her physical well-being had been reported to social services by neighbours and teachers (Department of Health and Social Security 1974).

14 Both RAD and X-rays require interpretation as to their meaning; the difference between X-rays and RAD as forms of evidence supporting the legitimacy of child protection measures is that the former has achieved consensus amongst practitioners in the clinical diagnosis of child abuse and is an accepted method of gaining evidence, the latter has not (see Pfohl 1977). See Latour and Woolgar (1979) on the stabilisation of scientific arguments.

15 Since the publication of Aries's book, there has been a range of historical work on childhood and family life. Anderson (1980) points to the diversity of western family forms and problems of the attempt to generalise to provide 'a' history of the western family. He identifies four approaches to this area: psychohistory (e.g. De Mause 1974), demographic approaches (e.g. Laslett 1972, 1977), sentiments approaches (e.g. Aries 1962; Flandrin 1979; Shorter 1976) and household economics approaches (e.g. Goody 1983). Each of these forms of historiography takes a different approach to the selection of problems, sources and use of evidence. Pollock (1983) and MacFarlane (1986) both offer alternative analyses to that provided by Aries.

16 Aries's original text *L'Enfant et la Vie Familiale sous l'Ancien Regime* (1960) uses the terms '*sentiment de l'enfance*' and '*sentiment familial*' which are not easy to translate into English. Baldick translates '*sentiment*' as 'idea' and 'concept', but this captures only one sense of the original meaning, which in French has both conceptual and sentimental connotations; '*notion*' and '*idee*', terms which can be more closely translated as 'idea' and 'concept', do not appear in the original text. See Wilson (1980).

17 On general problems with evidence in relation to the history of children and childhood, see Jordanova (1985, 1989) and Cunningham (1995). Historians have made a number of specific criticisms of Aries, for example in relation to his use of iconographic evidence (Jordanova 1989; Pollock 1983; Vann 1982; Wilson 1980). Aries presents iconographic material in a naïve fashion, as though it were possible simply to read off from a painting the status of childhood in a given era and social milieu. He pays no attention to developments in painting and the effects of this on the representation of children. Since Aries's book there have been more sophisticated readings of iconographic material in relation to children and families; for example see Higonnet (1998).

18 Apprenticeship, usually beginning at the age of 11 or 12, was one of the routes through which children were integrated into society through the middle ages (Cunningham 1995: 35).

19 See Hooper (1992) on the relation between feminism and social purity movements.

20 During the late nineteenth century, the first international conferences on child welfare were held, the first in Paris in 1882. 1896 saw the formation of the International Congress for the Welfare and Protection of Children (Rose 1991: 235). On the history of child protection in Britain from the New Poor Law 1834, through Victorian philanthropy to the establishment of twentieth century state-sponsored social work, see Bailey and Blackburn (1979), Corby (1993), Frost and Stein (1989), Parton and Jordan (1983), Packman (1981), Parton (1985a), Pinchbeck and Hewitt (1969, 1973). See Gittins (1985) on the family and social intervention. For recent work bringing together

the history of child health and welfare with consideration of the changing character of childhood and family see Cooter (1992), Hendrick (1990, 1994). For a discussion of the relationship between families and philanthropic organisations and the state which goes back further than the nineteenth century, see Cunningham (1995).

21 See Boswell (1988), Hanawalt (1977), Hoyles (1979), Hunt (1970), Pollock (1983), Thane (1981), Vann (1982) and Wilson (1980).

22 The same point is made by Wilson (1980) and by Pollock (1983).

23 Wilson (1980) challenges this simplistic assimilation of Aries as a theorist of 'modernisation'.

2 Dilemmas of liberalism: child, family and state through the public/private distinction

1 Nor is this a comprehensive analysis of the public/private distinction, this lies far beyond the scope of this chapter. See Benn and Gaus (1983); Boling (1996); Pateman (1988, 1989); Weintraub and Kumar (1997).

2 Kymlicka argues that the distinction drawn between public and private within liberalism is not a distinction between spheres, but a distinction between different responsibilities. He differentiates the domestic/public dichotomy from the public/ private dichotomy and argues that the former is inherited by liberalism rather than being central to it (Kymlicka 1990: 254, n 6).

3 See Gray (1989) and Macedo (1991), for recent discussions of these issues. Many of the issues discussed in this chapter are currently under intense scrutiny as the Human Rights Act, incorporated into English law in October 2000, works its way through institutions.

4 Dworkin provides a clear analytic expression of the foundational character of the public/private dichotomy within contemporary liberalism. For Dworkin this dichotomy is foundational because the concept of equality, a core principle of liberalism, requires that government be neutral with respect to diverse conceptions of the good. Government should therefore be organised around a universal framework of justice or 'right', and should neither penalise nor foster specific conceptions of the 'good' (1986: 191–2).

5 Though the idea of an inner world of conscience goes much further back than the seventeenth and eighteenth centuries in western culture, see Peter Brown (1987).

6 These differences might be specified in terms of different liberalisms' distinct justificatory strategies in natural rights arguments, Kantian constructivism, and utilitarianism. Picking up the arguments of Locke, Rawls and J.S. Mill later in this chapter we will see how, despite important differences, liberal thinkers pose a common problematic in relation to understanding childhood as a naturalised phase of dependence prior to the autonomy of adulthood and in relation to their provision of justifications for public intervention into the private sphere of the family.

7 The sovereignty of nation states took shape in the seventeenth century in response to, among other things, changing conditions of external trade. The Treaty of Westphalia (1648) established a principle of nonintervention between nation states, that is, states recognised each other as sovereign within their own territory (Hirst 1997; Spruyt 1994).

8 For an account of Locke's text as primarily directed against Filmer see Laslett's introduction to Locke's *Two Treatises* ([1967] 1988: 67–78).

9 Pateman (1988) goes further than this, arguing that a 'fraternal social contract' underpinned the shift from descending theses of political authority to accounts of political authority as founded on contract. She argues that while Locke is traditionally seen as refuting patriarchy and providing the basis for government based on equality and consent, the continued ownership and exchange of women through marriage subverts the claim of such contractarian political theory to be post-patriarchal. Instead she argues that, rather than being in opposition to patriarchy, contract is the form

through which modern patriarchy is constituted. For alternative accounts of the importance of these arguments, especially with reference to feminism, see Brown (1995) and Gobetti (1997). Gobetti in particular emphasises the ways in which developments in natural law arguments during the seventeenth century worked progressively to undermine ideas of proprietorship and absolute power in relation to persons.

10 See Dunn (1983) on common misreading of this as 'possessive individualism'.

11 The idea that liberalism articulates differently grounded spaces of rule is indebted to Valverde (1996).

12 Immediately prior to this Hobbes states:

> The Liberty of a Subject, lyeth therefore only in those things, which in regulating their actions, the Soveraign hath praetermitted: such as the Liberty to buy, and sell, and otherwise contract with one another; to choose their own aboad, their own diet, their own trade of life, and institute their children as they themselves think fit; and the like.
>
> ([1651] 1996: 148)

13 Transfer being necessary in order that Hobbes be able to arrive at a justification for absolutism from egalitarian and self-interested premises: once we have established the Leviathan we have no necessary right to resist, we have given up this right.

14 Rawls contests the idea that political liberalism is an individualist political conception, 'since its aim is the protection of the various interests in liberty, both associational and individual' ([1997] 1999: 603). However, as his own essay makes clear and as discussed later in this chapter, the individual endowed with certain basic inalienable rights is, on his account, prior to associations.

15 At least in the first instance, see below on the limits of parental authority. Liberal arguments also justify paternalism in relation to others designated 'faulty' reasoners, for example, those categorised mentally ill.

16 This formulation owes a great deal to conversations with James Brown.

17 Locke's account is a useful counterpoint to this. For Locke, freedom is the freedom of a rational individual in relation to the law of nature; from this position libertarian arguments for children's rights would appear to constitute abandonment:

> The *Freedom* then of Man and Liberty of acting according to his own Will, is *grounded on* his having *Reason*, which is able to instruct him in that Law he is to govern himself by, and make him know how far he is left to the freedom of his own will. To turn him loose to an unrestrain'd Liberty, before he has Reason to guide him, is not the allowing him the priviledge of his Nature, to be free; but to thrust him out amongst Brutes, and abandon him to a state as wretched, and as much beneath that of a Man, as theirs. This is that which puts the *Authority* into the *Parents* hands to govern the *Minority* of their Children.
>
> ([1698] 1988: II, §63, 309, emphasis in text)

Locke's argument also points up the Hobbesian character of libertarian conceptions of liberty. See Fox-Harding (1991) and Archard (1993, 1998) for contemporary critical responses to libertarian arguments.

18 Although, as already noted, in the current context parental rights of chastisement qualify this.

19 Locke continues:

> 'Let us therefore consider a *Master of a Family* with all these subordinate Relations of *Wife, Children, Servants* and *Slaves* united under the Domestick Rule of a Family; which what resemblance soever it may have in its Order, Offices, and Number too, with a little Common-wealth, yet is very far from it, both in its Constitution, Power and

End . . . the *Master of the Family* has a very distinct and differently limited *Power*, both as to time and extent, over those several Persons that are in it; for excepting the Slave . . . he has no Legislative Power of Life and Death over any of them, and none too but what a *Mistress of a Family* may have as well as he.

([1698] 1988: II, §86, 323, emphasis in text)

20 Locke oscillates between advocacy of 'parental' and 'paternal' authority (see [1698] 1988: II, §52, 303, §82, 321).

21 'A Father cannot alien the Power he has over his Child, he may perhaps to some degrees forfeit it, but cannot transfer it' (Locke [1698] 1988: I, §100, 214). A father cannot transfer his power because the child is not his property: 'The *Power of the Father doth not reach* at all to the *Property* of the Child, which is only in his own disposing.' ([1698] 1988: II, §170, 381, emphasis in text).

22 Archard takes this up to suggest that in the logic of Locke's account the state is only constrained by considerations of a child's best interests, and that this leaves wide scope for intervention depending on the definition of children's 'best interests' that is current (1993: 9–10).

23 For a discussion of the way in which Mill limits this account of liberty to a culturally specific understanding of individuals in the 'maturity of their faculties', see Valverde (1996).

24 His ideas are concomitant with the progressive legal separation of women and children from patriarchal authority in English law; see Smart (1992).

25 See O'Donovan (1985), Showstack-Sassoon (1987) and Lister (1997) for evidence that women's assumed responsibility for the family, for example, both restricts and structures the shape of their access to labour markets and to the public political sphere.

26 For example, Locke suggests that when disputes occur within a family the male head of household has authority to make decisions since man is the 'abler and the stronger' ([1698] 1988: II, §82, 321); yet both parents have relations of temporary authority over a child (a relation of trust) as they are both considered more rational and thus more autonomous than it.

3 From liberal to critical theory: child, family and state through the system/lifeworld distinction

1 Useful introductions to Critical Theory are provided by Outhwaite (1994), White (1988) and Wiggerhaus (1994).

2 Habermas argues that Weber separates his treatment of the rationalisation of purposive rational action from his investigation of cultural traditions, and therefore does not account for rationalisation in this second dimension, instead producing an overly pessimistic diagnosis of modernisation, see Habermas (1984 Chapter 2).

3 Some feminists have theorised this as a move from 'private' to 'public' patriarchy; see, for example, Hernes (1987), Walby (1990).

4 During 1987 and 1988, Marietta Higgs was depicted by the press variously as a crusading feminist and as the mother of four, see Campbell (1988).

5 PAIN advertises itself as 'Advising, counselling and supporting parents, children, family members, professional carers and others when a child is mistakenly thought to be at risk or to have been abused' (PAIN 1993). In its preface to comments on a draft guidance document on inter-agency cooperation for the protection of children, it states the following: 'PAIN has been founded by parents, who are innocent of child abuse or neglect, but have nevertheless found themselves involved in child abuse and care procedures' (1986). It publishes a range of materials on child abuse and child protection, organises workshops for practitioners, and has a resource centre of research on child abuse issues. It liaises with the media to inform the public about child care law

and policy, and is an advocate on behalf of parents, carers and children involved in child protection cases.

6 Habermas makes a consonant argument in his later work, with respect not to issues of child abuse but with regard to feminist demands for equality; see (1996: 418–27). In *The Theory of Communicative Action*, Habermas discusses feminist movements as 'struggles against patriarchal oppression' (1987a: 393), but he does not elaborate on this in terms of a concern with the privacy of familial relations.

7 Honneth notes that, subsequent to *The Theory of Communicative Action*, Habermas distinguishes 'agreement' and 'influence', suggesting that strategic action is an aspect of socially integrated action in the lifeworld; as Honneth notes, however, this is not decisive to Habermas's conceptual framework so that 'all presystemic processes of the constitution and reproduction of domination must fall out of view' (Honneth 1991: 301). In the same text, Honneth argues that this limitation is linked to Habermas's adoption of a systems theoretic perspective that is counterpoised in a dualistic manner with the communicative organisation of the lifeworld, so that both system and lifeworld are reified categories in Habermas's work. On this latter point, see also McCarthy (1985).

8 In *The Theory of Communicative Action*, Habermas had already drawn a distinction between 'law as medium' and 'law as institution', pointing in the direction of his later argument. In *Between Facts and Norms* this distinction is elaborated, but not maintained in the form originally specified, rather it is reformulated in terms of a distinction between instrumentalised law and legitimately grounded law (Habermas 1996: 562 n 48).

9 I have discussed Habermas's attempt to provide renewed legitimacy to the welfare state in more detail in Ashenden (1999).

10 This is in turn grounded in a moral theory that aims to clarify the conditions under which participants in discourses could find rational answers for themselves (Habermas 1993: 24).

11 Though for those directly interested to have decision-making power in such contexts should probably be seen as inimical to considerations of justice.

12 See Chapter 5 and Conclusion.

13 Though it is worthy of note that Dworkin (1986) makes a similar point without engaging in the strong idealising presuppositions required by Habermas's argument.

14 Habermas addresses the question of 'how autonomous the public is when it takes a position on an issue', and how far public opinion is a 'more or less concealed game of power'. He suggests that despite empirical studies, we do not know the answer to this question. He then suggests, 'But one can at least pose the question more precisely by assuming that public processes of communication can take place with less distortion the more they are left to the internal dynamic of a civil society that emerges from the lifeworld' (1996: 375). This is a huge assumption that grounds the possibility of Habermas holding on to the category difference between system and lifeworld in terms of an inside and outside of power.

15 I would like to thank David Owen for drawing my attention to the importance of Habermas's use of developmental psychology to my concerns.

16 Habermas builds on the developmental psychology of Kohlberg and Piaget to suggest a path of ego development, combining this with G.H. Mead's account of the intersubjective core of the self (1979 Chapter 2, 1992 Chapter 7). For Habermas, this is the path of individual and also of societal development: only under modern conditions of post-metaphysical reason do we, as competent participants in communicative interaction, achieve capacities for autonomous reasoning (1984 Chapter 1, Section 2, 1996: 71, 97–8, 113–18).

4 Reproblematising the governance of child sexual abuse: Foucault's practice of social criticism

1 Thanks to Paul Hirst for this formulation.

2 Foucault suggests that problematisation . . . 'doesn't mean representation of a pre-existing object, nor the creation by discourse of an object that doesn't exist' (1988c: 257).

3 'Apparatus' is one English translation of the French 'dispositif' (Gordon 1980); Dreyfus and Rabinow (1982) translate this as 'grid of intelligibility'.

4 The concept *dispositif* involves a recognition that discourses and practices are multiple and varied; consequently the task of genealogy is to uncover and specify particular sets of relations whereby specific aspects of modern subjectivity are constituted by mapping significant relations between diverse practices. Dreyfus and Rabinow clarify this in the following manner:

> *Dispositif* [. . .] encompasses the non-discursive practices as well as the discursive. It is resolutely heterogeneous, including 'discourses, institutions, architectural arrangements, regulations, laws, administrative measures, scientific statements, philosophic propositions, morality, philanthropy, etc.' [. . .] Drawing from these disparate components, one seeks to establish a set of flexible relationships and merge them into a single apparatus in order to isolate a specific historical problem. This apparatus brings together power and knowledge into a specific grid of analysis. Foucault defines *dispositif* by saying that when one has succeeded in isolating 'strategies of relations of forces supporting types of knowledge and inversely,' then one has a *dispositif.*
>
> (1982: 121)

5 O'Malley *et al.* characterise this as a 'practice of critique as a troubling of truth regimes' (1997: 507).

6 Rather than regarding genealogy as a form of nihilism, we can see genealogy as a way of overcoming nihilism, as a way of addressing the questions 'Who are we?' and 'What can we become?' without recourse to the kind of metaphysics that continues to haunt Habermas and which grounds his attempt theoretically to pre-determine the limits of reason and the practical possibilities of politics; see Owen (1995).

7 Genealogies are responses to problems in the present, but they are not presentist: past formations are not read in terms of the present or as necessary stages toward the present.

8 As against Marxist and other versions of ideology critique, where knowledge and truth are situated as the obverse of power.

9 See Chapter 3.

5 Governmentality and liberal political reason

1 Hacking (1991b) develops these ideas.

2 Foucault outlines the 'repressive hypothesis' as the assumption that modern power acts on sexuality fundamentally through the repression of 'natural instincts'.

3 Foucault argues that 'in the confession [. . .] truth and sex are joined, through the obligatory and exhaustive expression of an individual secret' (1979a: 61).

4 Nor is the concern with political rationalities a concern with processes of rationalisation understood in the sense that Habermas and a number of other social theorists use the term to designate an evolutionary process producing modern societies. Rather, Foucault's concern is with particular 'forms of rationality' (Foucault 1988a: 28) that produce grids of intelligibility that simultaneously make possible and delimit our forms of thinking and acting. Foucault's approach is clarified in an interview where he is asked about Habermas's praise concerning his description of 'the bifurcation of reason'

(1988a: 26), or the 'moment reason bifurcated' (1988a: 27). In response, Foucault takes pains to point out that his work has been concerned not with the bifurcation of reason at a particular moment, from which we can now perceive an authentic and an inauthentic relation to reason, but rather with the continuous splitting of reason and the analysis of the 'forms of rationality' to which this has given rise (Foucault 1988a: 28). Foucault clarifies the stakes of this with the following comment:

> Those who resist or rebel against a form of power cannot merely be content to denounce violence or criticize an institution. Nor is it enough to cast blame on reason in general. What has to be questioned is the form of rationality at stake. The criticism of power wielded over the mentally sick or mad cannot be restricted to psychiatric institutions; nor can those questioning the power to punish be content with denouncing prisons at total institutions. The question is: How are such relations of power rationalized? Asking it is the only way to avoid other institutions, with the same objectives and the same effects, from taking their stead.
>
> (Foucault [1979c] 2001: 324–5)

5 For Foucault the state is:

> no more than a composite reality and a mythical abstraction whose importance is a lot more limited than many of us think. Maybe what is really important for our modern times, that is for our actuality, is not so much the State-domination of society, but the 'governmentalisation ' of the State.
>
> (1979b: 20)

6 Hunter also takes issue with what he calls the 'philosophical scheme' of Foucault's treatment of liberalism in the *Governmentality* essay. He points out that Foucault's approach contains elements of a teleological narrative, for example in the suggestion that traditional mechanisms of sovereignty 'blocked' the governmental rationality that would attend population (Hunter 1998: 249).

7 Whilst Donzelot recognizes that the modern family is a site of conflict between its members, he does not draw out the tension between privacy and intervention engendered by the simultaneous recognition of the family as a juridical unit and locus and instrument of welfare.

8 All quotations from the latter text are the author's own translation.

9 Foucault suggests that nineteenth century penal mechanisms were the antithesis of eighteenth century jurisprudence; see Foucault ([1973b] 2001: 52–87). Projects such as the Gracewell Clinic, Birmingham (Wyre 1989, 1992), and other moves linking the punishment of offenders with therapeutic attempts to reform them, can be regarded as contemporary manifestations of this theme.

10 See the opening passages of Foucault (1977) for an illustration of this shift.

11 See Foucault ([1975] 1999: 135) on this as a voluntary organisation of family relations. Foucault points out the ambiguity of the notion of perversion, combining suggestions of culpability and of madness.

12 Foucault discusses in an earlier lecture in this series how, prior to this, if someone came from a 'good home' and murdered this was considered a sign of lack of reason ([1975] 1999: 17–18).

13 See Foucault (1977: 190) on the hospital as a laboratory, providing the conditions of possibility of observation and classification necessary to produce ideas of the normal.

14 For example, there is an emerging literature on 'victimology'. See Mawby and Walklate (1994).

15 See also Smart (1989), Hunt (1993) and Hunt and Wickham (1994) for alternative interpretations of Foucault on this.

16 Such a focus can be seen in current UK Government policy concerning sex offenders,

where the threat posed by such offenders within communities is seen to justify overriding their civil rights in certain prescribed ways. See Ashenden (2002).

17 Wraith and Lamb describe inquiries as, at their best, 'providing a genuine opportunity for popular participation in reaching local decisions' (1971: 354), something contested by both Wynne (1982) and Kemp (1985) in their respective analyses of the Windscale Inquiry, and by Sedley (1989) in his reflection on the role of inquiries in managing public controversy.

18 Local government inquiries have no statutory powers in the UK context.

19 Foucault discusses how the 'failures' of the prison system have been coterminous with the prison itself, describing how 'for a century and a half the prison has always been offered as its own remedy' in successive inquiries into its failures (1977: 268). That is, 'failure', rather than initiating a call to abandon the prison as a programme for the governance of its population, becomes an incentive for new efforts. In this sense, failure is part of the functioning of the prison system and of other disciplinary mechanisms, which call on themselves as their own remedy in processes that have what Foucault calls 'the element of utopian duplication' (1977: 271).

20 He suggests that whilst the inquiry as a relation to truth appeared for the first time in Ancient Greece, in the idea of witnessing, it is not until the twelfth century invention of new forms of judicial practice and procedure that the judicial inquiry emerges. See Foucault ([1973b] 2001: 42–50).

6 Reconstructing the liberal governance of child sexual abuse: the public inquiry into Cleveland (1987)

1 The Waterhouse Inquiry (2000) into abuse in children's homes is more recent but had a different focus, see Chapter 1, note 4.

2 The chapter does not focus on the problems of administration and management highlighted by the inquiry; though these were an important part of the inquiry's concerns and recommendations, see Butler-Sloss (1988).

3 The act referred to is the Children and Young Person's Act 1969.

4 The use of PSOs in Cleveland did contravene established guidelines. The proactive stance of workers in Cleveland emerged in the context of a series of child abuse 'errors' leading to child deaths during the 1980s, and can be seen as an attempt by social workers and paediatricians not to allow potentially abused children to escape their attention; see Chapter 1, also Howitt (1992).

5 For an assessment of the impact of this on the Children Act 1989, see Bainham (1990a, 1990b), Lyon and de Cruz (1993) and Fortin (1998).

6 The report comments that experts giving evidence to the inquiry:

> accepted that anal abuse may cause a range of signs, from surface skin damage, fissures, defects of anal verge, to severe lacerations, but that in our present state of knowledge, none of these in themselves, or in various clusters, establish with reasonable certainty that anal abuse has occurred. All are, or may be, open to alternative explanations. All, singularly and in various combinations were seen in the children in Cleveland in whom child sexual abuse was suspected.
>
> (Butler-Sloss 1988: 11.23, 189)

7 It is important to note that the inquiry found no evidence of routine screening for sexual abuse. It states that although RAD was given undue weight in medical examinations 'only in 18 cases out of 121 cases was it the sole physical sign and in no case was it the sole ground for the diagnosis' (ibid: 9.3.22, 165). Moreover, it states that 'in each case of a child attending hospital for "routine injuries and ailments" there were grounds in the professional judgement of the examining consultant for the investigation of the child for the possibility of sexual abuse' (ibid: 9.3.22, 165).

8 Commenting further on her approach to the diagnoses, Higgs states:

> I am not saying that I was not looking for it [RAD]. I certainly was looking in children where I thought sexual abuse was a differential diagnosis of their presenting problem, . . . if children present to me and I find evidence of sexual abuse then I cannot ignore it. The numbers are very worrying I agree . . . I think the sign itself is a very important sign. I believe it is a good indicator of sexual abuse and that is the diagnosis that we need to look into very carefully.
>
> (Butler-Sloss 1988: 8.8.61, 141)

9 According to the report, three factors gave Higgs disproportionate authority and produced the social workers' over-reliance on her judgement: meeting in Sue Richardson someone with shared views on the prevalence and seriousness of sexual abuse; social workers' statutory duties to protect children given firm diagnoses by a doctor; and the support of Mr Bishop for Higgs's view of the management of the cases (ibid: 8.8.77: 144).

10 The report does not take issue with the work at GOS, and comments that in any case in a high proportion of cases seen at this clinic 'there was clear evidence of abuse' (ibid: 12.21, 206).

11 There has been a great deal of work in the last decade to change the laws of evidence in criminal trials in order to enable younger children to act as witnesses and to make giving evidence less traumatising for children. As a result of the Pigot Committee's proposals (Pigot Committee 1989), video-recorded interviews have, since 1992, been allowed as evidence in chief in criminal trials in England. However, the Criminal Justice Act 1991, which effected these changes, left unchanged the provision of the Criminal Justice Act 1988 under which children still have to be available for oral cross-examination, sometimes behind screens or via television links to the court. The Pigot Committee found that young children were no more likely to give inaccurate or untruthful evidence than older witnesses (1989: 48).

12 This criticised outcome of disclosure or denial, failing to consider the possibility that abuse had not taken place, is similar to a range of criticisms of Masson's critique of Freud's work (see Malcolm 1985; Masson 1985; Miller 1985; Scott 1988). In a similar way to the way in which Masson closes interpretive options by using a flat, empiricist/physicalist definition of meaning (the idea that something must empirically have happened for there to be trauma) the disclosure interview appears to be predicated on a politics of the 'real event' (Scott 1988) and an inquisitorial process in which the subject (here a child) is assumed guilty (here abused), thus producing this as an outcome. In the dispute over disclosure interviews in Cleveland, one group close around the fact that something 'must' have happened and focus on denying the denial, the other staunchly deny the possibility of abuse – in this there is little room to consider the meaning of children's experiences and fantasy life. The inquiry attempts to negotiate this by stating that workers should listen to, but not necessarily believe, the child.

13 With regard to Cleveland it is important to note a reversal to the normal order of proof. The idea that the uncorroborated testimony of the alleged victim constitutes the 'gold standard' in assessing whether a child has been sexually abused reverses judicial preference for corroborative evidence in favour of the subject's own truth as a victim.

14 There are obvious links here with Foucault's analysis of the constitution of psychiatry through the claim to expertise in the detection of monomania ([1975] 1999). In this case, the inquiry plays an important role in encouraging the constitution of a new domain of expertise in the analysis of children's statements.

15 In this respect the child is viewed as a rational being capable of autonomous choice; however, this notion of the child is not always sustained in the report.

16 Following the Children Act 1989, police officers also have specific powers to protect children in emergency situations.

17 The test of 'real possibility' is lower than the standard of proof of 'balance of probability' (Butler-Sloss 1988: 16.45, 232).

18 See also Watson (1994) for an analysis of how the functions of law and order are combined within modern policing. Policing and social work practices both involve elements of discipline and normalisation, though they centre on different objects of government – the abuser and the abused child, respectively.

19 Such research is ongoing in a number of contexts. For examples, see Gobert 1992; Murray and Gough 1991; Sinason 1994; Spencer 1990; Spencer and Flin 1990.

7 Rearticulating the liberal governance of child sexual abuse: the press and Orkney 1991

1 The Orkney Inquiry (Clyde 1992) did not have the same impact as the Cleveland Inquiry with regard to child-care legislation and the issues concerned were extensively reported in press coverage.

2 For such analyses see work by the Glasgow University Media Group, in particular Kitzinger and Henderson (1991a, 1991b) and Kitzinger and Skidmore (1994).

3 Presentation of press coverage here includes page numbers for articles drawn from the *Daily Mail* and *The Scotsman* but not for *The Times*; CD Rom was used to gather *Times* reports and this does not provide page numbers.

4 La Fontaine, investigating the problem of organised abuse in England and Wales on behalf of the Department of Health, found no evidence of 'satanic' abuse in the period covered (1987–91), but several substantiated cases of 'ritual' abuse; however, she notes that 'in these cases the ritual was secondary to the sexual abuse which clearly formed the primary objective of the perpetrators' (La Fontaine 1994: 30).

5 A note on press representations of childhood is important at this point. Within press reporting, childhood is often presented as a time of innocence and dependence, requiring protection. However, along with the assumption of childhood innocence go three accompanying and contradictory notions: first, that children are or should be bearers of rights; second, that they are inherently suggestible, unreliable, more liable to fantasy and suggestive 'brainwashing' than adults; and third, that childhood is a corrupted condition that is a potential threat to social order. The latter conception has recently been articulated in press responses to the murder of James Bulger by Robert Thompson and Jon Venables, then aged 10, in England in 1993. Bulger's killers were widely represented by the press as monsters. See King (1997 Chapter 5); Scraton (1997); Diduck (1999). These contrary notions of childhood produce a situation in which the press criticise social workers for accepting children's statements, yet at the same time focus on the child as a bearer of rights denied in the denial of the right to attend panel hearings.

6 This theme is echoed in the *Daily Mail*, where coverage of the Orkney events coincides and competes with coverage of both the Gulf War and an explosion of concern over what the paper calls 'virgin births' – women outside relationships with men requesting artificial insemination. The first theme provides a picture of women and children waiting for men to come home from the conflict, the latter is constituted as a 'scare' story that the *Daily Mail* suggests is a threat to the institution of the family as 'we' know it. Both conjure potent images of 'the normal family' that reverberate with its coverage of Orkney.

7 Such interrogation techniques would be dismissed as 'oppressive' under s. 76 of the Police and Criminal Evidence Act 1984.

8 It is worth reflecting briefly on the similarities between the forms of reasoning employed by the social workers in Orkney and those concerned with the trial of witches in sixteenth and seventeenth century Europe:

The prevailing view of the writers of witchcraft manuals in the sixteenth and

> seventeenth centuries was that witchcraft was '*crimen exceptum*' because the difficulty of establishing guilt and the Satanic power behind the accused meant that normal rules of evidence and court procedure need not apply.
>
> (*Larner* 1980: 49)

The similarity with Orkney is especially borne out in terms of social workers' certainty concerning the veracity of the allegations, based on the similarity of children's statements; the assumption that, as children are saying the same things, these statements must be true. A similar circularity occurred during the witch-hunts of the sixteenth and seventeenth centuries, whereby those engaged in hunting witches transported ideas concerning 'signs' of maleficence to different contexts, then 'finding' similar acts of witchcraft in these different locations (Boyer and Nissenbaum 1974; Langbein 1976; Larner 1980, 1981; Peters 1978;). In Orkney, social workers appear to have overlooked the ways in which their own assumptions could produce such similarities, producing 'evidence' that perhaps had less to do with events than with the professional literature. The implications of this become even more grotesque when we note the assumptions of some of those involved in the treatment of child abusers; for example, Wyre has suggested that the criminal prosecution of abusers could be made less difficult, and certainly less traumatic for children, through eliciting confessions from alleged abusers and that this might take place within a therapeutic context (Wyre 1992).

9 On the other hand, a social worker involved, Michelle Miller, is reported stating that she 'believed they [the children] were still at risk. [. . .] "I think the risks have not been either addressed or the allegations discredited and, therefore, they must be outstanding"' (*The Times* 13.9.91). From this position law is seen rather differently, not as a source of objectivity but as a crucial site on which power relations are played out, with the parents' legal representatives using their legal knowledge to overpower the March hearing in a manner not appropriate to the context and effectively leaving the case beyond debate:

> Mrs Miller was questioned about the children's hearing on March 25th which, she said, had become uncontrollable. The parent's legal representatives were out of place at such a hearing, she said. 'They behaved in such a way that showed their expertise in terms of their legal professionalism and overwhelmed the panel members. They were using their legal jargon in a way one might expect them to behave in a court, in a setting that was not appropriate,' she said. Nigel Mann, QC, for the parents, asked her, 'should members of the public not be allowed to know what is going on in the name of the law?' Mrs Miller replied: 'I don't think they did know what was going on in the name of the law, they knew only the press's interpretation of the families' side of what was going on.'
>
> (*The Times* 13.9.91)

10 For an exact account of the remit and the limitations placed upon the inquiry, see Clyde (1992: 1.3, 1.10, 2, 4).

11 In this context comes a report of a call from the British Association for Social Work for an end to expensive inquiries, in an argument that they lead to public complacency, act as political pressure valves, and that the money spent on them would be better spent on providing services (*The Scotsman* 10.4.92, 12). This report stresses that 'It [BASW] wants to control the profession and handle complaints through a self-governing General Social Work Council [arguing that this would . . .] give a more considered response to problems' (*The Scotsman*: 10.4.92, 12).

Conclusion

1 This point draws on Dean's analysis of Habermas's work as an attempt to 'normalize democracy':

> Medicine is no less normalising when norms of health are derived from discursive contestation and the testing of existing medical models by citizens, social movements and other health professionals, than when they are simply imposed by medical experts alone. We might prefer one regime to another and even be able to elaborate grounds for that preference. But we don't need to fool ourselves that because we can raise questions about the validity of medical norms and force medical expertise to become discursive (in Habermas' normative sense of the word), we have escaped the power of the norm. Notions of accountability, transparency, democratic contestability, dialogue and so on are internal to the contemporary transformation of expertise, not to its overcoming.
>
> (Dean 1999c: 188)

Bibliography

Anderson, M. (1980) *Approaches to the History of the Western Family, 1500–1914*, London: Macmillan.

Archard, D. (1993) *Children: Rights and Childhood*, London: Routledge.

—— (1998) *Sexual Consent*, Boulder, CO: Westview Press.

Aries, P. (1962) *Centuries of Childhood: A Social History of Family Life*, trans. R. Baldick, New York: Jonathan Cape.

Armstrong, D. (1983) *Political Anatomy of the Body*, Cambridge: Cambridge University Press.

Arthurs, H.W. (1985) *Without the Law: Administrative Justice and Legal Pluralism in Nineteenth Century England*, Toronto: University of Toronto Press.

Ashenden, S. (1999) 'Habermas on discursive consensus: rethinking the welfare state in the face of cultural pluralism', in P. Chamberlayne, A. Cooper, R. Freeman, M. Rustin (eds) *Welfare and Culture in Europe*, London: Jessica Kingsley.

—— (2002) 'Policing perversion: the contemporary governance of paedophilia', *Cultural Values* 6 (1&2): 197–222.

Asquith, S. (1993) *Protecting Children – Cleveland to Orkney: More Lessons to Learn?*, Edinburgh: HMSO.

Bailey, V. and Blackburn, S. (1979) 'The Punishment of Incest Act: a case study of law creation', *Criminal Law Review* (November) 708–18.

Bainham, A. (1990a) *Children: The New Law: The Children Act 1989*, Bristol: Jordan.

—— (1990b) 'Privatization of the Public Interest in Children', *Modern Law Review* 53(2): 206–21.

—— (1991) 'Care after 1991 – a reply', *The Journal of Child Law* (April/June), 99–104.

Barrett, M. and McIntosh, M. (1982) *The Anti-Social Family*, London: NLB.

Bauman, Z. (1989) *Modernity and the Holocaust*, Cambridge: Polity Press.

Beck, U. (1992) *Risk Society*, London: Sage.

Bell, S. (1988) *When Salem Came to the Boro: The True Story of the Cleveland Child Abuse Crisis*, London: Pan Books.

Bell, V. (1993a) *Interrogating Incest: Feminism, Foucault and the Law*, London: Routledge.

Bell, V. (1993b) 'Governing childhood: neo-liberalism and the law', *Economy and Society* 22 (3): 390–405.

Bell, V. (2002) 'The vigilant(e) parent and the paedophile: the News of the World campaign 2000 and the contemporary governmentality of child sexual abuse', *Feminist Theory* 3(1): 83–102.

Bellamy, R. (1992) *Liberalism and Modern Society*, Cambridge: Polity Press.

Bellingham, B. (1988) 'The history of childhood since the "invention of childhood": some issues in the eighties', *Journal of Family History* 13(2): 347–58.

Benhabib, S. (1986) *Critique, Norm and Utopia: A Study in the Normative Foundations of Critical Theory*, New York: Columbia University Press.

—— (1992) *Situating the Self: Gender, Community and Postmodernism in Contemporary Ethics*, Cambridge: Polity Press.

—— (ed.) (1996) *Democracy and Difference: Contesting the Boundaries of the Political*, Princeton: Princeton University Press.

Benn, S.I. and Gaus G.F. (1983) *Public and Private in Social Life*, London: Croom Helm.

Bennett, F., Campbell, B. and Coward, R. (1981) 'Feminists – the degenerates of the social?', in *Politics and Power 3*, London: Routledge and Kegan Paul.

Berry, C. (1997) *Social Theory of the Scottish Enlightenment*, Edinburgh: Edinburgh University Press.

Boling, P. (1996) *Privacy and the Politics of Intimate Life*, Ithaca: Cornell University Press.

Boswell, J. (1988) *The Kindness of Strangers: the Abandonment of Children in Western Europe from Late Antiquity to the Renaissance*, Harmondsworth: Penguin.

Bowlby, J. (1951) *Maternal Care and Mental Health*, Geneva: World Health Organization.

Boyd, A. (1991) *Blasphemous Rumours: Is Satanic Ritual Abuse Fact or Fantasy? An Investigation*, London: Harper Collins.

Boyer, P. and Nissenbaum, S. (1974) *Salem Possessed*, Harvard: Harvard University Press.

Brown, P. (1987) *The Body and Society*, London: Faber.

Burchell, G. (1993) 'Liberal government and techniques of the self', *Economy and Society* 22(3): 267–282.

Butler, J. (1990) *Gender Trouble: Feminism and the Subversion of Identity*, London: Routledge.

Butler-Sloss, E. (1988) *Report of the Inquiry into Child Abuse in Cleveland 1987*, London: HMSO, Cmnd 412.

—— (1993) 'From Cleveland to Orkney', in Asquith (ed.) *Protecting Children – Cleveland to Orkney: More Lessons to Learn?* Edinburgh: HMSO.

Campbell, B. (1988) *Unofficial Secrets: Child Sexual Abuse – The Cleveland Case*, London: Virago.

—— (1991) 'From dangerousness to risk', in G. Burchell, C. Gordon, and P. Miller (eds) *The Foucault Effect: Studies in Governmentality*, Hemel Hempstead: Harvester Wheatsheaf.

Clarke, J. (ed.) (1993) *A Crisis in Care? Challenges to Social Work*, London: Sage.

Clyde, J. (1992) *The Report of the Inquiry into the Removal of Children from Orkney in February 1991*, Edinburgh: HMSO.

Collini, S. (1979) *Liberalism and Sociology: L.T. Hobhouse and Political Argument in England 1880–1914*, Cambridge: Cambridge University Press.

Cooter, R. (ed.) (1992) *In the Name of the Child: Health and Welfare, 1880–1940*, London: Routledge.

Corby B. (1993) *Child Abuse: Towards a Knowledge Base*, Buckingham: Open University Press.

Cunningham, H. (1995) *Children and Childhood in Western Society since 1500*, London: Longman.

D'Agostino, F. (1998) 'Two conceptions of autonomy', *Economy and Society* 27(1): 28–49.

Dean, M. and Hindess, B. (1998) 'Introduction: government, liberalism, society', in M. Dean and B. Hindess (eds) *Governing Australia: Studies in Contemporary Ratonalities of Government*, Cambridge: Cambridge University Press.

Dean, M. (1996) 'Putting the technological into government', *History of the Human Sciences* 9(3): 47–68.

—— (1999a) *Governmentality*, London: Sage.

—— (1999b) 'Risk, calculable and incalculable', in D. Lupton (ed.) *Risk and Sociocultural Theory*, Cambridge: Cambridge University Press.

—— (1999c) 'Normalising democracy: Foucault and Habermas on democracy, liberalism and law', in S. Ashenden and D. Owen (eds) *Foucault contra Habermas: Recasting the Dialogue Between Genealogy and Critical Theory*, London: Sage.

Department of Health and Social Security (1974) *Report of the Committee of Inquiry into the Care and Supervision Provided in Relation to Maria Colwell*, London: HMSO.

Department of Health (1991a) *Working Together under the Children Act 1989*, London: HMSO.

Department of Health (1991b) *Child Abuse. A Study of Inquiry Reports 1980–89*, London: HMSO.

De Mause, L. (ed.) (1974) *The History of Childhood*, New York: Psychohistory Press.

Diduck, A. (1999) 'Justice and childhood: reflections on refashioned boundaries', in M. King (ed.) *Moral Agendas for Children's Welfare*, London: Routledge.

Dominelli, L. (1986) 'Father–daughter incest: patriarchy's shameful secret', *Critical Social Policy* 16: 8–22.

Donzelot, J. (1979) *The Policing of Families*, trans. R. Hurley, London: Hutchinson.

Dreyfus, H.L. and Rabinow, P. (1982) *Michel Foucault: Beyond Structuralism and Hermeneutics*, Hemel Hempstead: Harvester Wheatsheaf.

Droisen, A. and Driver, E. (1989) *Child Sexual Abuse: Feminist Perspectives*, Basingstoke: Macmillan.

Dunn, J. (1983) 'From applied theology to social analysis: the break between John Locke and the Scottish Enlightenment', in I. Hont and M. Ignatieff (eds) *Wealth and Virtue: The Shaping of Political Economy in the Scottish Enlightenment*, Cambridge: Cambridge University Press.

Dworkin, R. (1986) *A Matter of Principle*, Oxford: Clarendon Press.

Eekelaar, J. (1984) *Family Law and Social Policy*, London: Weidenfeld and Nicolson.

Elshtain, J.B. (1981) *Public Man, Private Woman*, Oxford: Martin Robertson.

—— (1982) *The Family in Political Thought*, Brighton: Harvester.

—— (1997) 'The displacement of politics', in J. Weintraub and K. Kumar (eds) *Public and Private in Thought and Practice: Perspectives on a Grand Dichotomy*, Chicago: Chicago University Press.

Farson, R. (1978) *Birthrights*, Harmondsworth: Penguin.

Feminist Review (1988) 'Family secrets: child sexual abuse', Special Issue, Spring: 28.

Finkelhor, D. (1984) *Child Sexual Abuse: New Theory and Research*, New York: Free Press.

Flandrin, J.L. (1979) *Families in Former Times: Kinship, Household and Sexuality*, trans. R. Southern, Cambridge: Cambridge University Press.

Flax, J. (1990) *Thinking Fragments: Psychoanalysis, Feminism and Postmodernism in the Contemporary West*, Berkeley: University of California Press.

Fortin, J. (1998) *Children's Rights and the Developing Law*, London: Butterworths.

—— (1973a) *The Birth of the Clinic: An Archaeology of Medical Perception*, trans. A.M. Sheridan, London: Tavistock.

—— ([1973b] 2001) 'Truth and juridical forms', in J. D. Faubion (ed.) *Michel Foucault – Power: The Essential Works of Foucault, vol. 3*, trans. R. Hurley *et al.*, London: Penguin.

—— ([1975] 1999) *Les Anormaux: Cours au Collge de France 1974–1975*, F. Ewald and A. Fontana (eds), Paris: Seuil/Gallimard.

—— (1977) *Discipline and Punish: The Birth of the Prison*, trans. A.M. Sheridan-Smith, Harmondsworth: Penguin.

—— (1978a) 'About the concept of the "dangerous individual" in 19th-century legal psychiatry', trans. A. Baudot and J. Couchman, *International Journal of Law and Psychiatry* 1: 1–18.

—— (1978b) 'Lemon and milk', in J. D. Faubion (ed.) *Michel Foucault – Power: The Essential Works of Foucault, vol. 3*, trans. R. Hurley *et al.*, London: Penguin.

—— (1979a) *The History of Sexuality Volume 1: An Introduction*, trans. R. Hurley, Harmondsworth: Penguin.

—— (1979b) 'Governmentality', trans. P. Pasquino, *Ideology and Consciousness* 6: 5–21.

—— ([1979c] 2001) '*"Omnes et singulatum"*: toward a critique of political reason', in J. D. Faubion (ed.), *Michel Foucault – Power: The Essential Works of Foucault, vol. 3*, trans. R. Hurley *et al.*, London: Penguin.

—— (1980a) 'Two lectures', in C. Gordon (ed.) *Power/Knowledge: Selected Writings 1972–1977*, trans. C. Gordon, L. Marshall, J. Meplam and K. Soper, Hemel Hempstead: Harvester Press.

—— (1980b) 'Truth and power', in C. Gordon (ed.) *Power/Knowledge: Selected Writings 1972–1977*, trans. C. Gordon, L. Marshall, J. Meplam and K. Soper, Hemel Hempstead: Harvester Press.

—— (1980c) 'The confession of the flesh', in C. Gordon (ed.) *Power/Knowledge: Selected Writings 1972–1977*, trans. C. Gordon, L. Marshall, J. Meplam and K. Soper, Hemel Hempstead: Harvester Press.

—— (1980d) 'The politics of health in the eighteenth century', in C. Gordon (ed.) *Power/Knowledge: Selected Writings 1972–1977*, trans. C. Gordon, L. Marshall, J. Meplam and K. Soper, Hemel Hempstead: Harvester Press.

—— (1982a) 'The subject and power', in H. Dreyfus and P. Rabinow, *Michel Foucault: Beyond Structuralism and Hermeneutics*, trans. L. Sawyer, Brighton: Harvester Press.

—— (1982b) 'Is it really important to think?' *Philosophy and Social Criticism* 9(1): 31–5.

—— (1984a) 'What is enlightenment?', in P. Rabinow (ed.) *The Foucault Reader*, trans. C. Porter, Harmondsworth: Penguin.

—— (1984b) 'Nietzsche, genealogy, history', in P. Rabinow (ed.) *The Foucault Reader*, Harmondsworth: Penguin.

—— (1984c) 'Polemics, politics, and problematizations: an interview with Michel Foucault', in P. Rabinow (ed.) *The Foucault Reader*, trans. Lydia Davis, Harmondsworth: Penguin.

—— (1988a) 'Critical theory/intellectual history', in L. D. Kritzman (ed.) *Politics, Philosophy, Culture: Interviews and Other Writings 1977–1984*, trans. J. Harding, London: Routledge.

—— (1988b) 'Practicing criticism', in L. D. Kritzman (ed.) *Politics, Philosophy, Culture: Interviews and Other Writings 1977–1984*, trans. A. Sheridan, London: Routledge.

—— (1988c) 'The concern for truth', in L. D. Kritzman (ed.) *Politics, Philosophy, Culture: Interviews and Other Writings 1977–1984*, trans. A. Sheridan, London: Routledge.

—— (1988d) 'The political technology of individuals', in L. Martin *et al.* (eds) *Technologies of the Self: A Seminar with Michel Foucault*, London: Tavistock.

—— (1988e) 'Social security', in L. D. Kritzman (ed.) *Politics, Philosophy, Culture: Interviews and Other Writings 1977–1984*, trans. A. Sheridan, London: Routledge.

—— (1988f) 'Politics and reason', in L. D. Kritzman (ed.) *Politics, Philosophy, Culture: Interviews and Other Writings 1977–1984*, trans. A. Sheridan, London: Routledge.

—— (1989a) 'Space, knowledge and power', in S. Lotringer (ed.) *Foucault Live: Collected Interviews, 1961–1984*, trans. C. Hubert, New York: Semiotext(e).

—— (1989b) 'Problematics', in S. Lotringer (ed.) *Foucault Live: Collected Interviews, 1961–1984*, trans. L. Hochroth and J. Johnston, New York: Semiotext(e).

—— (1989c) 'The ethics of the concern for self', in S. Lotringer (ed.) *Foucault Live: Collected Interviews, 1961–1984*, trans. J. Johnston, New York: Semiotext(e).

—— (1991) 'Questions of method', in G. Burchell, C. Gordon, and P. Miller (eds) *The Foucault Effect: Studies in Governmentality*, Hertfordshire: Harvester Wheatsheaf.

—— (1994) 'Foucault, Michel, 1926–', in G. Gutting (ed.) *The Cambridge Companion to Foucault*, trans. C. Porter, Cambridge: Cambridge University Press.

—— (1992) *The Use of Pleasure – The History of Sexuality Volume 2*, trans. R. Hurley, London: Penguin.

—— (2000a) 'The Abnormals', in P. Rabinow (ed.) *Michel Foucault – Ethics: Essential Works of Foucault 1954–1984, vol. 1*, trans. R. Hurley *et al.*, London: Penguin.

—— (2000b) 'The Birth of biopolitics', in P. Rabinow (ed.) *Michel Foucault – Ethics: Essential Works of Foucault 1954–1984, vol. 1*, trans. R. Hurley *et al.*, London: Penguin.

Fox-Harding, L. (1991) *Perspectives in Child Care Policy*, London: Longman.

Franklin, B. (ed.) (1986) *The Rights of Children*, Oxford: Basil Blackwell.

Fraser, N. (1989) *Unruly Practices: Power, Discourse and Gender in Contemporary Social Theory*, Cambridge: Polity Press.

Fraser, N. and Nicholson, L. (1988) 'Social criticism without philosophy: an encounter between feminism and postmodernism', *Theory, Culture and Society* 5: 373–94.

Frost, N. and Stein, M. (1989) *The Politics of Child Welfare*, Hemel Hempstead: Harvester Wheatsheaf.

Ginsburg, N. (1992) *Divisions of Welfare*, London: Sage.

Gittins, D. (1985) *The Family in Question: Changing Households and Family Ideologies*, Basingstoke: Macmillan.

Gobert, J. (1992) 'The testimony of child victims of sexual abuse – the view from America', *Journal of Child Law* (January) 30–2.

Gobetti, D. (1997) 'Humankind as a system: Private and public agency at the origins of modern liberalism', in J. Weintraub and K. Kumar (eds) *Public and Private in Thought and Practice: Perspectives on a Grand Dichotomy*, Chicago: Chicago University Press.

Goody, J. (1983) *The Development of the Family and Marriage in Europe*, Cambridge: Cambridge University Press.

Gordon, C. (1980) 'Afterword', in C. Gordon (ed.) *Power/Knowledge: Selected Writings 1972–1977*, Hemel Hempstead: Harvester Press.

—— (1991) 'Governmental rationality: an introduction', in C. Burchell, C. Gordon, and P. Miller (eds) *The Foucault Effect: Studies in Governmentality*, Hemel Hempstead: Harvester Wheatsheaf.

—— (2001) 'Introduction', in J. D. Faubion (ed.) *Michel Foucault – Power: The Essential Works of Foucault, vol. 3*, trans. R. Hurley *et al.*, London: Penguin.

Granshaw, L. and Porter, R. (ed.) (1989) *The Hospital in History*, London: Routledge.

Gray, J. (1989) *Liberalisms: Essays in Political Philosophy*, London: Routledge.

—— (1995) *Liberalism*, 2nd edn, Buckingham: Open University Press.

Gregory, J. and Miller, S. (1998) *Science in Public: Communication, Culture and Credibility*, Cambridge, MA: Persens Publishing.

Habermas, J. ([1968] 1989) *The Structural Transformation of the Public Sphere: An Inquiry into a Category of Bourgeois Society*, trans. T. Burger and F. Lawrence, Cambridge: Polity Press.

—— (1976) *Legitimation Crisis*, trans. T. McCarthy, London: Heinemann.

—— (1979) *Communication and the Evolution of Society*, trans. T. McCarthy, London: Heinemann.

—— (1984) *The Theory of Communicative Action Volume 1: Reason and the Rationalization of Society*, trans. T. McCarthy, Boston: Beacon Press.

—— (1985) 'Questions and counter questions', in J. Bernstein (ed.) *Habermas and Modernity*, Cambridge: Polity Press.

—— (1987a) *The Theory of Communicative Action Volume 2: Lifeworld and System*, trans. T. McCarthy, Cambridge: Polity Press.

—— (1987b) *The Philosophical Discourse of Modernity: Twelve Lectures*, trans. F. Lawrence, Cambridge: Polity Press.

—— (1992) *Postmetaphysical Thinking*, trans. W. M. Hohengarten, Cambridge: Polity Press.

—— (1993) *Justification and Application*, trans. C. Cronin, Cambridge: Polity Press.

—— (1996) *Between Facts and Norms: Contributions to a Discourse Theory of Law and Democracy*, trans. W. Rehg, Cambridge: Polity Press.

Hacking, I. (1990) *The Taming of Chance*, Cambridge: Cambridge University Press.

—— (1991a) 'The making and molding of child abuse', *Critical Inquiry* (Winter) 17: 253–88.

—— (1991b) 'How should we do, the history of statistics?', in G. Burchell, C. Gordon, and P. Miller (eds) *The Foucault Effect: Studies in Governmentality*, Hemel Hempstead: Harvester Wheatsheaf.

—— (1994) 'Memoro-politics, trauma and the soul', *History of the Human Sciences* 7(2): 29–52.

—— (1999) *The Social Construction of What?* Cambridge, MA: Harvard University Press.

Hallett, C. (1989) 'Child abuse inquiries and public policy', in Stevenson, O. (ed.) *Child Abuse: Public Policy and Professional Practice*, Hemel Hempstead: Harvester Wheatsheaf.

Hanawalt, B. (1977) 'Childrearing among the lower classes of late medieval England', *Journal of Interdisciplinary History* 8: 1–22.

Hareven, T. (1987) 'Family history at the crossroads', *Journal of Family History* 12(1–3): ix–xxiii.

Harris, J. (1982) 'The political status of children', in K. Graham (ed.) *Contemporary Political Philosophy: Radical Studies*, Cambridge: Cambridge University Press.

Hendrick, H (1990) 'Constructions and reconstructions of British childhood: An interpretative survey, 1800 to the present', in A. James and A. Prout (eds) *Constructing and Reconstructing Childhood*, Brighton: Falmer.

—— (1994) *Child Welfare: England 1872–1989*, London: Routledge.

Hernes, H. (1987) 'Women and the welfare state: the transition from private to public dependence', in A. Showstack Sassoon (ed.) *Women and the State*, London: Hutchinson.

Higonnet, A (1998) *Pictures of Innocence: The History and Crisis of Ideal Childhood*, London: Thames and Hudson.

Hindess, B. (1996a) 'Liberalism, socialism and democracy: variations on a governmental theme', in A. Barry, T. Osborne, and N. Rose (eds) *Foucault and Political Reason: Liberalism, Neo-liberalism and Rationalities of Government*, London: UCL Press.

—— (1996b) *Discourses of Power: From Hobbes to Foucault*, Oxford: Blackwell.

—— (1997) *From Statism to Pluralism: Democracy, Civil Society and Global Politics*, London: UCL Press.

Hobbes, T. ([1651] 1996) *Leviathan*, R. Tuck (ed.), Cambridge: Cambridge University Press.

Holt (1975) *Escape from Childhood: The Needs and Rights of Children*, Harmondsworth: Penguin.

Hont, I. and Ignatieff, M. (eds) (1983) *Wealth and Virtue: The Shaping of Political Economy in the Scottish Enlightenment*, Cambridge: Cambridge University Press.

Honneth, A. (1991) *The Critique of Power: Reflective Stages in a Critical Social Theory*, trans. K. Baynes, Cambridge, MA: MIT Press.

Hooper, C. (1992) 'Child sexual abuse and the regulation of women: variations on a theme', in C. Smart (ed.) *Regulating Womanhood: Historical Essays on Marriage, Motherhood and Sexuality*, London: Routledge.

Howitt, D. (1992) *Child Abuse Errors: When Good Intentions Go Wrong*, Hemel Hempstead: Harvester Wheatsheaf.

Hoyles, M. (1979) 'Childhood in historical perspective', in M. Hoyles (ed.) *Changing Childhood*, London: Writers and Readers Publishing Cooperative.

Hunt, A. (1993) *Explorations in Law and Society: Toward a Constitutive Theory of Law*, London: Routledge.

Hunt, A. and Wickham, G. (1994) *Foucault and Law: Towards a Sociology of Law as Governance*, London: Pluto Press.

Hunt, D. (1970) *Parents and Children in History: the Psychology of Family Life in Early Modern France*, New York: Harper Row.

Hunter, M. (1998) 'Uncivil society: liberal government and the deconfessionalisation of politics' in M. Dean and B. Hindess (eds) *Governing Australia: Studies in Contemporary Ratonalities of Government*, Cambridge: Cambridge University Press.

Johnson, N. (1987) *The Welfare State in Transition: The Theory and Practice of Welfare Pluralism*, Brighton: Wheatsheaf.

Jordanova (1985) 'Fantasy and history in the study of childhood', *Free Associations: Psychoanalysis, Groups, Politics, Culture 2*, London: Free Association Books.

Jordanova, L. (1989) 'Children in history: concepts of nature and society', in G. Scarre (ed.) *Children, Parents and Politics*, Cambridge: Cambridge University Press.

Keenan, T. (1987) 'The "Paradox" of knowledge and power: Reading Foucault on a bias', *Political Theory* 15(1): 5–37.

Keeton, G.W. (1960) *Trial by Tribunal: A Study of the Development and Functioning of the Tribunal of Inquiry*, London: Museum Press.

Kelman, M. (1991) 'Reasonable evidence of reasonableness', *Critical Inquiry* 17: 798–817.

Kemp, R. (1985) 'Planning, public hearings and the politics of discourse', in J. Forrester (ed.) *Critical Theory and Public Life*, Cambridge, MA: MIT Press.

King, M. (1997) *A Better World for Children?* London: Routledge.

Kirkwood, A. (1993) *The Leicestershire Inquiry 1992*, Leicester: Leicestershire County Council.

Kitzinger, J. and Henderson, L. (1991a) 'The press coverage of Orkney', Report prepared for the Orkney Judicial Inquiry, Glasgow University Media Group.

Kitzinger, J. and Henderson, L. (1991b) 'The television news coverage of Orkney', Report prepared for the Orkney Judicial Inquiry, Glasgow University Media Group.

Kitzinger, J. and Skidmore, P. (1994) 'Playing safe: media coverage of child sexual abuse prevention strategies', *Child Abuse Review*

Kymlicka, W. (1990) *Contemporary Political Philosophy: An Introduction*, Oxford: Clarendon Press.

La Fontaine, J. (1990) *Child Sexual Abuse*, Cambridge: Polity Press.

La Fontaine, J. (1994) *The Extent and Nature of Organised and Ritual Abuse: Research Findings*, London: HMSO.

Laming, W. (2003) *The Victoria Climbié Inquiry*, London: Stationery Office.

Landes, J. (1998) *Feminism, the Public and the Private*, Oxford: Oxford University Press.

Langbein, J.H. (1976) *Torture and the Law of Proof*, Chicago: University of Chicago Press.

Larner, C. (1980) '*Crimen Exceptum?* The crime of witchcraft in Europe', in V.A.C. Gatrell *et al.*, *Crime and the Law*, Europa.

—— (1981) *Enemies of God*, London: Chatto and Windus.

Lasch, C. (1977) *Haven in a Heartless World: The Family Besieged*, New York: Basic Books.

Laslett, P. ([1967] 1988) 'Introduction', J. Locke *Two Treatises on Government*, Cambridge: Cambridge University Press.

—— (ed.) (1972) *Household and Family in Past Time: Comparative Studies in the Size and Structure of the Domestic Group over the Last Three Centuries in England, France, Serbia, Japan and Colonial North America*, London: Cambridge University Press.

—— (1977) *Family Life and Illicit Love in Earlier Generations: Essays in Historical Sociology*, Cambridge: Cambridge University Press.

—— (1987) 'The character of familial history, its limitations and the conditions for its proper pursuit', *Journal of Family History* 12(1–2): 263–84.

Latour, B. and Woolgar, S. (1979) *Laboratory Life: The Social Construction of Scientific Facts*, Beverley Hills: Sage.

Levy, A. and Kahan, B. (1991) *The Pindown Experience and the Protection of Children*, the Report of the Staffordshire Child Care Inquiry 1990, Staffordshire: Staffordshire County Council.

Lister, R. (1997) *Citizenship: Feminist Perspectives*, Basingstoke: Macmillan.

Locke, J. ([1698] 1988) *Two Treatises on Government*, P. Laslett (ed.), Cambridge: Cambridge University Press.

London Borough of Brent (1985) *A Child in Trust: Report of the Panel of Inquiry Investigating the Circumstances Surrounding the Death of Jasmine Beckford*, London: London Borough of Brent.

London Borough of Greenwich (1987) *A Child in Mind: Protection of Children in a Responsible Society: Report of the Commission of Inquiry into the death of Kimberley Carlile*, London: London Borough of Greenwich.

London Borough of Lambeth (1987) *Whose Child? The Report of the Panel Appointed to Inquire into the Death of Tyra Henry*, London: London Borough of Lambeth.

Luhmann, N. (1990) *Political Theory in the Welfare State*, Berlin: Walter de Gruyter.

Lyon, C. and de Cruz, P. (1993) *Child Abuse*, Bristol: Jordan Publishing.

Macedo, S. (1991) *Liberal Virtues: Citizenship, Virtue and Community in Liberal Constitutionalism*, Oxford: Clarendon Press.

MacFarlane, A. (1986) *Marriage and Love in England: Modes of Reproduction 1300–1840*, Oxford: Basil Blackwell.

MacKinnon, C. (1989) *Toward a Feminist Theory of the State*, Cambridge, MA: Harvard University Press.

Malcolm, J. (1985) *In the Freud Archives*, New York: Vintage.

Masson, J. (1985) *The Assault on Truth: Freud's Suppression of the Seduction Theory*, Harmondsworth: Penguin.

Mawby, R. and Walklate, S. (1994) *Critical Victimology*, London: Sage.

—— (1985) 'Complexity and democracy, or the seducements of systems theory', *New German Critique* 35: 27–53.

McNay, L. (1992) *Foucault and Feminism*, Cambridge: Polity Press.

Mearns, A. (ed.) ([1883] 1970) *The Bitter Cry of Outcast London*, A.S. Wohl (ed.), London: Leicester University Press.

Mill, J.S. ([1859] 1989) 'On liberty', in S. Collini (ed.), *On Liberty and Other Essays*, Cambridge: Cambridge University Press.

Mill, J.S. [1869] 1989) 'The subjection of women', in S. Collini (ed.), *On Liberty and Other Essays*, Cambridge: Cambridge University Press.

Miller, A. ([1953] 2000) *The Crucible*, London: Penguin.

Miller, A. (1985) *Thou Shalt Not be Aware: Society's Betrayal of the Child*, London: Pluto Press.

Miller, P. and Rose, N. (1990) 'Political rationalities and technologies of government', in S. Hanninen and K. Palonen (eds) *Texts, Contexts, Concepts: Studies on Politics and Power in Language*, Helsinki: Finnish Political Science Association.

Millett, K. (1977) *Sexual Politics*, London: Virago.

Mishra, R. (1984) *The Welfare State in Crisis*, Brighton: Harvester.

Murray, K. and Gough, D.A. (1991) *Intervening in Child Sexual Abuse*, Edinburgh: Scottish Academic Press.

National Institute for Social Work (1982) *Social Workers: Their Role and Tasks* (Barclay Report), London: Bedford Square Press.

Nicholson, L.J. (1986) *Gender and History: The Limits of Social Theory in the Age of the Family*, New York: Columbia University Press.

Nicholson, L.J. (ed.) (1990) *Feminism/Postmodernism*, Routledge: London.

Oakeshott, M. (1975) *Hobbes on Civil Association*, Oxford: Blackwell.

O'Donovan, K. (1985) *Sexual Divisions in Law*, London: Wiedenfeld and Nicolson.

O'Donovan, K. (1993) *Family Law Matters*, London: Pluto Press.

Offe, C. (1984) *Contradictions of the Welfare State*, London: Hutchinson.

O'Malley, P., Weir, L. and Shearing, C. (1997) 'Governmentality, criticism, politics', *Economy and Society* 26(4): 501–17.

O'Neill, O. (1989) *Constructions of Reason: Explorations of Kant's Practical Philosophy*, Cambridge: Cambridge University Press.

Osborne, T. (1998) *Aspects of Enlightenment: Social Theory and the Ethics of Truth*, London: UCL Press.

Outhwaite, W. (1994) *Habermas: A Critical Introduction*, Oxford: Polity in association with Blackwell.

Owen, D. (1995) 'Genealogy as exemplary critique: reflections on Foucault and the imagination of the political', *Economy and Society* 24(4): 489–506.

Packman, J. (1981) *The Child's Generation: Childcare Policy from Curtis to Houghton*, Oxford: Blackwell.

Parents Against Injustice (1986) *A Response to Child Abuse – Working Together*, Bishop's Stortford, Herts.

—— (1993) *Newsletter*, Riverside Business Park, Stansted, Essex.

Parton, N. (1985a) *The Politics of Child Abuse*, Basingstoke: Macmillan.

—— (1985b) 'Children in care: recent changes and debates', *Critical Social Policy* 5: 107–17.

—— (1992) 'The contemporary politics of child protection', *Journal of Social Welfare and Family Law* 2: 100–13.

Parton, N. and Jordan, B. (eds) (1983) *The Political Dimensions of Social Work*, Oxford: Blackwell.

Pateman, C. (1988) *The Sexual Contract*, Cambridge: Polity Press.

—— (1989) *The Disorder of Women*, Cambridge: Polity Press.

Peters, E. (1978) *The Magician, The Witch and The Law*, Brighton: Harvester.

Pfohl, S.J. (1977) 'The "discovery" of child abuse', *Social Problems* 24: 310–23.

Phillips, A. (1991) *Engendering Democracy*, Cambridge: Polity Press.

—— (1995) *The Politics of Presence*, Oxford: Clarendon Press.

Pigot Committee (1989) *Report of the Advisory Group on Video Evidence*, London: Home Office.

Pinchbeck, I. and Hewitt, M. (1969) *Children in English Society Volume One*, London: Routledge.

—— (1973) *Children in English Society Volume Two*, London: Routledge.

Pollock, L.A. (1983) *Forgotten Children: Parent–Child Relations from 1500 to 1900*, Cambridge: Cambridge University Press.

Ransom, J.S. (1997) *Foucault's Discipline: The Politics of Subjectivity*, Durham: Duke University Press.

Ray, L.J. (1993) *Rethinking Critical Theory*, London: Sage.

Rawls, J. (1973) *A Theory of Justice*, Oxford: Oxford University Press.

—— ([1997] 1999) 'The idea of public reason revisited', in S. Freeman (ed.) *John Rawls: Collected Papers*, Cambridge, MA: Harvard University Press.

Renvoize, J. (1993) *Innocence Destroyed: A Study of Child Sexual Abuse*, London: Routledge.

Rose, L. (1991) *The Erosion of Childhood*, London: Routledge.

Rose, N. (1985) *The Psychological Complex: Psychology, Politics and Society in England 1869–1939*, London: Routledge and Kegan Paul.

—— (1987) 'Beyond the public/private division: Law, power and the family', *Journal of Law and Society* 14(1): 61–76.

—— (1989) *Governing the Soul*, London: Routledge.

—— (1993) 'Government, authority and expertise in advanced liberalism', *Economy and Society* 22(3): 283–99.

—— (1996) 'Governing "advanced" liberal democracies', in A. Barry, T. Osborne, and N. Rose (eds) *Foucault and Political Reason: Liberalism, Neo-liberalism and Rationalities of Government*, London: UCL Press.

—— (1999a) *Powers of Freedom: Reframing Political Thought*, Cambridge: Cambridge University Press.

—— (1999b) *Governing the Soul*, 2nd edn, London: Free Association.

Rush, F. (1980) *The Best Kept Secret: Sexual Abuse of Children*, New York: McGraw-Hill.

Sawicki, J. (1991) *Disciplining Foucault: Feminism, Power and the Body*, London: Routledge.

Schmidt, J. (ed.) (1996) *What is Enlightenment? Eighteenth Century Answers and Twentieth Century Questions*, Berkeley: University of California Press.

Scott, A. (1988) 'Feminism and the seduction of the "real event"', *Feminist Review* 28: 88–102.

Scraton, P. (ed.) (1997) *'Childhood' in 'Crisis'?* London: UCL Press.

Search, G. (1988) *The Last Taboo: Sexual Abuse of Children*, Harmondsworth: Penguin.

Sedley, S. (1989) 'Public inquiries: a cure or a disease?' *Modern Law Review* 52: 469–79.

Seligman, A. (1992) *The Idea of Civil Society*, New York: Free Press.

Sennett, R. (1978) *The Fall of Public Man: On the Social Psychology of Capitalism*, New York: Vintage.

Shorter, E (1976) *The Making of the Modern Family*, London: Collins.

Showstack Sassoon, A. (ed.) (1987) *Women and the State*, London: Hutchinson.

Sinason, V. (1994) *Treating Survivors of Satanist Abuse*, London: Routledge.

Skinner, Q (1989) 'The state', in T. Ball, J. Farr and R. Hanson (eds) *Political Innovation and Conceptual Change*, Cambridge: Cambridge University Press.

Smart, C. (1989) *Feminism and the Power of Law*, London: Routledge.

Smart, C. (ed.) (1992) *Regulating Womanhood: Historical Essays on Marriage, Motherhood and Sexuality*, London: Routledge.

Smith, A. ([1776] 1981) *An Inquiry into the Nature and Causes of the Wealth of Nations*, R. H. Campbell, A. S. Skinner and W. B. Todd (eds) Indianapolis: Liberty Fund.

Spencer, J. (1990) 'Children's evidence and the Criminal Justice Bill', *New Law Journal* (December): 1750–1.

Spencer, J.R. and Flin, R. (1990) *The Evidence of Children: The Law and Psychology*, London: Blackstone.

Spruyt, H. (1994) *The Sovereign State and its Competitors: An Analysis of Systems Change*, Princeton: Princeton University Press.

Strauss, L. (1963) *The Political Philosophy of Hobbes: Its Basis and its Genesis*, Chicago: University of Chicago Press.

Teubner, G. (ed.) (1985) *Dilemmas of Law in the Welfare State*, Berlin: Walter de Gruyter.

Thane, P. (1981) 'Childhood in history', in M. King (ed.) *Childhood, Welfare and Society*, London: Batsford.

Valverde, M. (1996) '"Despotism" and ethical liberal governance', *Economy and Society* 25(3): 357–72.

Vann, R. (1982) 'The youth of centuries of childhood', *History and Theory* 21: 279–97.

Walby, S. (1990) *Theorizing Patriarchy*, Oxford: Basil Blackwell.

Warnock, M. (1992) 'The good of the child', in M. Warnock (ed.) *The Uses of Philosophy*, Oxford: Blackwell.

Waterhouse, R. (2000) *Lost in Care. The report of the Tribunal of Inquiry into the abuse of children in the former County Council areas of Gwynedd and Clwyd since 1974*, London: The Stationery Office.

Watson, S. (1994) 'Symbolic antagonism, police paranoia and the possibility of social diversity', in J. Weeks, (ed.) *The Lesser Evil and the Greater Good: The Theory and Politics of Social Diversity*, London: Rivers Oram Press.

Weber, M. ([1918] 1991) 'Science as a Vocation', in *From Max Weber: Essays in Sociology*, trans. and ed. H. H. Gerth and C. Wright Mills, London: Routledge.

Weintraub, J. and Kumar, K. (eds) (1997) *Public and Private in Thought and Practice: Perspectives on a Grand Dichotomy*, Chicago: Chicago University Press.

White, S. K. (1988) *The Recent Work of Jurgen Habermas*, Cambridge: Cambridge University Press.

Wiggerhaus, R. (1994) *The Frankfurt School: Its History, Theories and Political Significance*, trans. M. Robertson, Cambridge: Polity Press.

Williams, G. and McCreadie, J. (1992) *Ty Mawr Community Home Inquiry*, Gwent: Gwent County Council.

Williams, R. (1976) *Keywords: A Vocabulary of Culture and Society*, London: Fontana.

Wilson, A. (1980) 'The infancy of the history of childhood: an appraisal of Philippe Aries', *History and Theory* 19: 132–53.

Wolmar, C. (2000) *Forgotten Children: the Secret Abuse Scandal in Children's Homes*, London: Vision Paperbacks.

Wolin, S. (1960) *Politics and Vision: Continuity and Innovation in Western Political Thought*, Boston: Little Brown.

Wraith, R.E. and Lamb, G.B. (1971) *Public Inquiries as an Instrument of Government*, London: Allen and Unwin.

Wynne, B. (1982) *Rationality and Ritual: The Windscale Inquiry and Nuclear Decisions in Britain*, Chalfont St Giles: British Society for the History of Science.

Wynne, J. and Hobbes, C. (1986) 'Buggery in childhood – a common syndrome of child abuse', *The Lancet*, 4 October.

Wyre, R. (1989) 'Gracewell clinic', in W. Stainton Rogers, D. Hevey and E. Ash (eds) *Child Abuse and Neglect: Facing the Challenge*, London: Batsford.

Wyre, R. (1992) 'Our developing understanding of the sex offender and the need for resources', paper presented at the conference, Sexual Abuse: Past, Present, Future, Keele University, 24 September.

Young, I.M. (1990) *Justice and the Politics of Difference*, Princeton: Princeton University Press.

Zelizer, V. (1985) *Pricing the Priceless Child: The Changing Social Value of Children*, New York: Basic Books.

Index